THE GREAT THEFT

T H E

GREAT THEFT

*Wrestling Islam
from the Extremists*

KHALED ABOU EL FADL

HarperSanFrancisco
A Division of HarperCollinsPublishers

HarperCollins books may be purchased for educational, business, or sales promotional use. For information please write: Special Markets Department, HarperCollins Publishers, 10 East 53rd Street, New York, NY 10022.

HarperCollins Web site: http://www.harpercollins.com
HarperCollins®, ®, and HarperSanFrancisco™ are
trademarks of HarperCollins Publishers.

FIRST HARPERCOLLINS PAPERBACK EDITION
PUBLISHED IN 2007

Designed by Joseph Rutt

Library of Congress Cataloging-in-Publication Data is available.

ISBN: 978–0–06–118903–6
ISBN-10: 0–06–118903–0

07 08 09 10 11 RRD(H) 10 9 8 7 6 5 4 3 2 1

This book is dedicated to my teachers,
who taught me beauty, compassion, and mercy,
and that the true Islam is the Islam of moderation.

CONTENTS

Contents

INTRODUCTION

Recently, a rather well-known Islam-basher wrote an article accusing me of being a "stealth Islamist." By this, I think he meant that although I pretend to be a moderate Muslim, in truth I am an extremist who promotes a militant agenda. The secretive and conspiratorial tone pervading the article bordered on the paranoid, and yet, other than the ad hominem attacks on me, the article raised issues that have become matters of general importance, namely, the credibility of the Muslim voice in the West. The issue raised by the article and the problem that has become of more general importance is: When are Muslims truthfully representing the true nature of their beliefs and convictions? What has contributed to the confusion is the lack of any clear demarcating points between extremist and moderate beliefs in Islam. Since it is not likely that any Muslim would describe himself or herself as militant or extremist, how can we really know if a particular Muslim writer or group holds fanatical or immoderate, as opposed to mainstream or moderate, convictions and beliefs about Islam? But even more urgently, the challenging question raised by the article attacking me is: Who in the West or the United States gets to decide what are to be considered fanatical, extremist, and militant as opposed to moderate, reasonable, and ultimately, acceptable Muslim beliefs.

Particularly after 9/11, there has been a virtual flood of materials published about Muslims, their beliefs, and loyalties, and yet it is fair to say that at no other time has there been as much confusion about Muslims and their beliefs, and Islam and its legacy. Despite President George W. Bush's assurances that Islam is a peaceful religion and that Muslims are a peace-loving people, and despite his assurances that all good Muslims hunger for democracy, the confusion persists. Many non-Muslims in the West seem unwilling to leave matters there and move on. In large measure, what feeds this confusion is the flood of printed materials and deluge of talking-heads who clutter the field with often contradictory statements about militant Islam, extremist Muslims, political Islam, liberal Islam and so-called moderate Muslims. To make things worse, added to this chaotic state are pundits who urge people to watch out for subversive discourses, hidden motives, sinister plots, and double-talking Middle Easterners.

When it comes to the subject of Islam, there are many political interests at stake, and, as history repeatedly teaches us, nothing is as corrupting of religion as politics. This is not to say that Islam, as a religion, has become corrupted by politics. Instead, I am saying that politics and political interests have obfuscated and corrupted our ability to see Islam as a faith that is followed by well over a billion adherents in the world. Islam is the second-largest religious faith in the world, and the reality is that even in liberal and secular democracies, Islam has become the chosen faith of millions. Regardless of how much religious bigots may hate this fact, like Christianity and Judaism, Islam will continue to inspire and guide the convictions and actions of millions of adherents in every developed and underdeveloped country in the world. The only question is: What particular type or brand of Islam will tend to predominate and prevail in each setting? Understanding Islam has become an absolute imperative because achieving such an understanding will determine the type of people we are—whether tolerant or bigoted, whether enlightened or ignorant.

In teaching, I am often asked by well-intentioned non-Muslim students, "How can we contribute to a peaceful coexistence with Muslims?" My response is that merely to resist the temptation to believe those who preach hate, dwell on uncontrollable rages, and speculate about inevitable historical showdowns is already doing a lot. In most cases, such language and paradigms are sensationalistic and lazy replacements for the hard work of achieving a genuine understanding. No one is born blistering with hate and outrage, and often what appears to be hate is in reality thinly concealed fear. The only ethically acceptable choice is to seek to understand.

The problem, however, is that there are elements that make understanding the current Muslim condition particularly challenging. The first and foremost must relate to what I call acts of ugliness surrounding the Muslim context. It is perhaps elementary that the vast majority of Muslims are not terrorists, and do not condone terrorism. Yet hardly a time passes without a group of extremist Muslims featured in the news, typically because of an act of violence that shocks the world. For those who know Islam only through the media, the legacy of modern Muslims seems to be a long sequence of morally repugnant acts. The list of such acts is long and onerous: hostage taking in Iran and Lebanon, death threats against and persecution of writers and thinkers, acts of extreme intolerance against women and religious minorities committed by the Taliban in Afghanistan, suicide bombings in different parts of the world, and the list goes on. As a result, it is not an exaggeration to say that in the minds of many in the world, Islam has become intimately associated with what can be described as ugliness—intolerance, persecution, oppression, and violence. Whether one believes this view of Islam and Muslims is justified or not, it has become an undeniable fact that in many parts of the world, the very word *Islam* arouses negative sentiments that range from suspicious indifference to fear or intense dislike.

For a Muslim who cares about his or her faith, this reality arouses intense feelings of hurt and anguish. More than a billion people find in Islam their emotional and spiritual sustenance and fulfillment. For those Muslims, Islam is their source of serenity and spiritual peace, and Islam offers moral and ethical guidance that, instead of ugliness, fills their lives with beauty. How does a Muslim reconcile between the faith he or she lives and experiences and the prevalent public perceptions in the non-Muslim world?

I believe that it has become imperative for Muslims to take a self-critical and introspective look at their own tradition and system of beliefs. The reason for such an introspective and self-critical look is to ask: Does the tradition of Islam, with its inherited system of beliefs and convictions, contribute to the commission of these acts of ugliness? Are the Muslims who commit acts of terrorism or who persecute women and religious minorities inspired by the doctrines and dogma of the Islamic religion? Stated in a more stark and blatant fashion: Did something go wrong with contemporary Islam, and if so, what?

As Muslims, we can no longer afford to refuse to critically engage our tradition. We have reached a critical stage in the history of our faith and we must have the will-power and courage to reclaim and reestablish Islam as a humanistic moral force in the world today.

The point of this book is not to set out a systematic program for reform but to identify and delineate the reality of Muslim thought as it currently exists. Before we can speak about the need for reform it is imperative that we first get a firm handle on the current Muslim condition and seek to understand the world of ideas that chart the divides within the Muslim mind.

The objective of this book is to argue that there is an already-existing schism in Islam between Muslim moderates and what I will call the Muslim puritans. Both moderates and puritans claim to represent the true and authentic Islam. Both believe that they represent the Divine message as God intended it to be, and both believe that their convictions are thoroughly rooted in the Holy Book, the Qur'an, and in authentic traditions of the Prophet Muhammad, who was God's final prophet and messenger to humanity. Puritans, however, accuse the moderates of having changed and reformed Islam to the point of diluting and corrupting it. And moderates accuse the puritans of miscomprehending and misapplying Islam to the point of undermining and even defiling the religion.

Observers of the current Islamic condition, such as the average journalist, politician, or layperson who are not specialized in Islamic studies, often find the situation confusing and even chaotic. These observers hear many competing and contradictory versions of what Islam is or should be, and it is never clear who among Muslims believes in what, and why. In addition, it is rarely clear whether all the competing claims about Islamic tenets are legitimately anchored in Islamic theology and law. Perhaps the most common inquiry and source of confusion is: To what extent do Islamic theology and law encourage and promote terrorism?

In my view, the equally compelling question is: Is there in fact an existing, reformed vision of Islam competing with a more conservative and strict version of the religion?

In this book, I will argue that indeed Islam is at the current time passing through a transformative moment no less dramatic than the Reformation movements that swept through Europe at one time, and led to long and bloody religious wars. Although this transformative moment is no less dramatic than the European reformations, in the Islamic context at the present time it is not as developed or acute.

Nevertheless, there is a significant rift between the belief system of the reformed moderates and the more conservative and strict puritans. We understand the difference between Islam as it is understood by puritans like the Taliban and Bin Laden, and Islam as it is understood by what I will argue are the majority of less visible Muslims. Moderates constitute the silent majority of Muslims in the world, but puritans have an impact upon the religion that is wildly disproportionate to their numbers. Regardless of the present constitution of the Islamic world, the transformative moment of which I speak is embodied by the fact that there are two paradigmatically opposed worldviews that are competing to define the truth of the Islamic faith.[1] By "truth of the Islamic faith," I mean what becomes the accepted precepts and axioms about the place of Islamic history in the Muslim psyche, the foundational message of the Qur'an, the quintessential lessons taught by the Prophet Muhammad, the moral priorities of the individual believer, and the ethical parameters that guide Muslims in interacting with others. Puritans and moderates not only disagree on all these issues, but they also each struggle to make their paradigms and worldviews the overwhelmingly dominant and long-lasting truth of Islam. In their most pure and unadulterated forms the views of the two groups are irreconcilable, and therefore, although some form of coexistence might be possible, the two views tend to clash and compete. It might be possible for each view to exist as a school of thought within Islam and to tolerate and perhaps respect the other, but this is becoming increasingly difficult. The acts of terrorism and violence committed by the puritans are increasing the pressure for confrontation and for a decisive transformation in Islamic history. The recent violent showdowns in Saudi Arabia between some of the most prominent puritan thinkers and the Saudi government are an example of this process. For better or worse, when all is said and done and the transformation is complete, as one of these orientations earns the consensus and near-total commitment of Muslims, it will clearly possess the formidable power of definition—the power to define Islam for what might turn out to be a considerably long time.

PART ONE

THE
BATTLEGROUND
FOR
FAITH

Muslim: follower of Islam

Islam: religion is Muslims as
         Specified by the Koran

ONE

ISLAM TORN BETWEEN EXTREMISM AND MODERATION

Not too long ago, at the end of an invited lecture, I was asked to name the most emphatic moral values taught by Islam. The answer was easy enough—it would have to be mercy, compassion, and peace. After all, these are the values that each practicing Muslim affirms in prayer at least five times a day. Imagine my surprise and chagrin when some members in the audience chuckled as if to say: "Come on, get real!" In a similar experience, after President Bush appointed me to serve on the U.S. Commission on International Religious Freedom, mingled with the messages of congratulations from well-wishers were messages from people I did not know asking: What could a Muslim possibly have to contribute to the cause of religious freedom and tolerance in the world?

These personal experiences are not anomalies: every Muslim will have her or his own stories to tell about how Islam is poorly perceived. Confronted with such negative perceptions of their religion, Muslims have a choice. They could complain and cry about it and grow old in silent bitterness. Alternatively, they could decide to teach others about their faith, but this assumes they are sufficiently educated and well-informed about their own religion. The problem, however, is that many Muslims are woefully ignorant about their own religion. This

[margin, handwritten: Most stressed i significant]

forces Muslims to consider a third relevant option, and that is to engage in study and thought not just to better understand the Islamic religion but also to try to understand how and why so many non-Muslims have come to have such a negative impression of Islam. Before trying to educate others about Islam we must first reflect upon the sources and reasons for the pervasive misunderstandings and misinformation.

For a believing Muslim, asking what if anything went wrong with the Islamic faith is an uncomfortable question. A Muslim cannot help but feel that he or she is somehow playing into the hands of Islam's enemies. All religions at one time or another have played a role in inspiring intolerance and violence, so why should Islam be singled out for special scrutiny? It is tempting for the faithful to absolve the Islamic faith of any possible fault and instead blame Muslims. In fact, many Muslims argue that Islam, as a set of beliefs and ideals, should not be blamed for the malfeasance of its followers. The fact that certain people who call themselves Muslims commit acts of ugliness is due, this argument says, to economic, political, and sociocultural factors that breed violence and intolerance, not to Islam. From this perspective, it is a mistake to attempt to critically examine Islamic doctrines, beliefs, or history when evaluating the contemporary problems that plague Muslims. Instead, one ought to ask what, if anything, went wrong with Muslims.

Although this argument does have some merit, as a general approach it is not a satisfying way of addressing the challenges that confront Muslims in the modern age. There are several reasons why this approach is both dishonest and dangerous. It is understandable that out of love and care for their religion some Muslims would be eager to defend their faith by pointing the finger away from Islam. A call for critical introspection, in the view of these Muslims, is tantamount to accusing

Islam of being deficient or flawed, and understandably they take great offense at such an insinuation. Muslims who believe that Islam is perfect and immutable regard a call for introspection with considerable suspicion and perhaps even hostility. Furthermore, in light of the historical conflicts between Islam and the West, calls for introspection are often seen as nothing more than poorly veiled attempts at appeasing the West by maligning Islam. A considerable number of Muslims believe wholeheartedly that fellow Muslims who attempt to adopt a critical stance toward the Islamic tradition are nothing more than self-promoters seeking to placate the West at Islam's expense.

These objections have merit, and I sympathize with those who believe that Islam is maligned enough as it is. The modern Muslim is exposed to a barrage of bad news and negative media coverage on a daily basis. It is undeniable that there is no short supply of Islam-haters, in the Western and non-Western worlds alike, who seem eager to malign the Islamic faith at every opportunity. In fact, I believe that the anti-Muslim sentiment in the modern age has reached a level of prejudice every bit as sinister and endemic as racism and anti-Semitism. As a consequence, the temptation is enormous for Muslims to adopt a defensive posture by insisting that Islam is perfect and that the inherited doctrines and dogmas of the Islamic tradition do not in any way contribute to the plight of Muslims in the modern age. Understandable though this defensive posture might be, it is a position that has its costs, and I believe that these costs have become oppressively prohibitive. In fact, the only way that Muslims can remain true to the moral message of their religion and at the same time discharge their covenant with God is through introspective self-criticism and reform.

Although the schism between moderate and puritan Muslims has become distinct, pronounced, and real, this division is

Jl Kot umy

not explicitly recognized in the Muslim world. The dichotomy between the two groups is a lived and felt reality, but there has been no attempt to recognize the systematic differences between the two contending parties. In fact, many Muslims have been reluctant to speak openly of two primary orientations juxtaposed against each other within modern Islam. The failure to acknowledge the existence of such a division has contributed to the confusion about who in Islam believes in what, and it may also be responsible for the widespread misconceptions about the teachings and doctrines of the religion.

The reluctance of many Muslims to recognize the existence of a schism within the faith is in many ways due to the powerful influence of the dogma of unity in modern Islamic thought. For reasons discussed later, contemporary Islamic thinkers and activists heavily emphasize the compelling need for unity among Muslims, demanding that all Muslims should regard themselves as a single person. The tenets of the Islamic faith emphasize that there is a straight path leading to God, and that Muslims should unite in pursuit of the Lord's path and not divide. Therefore, many Muslims feel uncomfortable admitting that there is a split that divides the religion. But at the same time, Islam teaches that it is the solemn duty of each and every Muslim to bear witness and testify to the truth, even if such testimony be against one's kin or coreligionists. Simultaneous to the strong emphasis on Muslim unity and the importance of truth is a long-established tradition in Islamic theology and law of tolerating differences of thought and opinion.

All of these teachings put this book in a rather odd position. By recognizing that there is a fundamental schism within contemporary Islam, I am discharging what I believe to be my religious obligation, but I am also offending many who believe that it is better not to dwell upon potentially seditious and divisive issues. To be divisive and to contribute to breaking the unity and harmony of Muslims is to cause *fitna* (sedition and divisiveness), and this word, *fitna,* fills the hearts of the pious with woe and dread. As sinful as *fitna* might be, I believe that what is at risk in the ongoing conflict between the moderates and puritans is nothing less than the very soul of Islam. Therefore, it is a greater act of sin for Muslims to indulge in a state of apathetic indifference.

In order to differentiate between the militant and fanatic minority and the silent majority of Islam, I am forced to compare and contrast two main groups: the moderates and the puritans. However, it is important to keep in mind that the modern world of Islam cannot be summed up in just those two categories. The reality of Islam today is far more complex, and to speak in terms of two juxtaposed groups is an inadequate oversimplification. For example, there are some orientations, such as the Sufis and the self-described secularists, that this book does not deal with. Nevertheless, I speak in terms of two competing groups to emphasize the fundamental difference between the two ends of the spectrum that are most likely to play a critical role in defining Islam's future. Few Muslims are going to be thoroughly moderate or thoroughly puritan. Most will fall somewhere between the two extremes, with the majority leaning toward moderation. The model articulated here will, I hope, give non-Muslims an understanding of the range of beliefs and convictions adopted by Muslims, and help Muslims evaluate their own relationship to Islam as they consider their place on this spectrum of ideas and convictions.

It is important to note that the two orientations described in this book cut through the Sunni and Shi'i sectarian divide. I have not attempted to describe the differences between Sunni and Shi'i theology here because there is an abundance of published material that discusses those differences, and because those differences are not relevant to the puritan-versus-moderate divide. Sunnis can be puritan or moderate according to the same criteria and distinguishing characteristics as Shi'is. A puritan Sunni tends to believe in the same ideas and come to the same conclusions as a puritan Shi'i. The same is true of Shi'i and Sunni moderates.

MODERATES AND PURITANS: WHY THIS TERMINOLOGY?

Choosing the right terminology to label a set of beliefs and convictions is always difficult. Labels do not just *describe;* they also *judge.* Moreover, what seems moderate to one person could appear extreme to another.

I chose the terms *moderate* and *puritan* largely by a process of exclusion. The Qur'an, the Holy Book of Islam, enjoins Muslims to be a moderate people. Moreover, the traditions of the Prophet Muhammad report that when confronted by two extremes, the Prophet would always choose the middle. In other words, the Prophet of Islam was always described as a moderate man who tended to avoid falling into extremes. Hence, the word *moderate* has roots in the Islamic tradition, and it conveys the normative disposition that the vast majority of Muslims are supposed to have.

Those I am labeling as *moderates* have been variously described as *modernists, progressives,* and *reformers.* None of these labels works as well, for me, as *moderates.*

The term *modernists* implies that a particular group deals with the challenges of modernity while others are reactionary—living in the past or seeking to return to the past. The fact is, however, that the relationship of all Islamic thinkers and activists with the past is a complex matter. (Islamic thinkers and activists, as opposed to secularists, are those who pursue private or public political, sociological, or economic agendas while considering Islam to be their authoritative, but not necessarily exclusive, frame of reference.) From a sociological perspective, fundamentalist Islamic groups are thoroughly a product of modernity, and of modernist ideologies such as nationalism. Furthermore, whether the so-called fundamentalists are rooted in the Islamic tradition is highly disputed. All Islamic groups, regardless of their orientation, are part of a modern reality which they, for better or worse, help shape and define.

The terms *progressives* and *reformers* are helpful, but they have serious shortcomings as well. Many moderates claim to reflect the true and authentic Islam. In one way or another, they contend that they do not change the religion for the better but instead attempt to call Muslims back to the original faith. There is no question that the positions of such Muslims tend to be liberal rather than conservative, but the relationship of liberalism to progress or reform is a complicated philosophical question that cannot be exhaustively treated in this book. Liberalism typically connotes the adoption or pursuit of values that are oriented toward greater individual liberty. However, there is no predictable relationship between liberalism and reform or progress. Some of the worst dictators in history, such as Joseph Stalin and Gamal 'Abd al-Nasser, implemented reforms that led to socioeconomic progress in their countries, and yet these dictators were not liberal-minded in any sense of the word. Ironically, liberal values are not always achieved by moving forward; sometimes they are achieved by harkening back to tradition. For example, certain aspects of the Islamic tradition are far more liberally oriented than modern ideas accepted by Muslims.

Aside from the issue of liberalism and its relation to reform and progress, there are other reasons that dissuade me from using the terms *reformers* and *progressives*. It might be that a minority of Muslims are reformers or progressives, but in terms of Islamic theology and law, the *majority* of Muslims are moderates. Progressiveness and reformism are positions often adopted by an intellectual elite, but moderation more aptly describes the religious convictions of the majority of Muslims.

Those I am calling *puritans* have been described by various writers as *fundamentalists, militants, extremists, radicals, fanatics, jihadists,* and even simply *Islamists.* I prefer the label *puritans,* because the distinguishing characteristic of this group is the absolutist and uncompromising nature of its beliefs. In many ways, this orientation tends to be purist, in the sense that it is intolerant of competing points of view and considers pluralist realities to be a form of contamination of the unadulterated truth.

Although many have used the label *fundamentalists,* it is clearly problematic. *All* Islamic groups and organizations claim to adhere to the fundamentals of Islam. Even the most liberal movement will insist that its ideas and convictions better represent the fundamentals of the faith. In the Western context, using the term *fundamentalists* to describe extremist Christian groups that insist on the literal meaning of scripture, regardless of the historical context of a text, appears to be quite reasonable. But as many Muslim researchers have noted, the term *fundamentalist* is ill-fitted for the Islamic context because in Arabic the word becomes *usuli,* which means "one who relies on the fundamentals or basics." So the expression *Islamic fundamentalism* conveys the unavoidable misimpression that only fundamentalists base their interpretations on the Qur'an and the traditions of the Prophet—the basic or fundamental sources of Islamic theology and law. However, many liberal, progressive, or moderate Muslims would describe themselves as *usulis*, or fundamentalists, without thinking that this carries a negative connotation. In the Islamic context, it makes much more sense to describe the fanatical reductionism and narrow-minded literalism of some groups as *puritanical* (a term that in the West invokes a particular historical experience that was not necessarily negative).

The terms *extremists, fanatics,* and *radicals* do offer reasonable alternatives. Most certainly, the Taliban and al-Qa'ida are extremists, fanatics, and radicals; and linguistically, extremism is the opposite of moderation. Nevertheless, considering the thought of these groups on a range of issues, it appears that they are consistently and systematically absolutist, dichotomous, and even idealistic. On certain issues, such as how they interpret the legacy of the Prophet and his Companions, these groups tend to be absolutist, unequivocal, and puritanical, not extremist or radical. In other words, the groups I am discussing in this book are not always, and on every issue, fanatical, radical, or extremist, but they are always puritanical. The earmark of their thinking is its absolutist and unequivocal quality, not its fanatical, radical, or extremist nature.

Although words connoting a level of extremism or fanaticism have their appeal, the term *militant* is clearly misguided. If by this term one means the willingness to use force, this designation is not very helpful. Islam, Christianity, and Judaism all accept that under certain circumstances the use of force is justified. On the other hand, if by *militant* one means the tendency to use excessive force, this label is so broadly applicable as to be unhelpful: it would apply to some Islamic groups, yes, but also to the policies of many factions and nations. If by *militant* one means the willingness to use offensive and aggressive, instead of purely defensive, force—well, practically *everyone* claims to use force only in self-defense. Furthermore, militancy is not helpful in describing the attitudes of these groups toward women or minorities, for instance.

Recently, some writers have started to use the word *jihadists* to describe people like the Taliban and al-Qa'ida. I will discuss the issue of jihad later, but as a label it is misguided, lending confusion instead of clarity to understanding the uniqueness and particularity of the puritan orientation.

Some commentators have tried to differentiate between Muslims and Islamists (meaning those who believe in political Islam), and typically these commentators try to brand Islamism as the source of danger to civilized societies. Both expressions—*Islamism* and *political Islam*—are vague and broad enough to cover any form of Islam that a particular commentator might wish to disparage. In general, Islamists are Muslims who believe that Islamic theology and law should serve as an authoritative frame of reference in any social or political condition. But using Islamic theology and law as an authoritative frame of reference does not necessarily mean believing in a theocratic state or imposing draconian laws upon an innocent group of people. It could simply mean drawing inspiration from Islamic ethics and morals in matters of public concern, and adopting positions endorsed or inspired by Islamic jurisprudence regarding a public issue. In short, using Islam as a source of authority could range widely from the most benign and noncoercive situations to a full-fledged theocratic state that dominates how people think and act.

Nevertheless, commentators who disparagingly use the labels *political Islam* or *Islamist* draw a line between the private and public sphere: Islam practiced privately is deemed acceptable, but any intrusion into the public sphere is treated as dangerous and unacceptable. Many Muslims would say that this amounts to proclaiming that Muslims may practice their religion but that they may not take their religion too seriously. Muslims are permitted to practice their religion within the confines of their private lives, but they may not intrude with their religion upon the public sphere. The exact role that religion should play in the public arena is far from a settled issue in either democratic theory or democratic practice. Religion may play a variety of roles in the public arena without the polity becoming a theocracy. Consider, for instance, the prominent roles that religious parties play in Israeli politics, and yet Israel is not a theocratic state. Even a country like the United States, which in comparison to the majority of Western liberal democracies has adopted the least compromising version of the doctrine of separation between church and state, is not immune. Recently, we have seen Christianity's influence in the public sphere increase markedly because of the strong religious convictions of high-ranking officials in the executive branch of the U.S. government. The idea that religion must be kept within the strict confines of the private sphere in order for a worthwhile democracy to exist is too simplistic, and it does not reflect the reality of successful democracies. Imposing this dichotomy between the private and public spheres upon Muslims and demanding that they adhere to a strict separation between church and state, otherwise disparagingly referring to them as Islamists or political Islamists, can only be described as arrogant, if not imperialist.

Curiously enough, Islam does not even have a church per se that can authoritatively set down the true canonical Islam; therefore, the doctrine of separation of church and state, strictly speaking, is not applicable to the Islamic context. The origins of Western democratic theory were based on preventing the Catholic Church from controlling and monopolizing the public sphere.

Early Western secularists of the seventeenth and eighteenth century wished to sharply curtail the powers of the Catholic Church, and in fact, several Western theorists thought that the Reformation and particularly Protestant theology was an adequate solution to the problem of religious hegemony over the public sphere and to horrendous atrocities such as the Inquisition, witch hunts, and the killing of heretics.

Islam, however, has had a very different experience with religion. In Islamic history, the absence of an institutional church ensured that religion could not monopolize or control the public sphere. Rather, religion or the representatives of Shari'a law were always forced to compete to influence the public sphere in a variety of ways. Importantly, throughout Islamic history there has never been a single voice that represents the Shari'a law or the canons of religion. Historically, the Islamic faith and Shari'a law have been represented by several competing schools of theological and jurisprudential thought, the most powerful and notable of these organized into privately run professional guilds. Although the state often claimed to rule in God's name, the legitimacy of such claims were challenged by these professional guilds.

The Protestant Reformation did not seek to remove religion from the public sphere altogether but to challenge the monopoly and religious despotism of the Catholic Church. Interestingly, among other things, this Reformation sought to bring to Europe a religious and political dynamic that already existed in Islam. Even most European democratic theorists of the seventeenth and eighteenth centuries did not envision that there would be a complete divorce between the state and religion.[1] After the French and American revolutions, secular theorists developed democratic theory in ways that would have been entirely unrecognizable and even shocking to the thinkers of the Protestant and Catholic Reformations. This historical overview underscores an important fact that is lost on many Muslims and non-Muslims in the modern age: theocratic government—in other words, government that rules in God's name and that, so to speak, represents God and His law in the public sphere—is anathema to Islamic history and theology. A true theocracy would necessarily mean that there is only one correct point of view in Islamic theology and law, and all the rest are erroneous or illegitimate. Instead of Shari'a being represented by various competing schools or guilds, with all of them having an equal claim to legitimacy, the state would effectively become a church, dictating the canon of the faith and treating all who disagree as heretics.

For the first time in Islamic history, the state is in a position to do just that, because the institutions that have historically represented Islamic theology and law have become co-opted and are now closely controlled by the state. In the past, the autonomy, plurality, and diversity of religious institutions made this kind of theocratic state difficult to achieve, but today the powers of the state in most of the Muslim world are vast and dominant. A theocratic state such as Saudi Arabia, for instance, is a genuine novelty in Islamic history.

Medieval Muslim jurists believed that it was the solemn duty of the state to protect Islam; and as long as the state did so, its legitimacy was not to be questioned or challenged. Interestingly enough, they also believed that Christians and Jews living in Muslim territory ought to be given the means to protect their religions as well. Medieval Muslim jurists envisioned that in order for the state to protect religion it was obligated to build mosques, collect and disperse alms, pilgrimage to the holy sites of Mecca, Medina, and Jerusalem, ban public acts of indecency, and punish those who maliciously defamed the Prophet or sought to corrupt the faith. At the same time, the state was obligated to afford protection to the diverse schools of thought and not to favor one interpretation of the faith over another.

That medieval legacy has left modern Muslims with extremely challenging questions. What is the difference between the state protecting religion, on the one hand, and the state representing religion, on the other? Can the state protect religion without undermining a democratic political order? England, for instance, has several statutes and common law doctrines that obligate the state to protect the Christian faith from malicious slander; Israel has various ordinances that protect Orthodox practices and observances in certain areas of the country, such as Jerusalem; Italy has a complex system of concessions and protections afforded to the Catholic Church; and Ireland, as well as other European states, is constitutionally obligated to preserve the Catholic identity of the state. Yet there is a significant difference between the state playing some role in protecting religion and the state becoming the representative and enforcer of religion, as in the Saudi model.

The formidable questions that confront Muslims today are whether democracy is reconcilable with Islam, whether Islam has its own unique system of government, and whether the historical caliphate should be restored and revitalized so that it can unite most Muslims under a single polity. The current debates among Muslims are not whether Islam can be political or not. But the exact role that Shari'a should play in a modern state, the role of Islamic jurists (*fuqaha*), the relationship of the state to God, legislative sovereignty, constitutional limitations on the actions of the legislature, and even the desirability of liberal democracies as well as the place of human rights in a Muslim polity are all hotly contested issues in modern Islam. The spectrum of ideas on all these issues ranges from strongly puritanical on the one end to moderate on the other. These issues are but examples of the many problems that increasingly divide the two main groups wrestling for the soul of Islam.

The range of ideas explained in this book is based on my long engagement with the problems, issues, and doctrines of Islam and Muslims in a large number of Muslim and non-Muslim countries. The battle over these ideas is waged in the nations of the Middle East in particular, but it is certainly not limited to that region of the world. The battle for the soul of Islam takes place in every country, Muslim or non-Muslim, where puritans have clashed with moderates and have managed to make inroads. For most of my life, I have been a student of Islamic theology and law, and at different times I have moved along the spectrum of ideas presented in this book, and have experienced them both as an activist and as an academic. At this point I must confess that after years of reading Islamic sources on theology and jurisprudence, I have become convinced that the puritan end of the spectrum empties Islam of its moral and ethical content. And I have become convinced that a nonhumanistic Islam is a false Islam—that Islam is a message of compassion, mercy, love, and beauty and that these values represent the core of the faith. Nevertheless, my training as an Islamic jurist, a secular academic, and a lawyer has taught me to represent positions and points of view I do not agree with. I will strive to do justice to both ends of the spectrum, even if I not only disagree with one of those ends but also find it morally repugnant.

Far from being dry scholastic theological disputes, disagreements over these issues have far-reaching real-life consequences and implications. The issue that confronts us is no less important than the following: Between the puritans and moderates, which of the two groups is more likely to define the meaning and role of the world's second-largest religion in the future?

TWO

THE ROOTS OF
THE PROBLEM

All religions, like all sociological and political movements, have a process or method for generating and defining authority. Authority can be formal or informal, but either way, authority defines for people what is official, formal, and binding. Fundamentally, it defines what can be relied upon and what ought to be followed. In the Islamic context, the authoritative communicates to believers what is objectionable, what is acceptable, and what is binding, and also what is formally a part of their religion.

However, in the modern era, Muslims have suffered a crisis of authority that has deteriorated to the point of full-fledged chaos. There are reasons for this that I will explain, but for now it is important to note that in the house of Islam, which includes any area where Muslims live, whether in Muslim countries or not, there are numerous parties who pretend to speak on God's behalf but too few who are willing to listen.

A brief aside is necessary here. Modernity, as a concept, is highly contested by social theorists, but by *modern era* I mean the twentieth and twenty-first centuries, especially after the 1950s. The deterioration in religious authority started with the age of colonialism in the eighteenth century, especially with Bonaparte's invasion of Egypt in 1798. But even back then the *ulama* (religious scholars or jurists) were able to mobilize the population into waging a vast rebellion against the French. By the twentieth century and onward, however, the *'ulama* ceased to have that kind of influence in most of the Muslim world, and the crisis in religious authority was in full effect.

Westerners often complain that it is difficult to learn whether Islam endorses or condemns a particular position or practice, such as hostage-taking, suicide bombings, and the veiling of women. The same complaint is made by Muslims living in practically every part of the globe. Many Muslims in numerous venues, ranging from books and newspapers to call-in television and radio programs, complain that on a very wide range of issues—from those named above, as well as the legality of secret marriages and certain types of divorce, to interest on bank loans, house mortgages, fighting the Americans in Iraq or Afghanistan, and the duty of Muslims toward those suffering occupation in Chechnya and Kashmir—they find many contradictory statements about what is Islamically legitimate or condemnable. The phenomenon described here is not limited to the Middle East or to one part of the Muslim world. I have received a large amount of correspondence from Muslims living in several non–Middle Eastern countries, including Malaysia, Indonesia, Pakistan, India, Bangladesh, Australia, and several South American and sub-Saharan African countries, lamenting the same problem and asking if there is some way that a Muslim can ascertain the incontrovertible and true Islamic position on any of the issues mentioned above.

The reality is that in the modern age, there are many contradictory claims made in Islam's name, and when it comes to Islamic law, the response one gets about any particular issue depends on whom one asks. This reality was keenly felt after the terrorist attacks of 9/11, but it has been evident in numerous controversies, such as the Salman Rushdie affair, the practices of the Taliban against women and historical and religious monuments, the stoning of women in Nigeria, the taking of hostages in Iran and Lebanon, the treatment of women in Saudi Arabia, the ejection of veiled Muslim girls from public schools in France, and the presence of women as religious leaders and advisers in Egypt, Canada, South Africa, and China.

JURISTS AND THE ONGOING BATTLE FOR RELIGIOUS AUTHORITY

There is no church in Islam, as was noted earlier, and although this contributes to the chaos, it does not fully explain it. There is likewise no clergy, in the Western sense; there is nothing in Islam that comes close to the papacy in Rome or the institution of the priesthood. There is, however, a class of people who attend something like a seminary, where they study the religious sciences and Islamic law. In Islam, they are given various names—in Arabic, *'alim* (pl. *'ulama*), *faqih* (pl. *fuqaha*), *mulla, shaykh,* or *imam.* Because of the nature of their technical legal training and their historical role as lawyers and experts in jurisprudence, I will call them *jurists* throughout the book. Today, these individuals play a role quite similar to that of rabbis in the Jewish faith, in that they give counsel, conduct marriages, conduct the last rites for the deceased, and in some cases serve as judges in a religious court.

The opinions of these jurists carry persuasive authority, but they are not mandatory or binding. These opinions, known as *fatawa* (sing. *fatwa*), may address either a specific problem of interest to a particular person or a matter of public concern. In the classical age, Muslim scholars set strict qualifications that a jurist had to meet before becoming qualified to issue a *fatwa,* and the more serious the subject the higher the qualifications demanded of a jurist. In the contemporary age, the institutions that enforced this system of qualifications have crumbled and disappeared. Today, practically anyone can appoint himself a *mufti* and proceed to spew out *fatawa*, without either a legal or a social process that would restrain him from doing so.

A *fatwa* may be authoritative for some Muslims but not others. The decision to accept or reject a *fatwa* is entirely up to each individual Muslim. One group of Muslims may defer to one jurist and abide by his *fatwa* because they respect his learning and judgment, while another group may completely ignore it because, for whatever reason, they do not believe his *fatwa* to be correct. A Muslim's decision to accept or reject a *fatwa*, however, is not supposed to be based on whim or mood; every Muslim is expected to reflect upon and ponder each *fatwa* and abide by it only if he or she believes that it truly and accurately represents the will of God. Although each *fatwa* reflects the opinion of a learned person about what God desires or wills, it is up to the recipients of the *fatwa* not to follow it blindly or unthinkingly. According to Islamic law, practicing Muslims must exert a degree of due diligence in researching the qualifications of the jurist issuing the *fatwa*, and also the evidentiary basis for the jurist's opinion, before deciding to follow or reject any particular *fatwa*. Today, with the explosion in self-declared experts in Islamic law, and the absence of credible institutions that can discredit or vouch for the qualifications of *fatwa* issuers, there is complete chaos in the world of Islamic law. Especially since the advent of the Internet, most *fatawa* are authored by people trained as doctors, engineers, and computer scientists rather than Islamic scholars.[1] This jurisprudential chaos is confusing and even torturous to the conscientious Muslim, let alone the average non-Muslim.

In the precolonial age, particularly from the ninth to the eighteenth centuries, jurists played the most pivotal role in providing authority in Islam. Although there was a long tradition of plurality of opinions within the juristic class and a practice of disputation and disagreement, juristic institutions provided the power of definition in Islam; collectively the juristic class determined what was orthodox and legitimate within the religion. Throughout the Muslim world, there were private religious endowments (known as the *awqaf* [sing. *waqf*]) that funded a network of seminaries. For the most part, these religious endowments were established by private philanthropists, many of whom were women. For all practical purposes, these seminaries functioned like law schools, providing jurists with rigorous training in Islamic jurisprudence.

Islamic jurisprudence is a legal system every bit as complex as the civil law, common law, and Jewish law legal systems. It is customary for Western scholars to distinguish between secular legal systems and Islamic law by claiming that secular law is based on the command of a *human* sovereign, while Islamic law is based on the command of a *Divine* sovereign. At the purely theoretical level, this claim is true to an extent, but it is an oversimplification that tends to understate the role of human agency in the production of Islamic law. Unlike secular law, Islamic jurisprudence covers matters pertaining to the relationship between God and human beings—this has to do with ritual practices such as praying, fasting, giving alms, and making pilgrimage (these are known as *'ibadat* laws). But, like secular law, Islamic jurisprudence also deals with matters relating to social and political interactions and to the relationship of human beings to one another (these are known as *mu'amalat* laws). These laws address a wide range of issues, such as marriage and divorce, inheritance, criminal offenses, contracts and commercial transactions, constitutional law, and international law. According to Islamic jurisprudential theory, all laws in either category must be geared toward achieving the welfare of people, establishing justice, and enjoining what is good while forbidding what is evil. These are the ultimate objectives of the law or, as some have called them, the constitutional purposes, of Islamic jurisprudence. As such, Muslim jurists are instructed to serve and promote these ultimate purposes.

Unlike secular legal systems, Islamic law is not based on positive commands issued by a government. Rather, Islamic law is produced by jurists interpreting textual sources and applying particular methodologies according to a fairly complex set of rules. The sources of Islamic law are the Qur'an, which Muslims believe is the literal, unadulterated word of God; the Sunna, which is a body of oral traditions describing what the Prophet and his Companions said and did; rule by analogy, which is effectively the following of precedents so that a judgment in an old case is adhered to in a similar new case; and consensus of the jurists (or, according to some, consensus of the Prophet's Companions, and according to still others, consensus of Muslims in general, as opposed to jurists). Other than these main sources, a ruling in Islamic law could be based on equity, public interest, or custom. This, of course, is a general overview of the sources that Muslim jurists relied upon in constructing and building the Islamic legal system. But it ought to be noted that there were extensive debates and disagreements about the exact meaning and application of each these sources. For example, many jurists, particularly Shi'is, believed that reason is an independent source of law.

Like in the common law system, Muslim jurists exercised the dominant role in producing the set of judgments and rulings that we now know as Islamic law. In theory, Muslim jurists searched and interpreted the Divine law, and they exercised considerable leeway and discretion in deciding what is valid or invalid, what is legitimate or illegitimate, what to count and what to abjure, what to rely on and what to exclude. Because most of Islamic law is the product of juristic reasoning and interpretive activity, on any significant issue one will find multiple legal opinions all claiming to be correct. In the first couple centuries of Islam, well over thirty schools of legal thought, organized along the lines of methodological and interpretive differences, competed for the hearts and minds of Muslims. Although the competition among the various schools of thought was often intense, all schools were considered equally legitimate and orthodox. The sum total of all the legal opinions according to the various schools of thought, in addition to the principles and methodologies, were known collectively as the Shari'a (the holy law of God). In the classical age the state could not produce Shari'a law; only the jurists could do so. Laws passed by the state were considered regulatory rules not included as part of Shari'a law.

By the tenth century, most Islamic jurists received training in one of four Sunni schools of thought: Shafi'i, Maliki, Hanafi, or Hanbali. Each of the four schools was considered equally orthodox, and the laity could choose to follow any of them. (The many other schools existing earlier for various complicated reasons had become extinct.) Shi'i jurists, depending on their theological affiliation, trained in the Ja'fari or Zaydi schools, and at times they also trained in one of the Sunni schools of law.[2]

After many years of study in a law school or with distinguished jurists, a student would receive a sufficient number of licenses (*ijazas*) from professional mentors, until reaching the status of a jurist, or expert in Shari'a. Trained in Islamic jurisprudence, such a graduate enjoyed many career opportunities, all of which would have earned him a high level of social esteem. Jurists could work as professors of law, as judges, as court clerks, or in other high-level administrative positions within the state bureaucracy. Importantly, however, regardless of their official or governmental post, jurists who earned the greatest trust, respect, and loyalty of the public through their teaching and writing also enjoyed the greatest level of social esteem and exercised the greatest influence on defining Islamic orthodoxy.

The Shari'a was richly diverse. Indeed, it is difficult to convey to modern readers the degree of richness and diversity that the Shari'a enjoyed. The only legal tradition that I am aware of that comes close to the richness of the Shari'a tradition is the Jewish Rabbinic tradition, with its multi-interpretive methods and various competing interpretations. As in the Rabbinic tradition, the students of Islamic law considered a wide range of alternative interpretations and opinions on any particular point of law, and the various sages of Islamic law worked hard to earn the respect and loyal following of a number of students, who in turn worked to spread and develop their master's intellectual heritage. The Rabbinic tradition, with all its various sages, methodologies, and legal determinations, collectively represented Jewish law. Likewise, the Shari'a contained a wide range of ethical and moral principles, legal methodologies, and many conflicting and competing judgments. This rich and diverse matrix of opinions and judgments was collectively considered to be God's law.

In fact, to help visualize the phenomenon that I am describing, perhaps I should mention my own personal library on Islamic law. It contains about fifty thousand titles, the vast majority of which were written before the sixteenth century and as early as the ninth century. The books in this library represent a variety of approaches, schools of thought, and opinions written over the course of several centuries. Many of the titles are multivolume—in fact, some titles contain as many as fifty volumes in print. As I repeatedly remind my students, the fifty thousand titles do not simply present the same ideas and doctrines over and over again. Rather, each book is unique and special in terms of the ideas and doctrines presented. Legally speaking, the diversity reflected in these books could make a world of difference in terms of results: some jurists, for instance, barred women from serving as judges while others allowed it; many jurists banned women from leading prayer while a few permitted it. But as much diversity and richness that is contained in my library as it stands, there are hundreds (if not thousands) of other texts that I dream of acquiring someday, because there are yet many other opinions and views that I am eager to learn. Unfortunately, many of these texts are not published and remain in manuscript form. Nevertheless, all these books together, those I have acquired and those I dream of acquiring, the published and unpublished, collectively represent what we call the Shari'a.

The Shari'a—as a symbol to the Divine path and as the representative of the collective effort of Muslims at understanding what God wants from human beings—functioned like the symbolic glue that held the diverse Muslim nation together, despite its many different ethnicities, nationalities, and political entities. Shari'a became a symbol of unity and commonality for Muslims around the world, and jurists were the Shari'a's guardians and protectors. Throughout the classical period, the Islamic Empire became divided into many principalities and kingdoms ruled by different emirs, sultans, or caliphs that at times were in military conflict with each other. But the Shari'a remained the transcendent symbol of unity, and the jurists, as its articulators and protectors, stayed above the petty political and military conflicts and struggles for power. As such, the jurists, although belonging to a variety of schools of thought, provided the quintessential source of religious authority in the Muslim world.

This whole complex edifice that supplied religious authority in Islam started to crumble with the entry of Western colonialism in the eighteenth century. Domestic elements not related to colonialism, such as inefficient taxation systems and poorly organized militaries, had already started the process of deterioration well before the eighteenth century, but those elements would likely have self-corrected had it not been for the sharp blow that colonialism dealt to the institutions of Shari'a after repeated military defeats of Ottoman and other Muslim forces across the Islamic world. Slowly but surely, the jurists lost their privileged position in society; and with the deterioration in their status, the place of Shari'a in Muslim society was seriously compromised as well.

Colonialism, under the auspices of modernization, generated new elites of Western-educated secular professionals. Under the guise of reform, Shari'a law was replaced with Western-based legal systems, and with that shift emerged a class of lawyers trained in Western-styled law schools. Nevertheless, the real damage to the status of jurists and the place of Shari'a was done by native rulers installed by colonial powers in the postcolonial period. Especially in the 1950s and 1960s, many of the rulers of Muslim countries were military men, trained in secular armies organized along Western military doctrines; in short, they were, for the most part, Western-educated, secular, and nationalistic. The impact of this was nothing short of devastating. The religious endowments that funded the Shari'a schools were nationalized and became state-owned property. In most countries the role of Shari'a was severely narrowed down and replaced with Western-based secular legal systems. Many of the Shari'a schools were closed down, and today most of them function as poorly preserved tourist attractions. Shari'a schools, such as the Azhar in Egypt, became state-owned schools in which the state appointed and fired the faculty.

With these changes, career opportunities for those trained in the Shari'a schools became severely limited. Increasingly, jurists were perceived as state functionaries who were entirely controlled and directed by the state. But there was another development that has escaped the attention of many contemporary scholars. The curricula of the Shari'a schools were carefully redefined by the state, and the training of the students enrolled in these schools was completely overhauled in order to limit the jurists' ability to provide intellectual leadership to society. The *'ulama* (jurists) were trained to perform limited functions in society such as leading prayers in mosques, delivering Friday sermons, and at most, serving as judges in personal law courts. In order to limit the jurists' social and political functions, the state followed the dual policy of enforcing poor educational standards and paying low wages. In most Muslim countries the state aspired to be the gatekeeper controlling the access of the *'ulama* to the Islamic intellectual heritage by eliminating certain chairs, banning particular subjects or books, and firing jurists who stepped out of line or defied the state in any way. In addition, by lowering the educational standards and limiting the earning potential of the jurists, the state ensured that the religious schools only attracted the least able and bright students. The material taught in the religious schools no longer included studying jurisprudential theory, legal maxims, legal precedents, hermeneutics, rhetoric, procedural theory, or any of the kind of subjects normally encountered in schools of law. As a result, those graduating from these schools were no longer jurists or legal experts in any sense. Effectively, the *'ulama* became more like Western-styled ministers, who functioned at the margins of society as religious advisers without being able to influence social or political policy in any meaningful way. After most Muslim countries adopted Western-based legal systems, the state took away the power of defining and enforcing the law from the jurists and gave it to lawyers educated in Western-styled secular law schools.[3]

This process left a vacuum in religious authority in modern Islam. The disintegration of the traditional institutions of Islamic learning and authority meant a descent into a condition of virtual anarchy in regard to the mechanisms of defining Islamic authenticity. In the nineteenth and early twentieth centuries, noticing that Shari'a law was losing its prominence in society, a number of jurists, including Rifa'a al-Tahtawi (d. 1873), Muhammad 'Abduh (d. 1905), Rashid Rida (d. 1935), 'Abd al-Rahman al-Kawakibi (d. 1902), Jamal al-Din al-Afghani (d. 1897), 'Ali Jalal al-San'ani (d. 1810), Muhammad al-Shawkani (d. 1834), Mustafa al-Maraghi (d. 1945), and Muhammad Iqbal (d. 1938), attempted to stem the disaster by promoting liberal programs for Shari'a reform. These thinkers tried to reinterpret Islamic law in order to make it more responsive to modern challenges, such as women's rights, civil and human rights, democratic governance, and economic equity.[4]

Although their intellectual efforts were formidable, it is difficult to assess the exact impact of these liberal reformers on the history of Islam. Institutionally, the political developments of the time pushed their reforms to the side, and rendered them marginal. The reformers, for the most part, were scholars and jurists who did not lead mass movements. The vacuum in religious authority that they were working to address was quickly filled by popular movements led by men who had neither the training nor the education of the liberal jurists. Examining their impact in the short term, one would be tempted to conclude that the liberal reformers did not make much of a

difference in the Muslim world. However, I think such a conclusion would be too hasty. The original liberal reformers inspired others, such as 'Abd al-Majid Salim (d. 1954),
Mahmud Shaltut (d. 1963), Muhammad al-Ghazali (d. 1996),
Muhammad 'Umara, Subhi al-Mahmassani, 'Abd al-Razzaq
al-Sanhuri (d. 1971), Salim al-'Awa, Ahmad Hasan (d. 1958),
Fazlur Rahman (d. 1988), and others, who have built upon
the efforts of their predecessors in every decade since the early
twentieth century. The reformers have had a significant impact
upon moderate trends in contemporary Islam. For instance,
some of the ideas that raised enormous controversy when
originally proposed are now taken for granted by moderate
Muslims. While the liberal reformers did not fill the vacuum
of authority created in the postcolonial age, their ideas have
inspired and shaped the thought of what I call moderate
Islam. Today, it is the moderates who stand against the puritans aspiring to fill the vacuum of authority plaguing contemporary Islam.[5]

THE NATURE OF THE VACUUM

In 1933, the prominent jurist Yusuf al-Dijjawi (d. 1365/1946)[6]
decried with great chagrin that various puritan orientations
were deprecating the Islamic tradition by enabling people with
a very limited education in Islamic jurisprudence to become
self-proclaimed experts in Shari'a.[7] The fears of al-Dijjawi
were not only well founded, but things were to become much
worse than he could have ever imagined. The vacuum in authority meant not so much that *no one* could authoritatively
speak for Islam, but that virtually *every* Muslim with a modest
knowledge of the Qur'an and the traditions of the Prophet
was suddenly considered qualified to speak for the Islamic tra-

dition and Shari'a law—even Muslims unfamiliar with the precedents and accomplishments of past generations. Often these self-proclaimed experts were engineers, medical doctors, and physical scientists. In fact, the leaders of most Islamic movements, such as the Muslim Brotherhood and al-Qa'ida, have been engineers or medical doctors.

As these self-proclaimed and self-taught "jurists" reduced the Islamic heritage to the least common denominator, Islamic intellectual culture witnessed an unprecedented level of deterioration. The sad reality is that Islamic law and theology in the contemporary age were reduced to the extracurricular hobby of pamphlet readers and writers. Marginalized and displaced, Islamic law was now a field ripe for pietistic fictions and crass generalizations, rather than a technical discipline of complex interpretive practices and sophisticated methodologies of social and textual analysis.

To bring the problem closer to mind, imagine Rabbinic law being suddenly usurped by Jewish engineers and medical doctors. Soon nothing would remain of the Rabbinic tradition except unsystematic anecdotes and meditative speculations. Regardless of how interesting the collective outcome might be, the Rabbinic tradition, as a cohesive legacy, would be gone.

The role played in Islam by self-proclaimed experts is partly explained by the paradoxical nature of Shari'a itself. As noted earlier, Shari'a is, on the one hand, the sum total of technical legal methodologies, precedents, and decisions; it is also, on the other hand, a powerful symbol of the Islamic identity. For the trained jurist, Shari'a is a legal system full of complex processes and technical jargon, but for the average Muslim, Shari'a is a symbol for Islamic authenticity and legitimacy. Throughout Islamic history, the layperson (who in all likelihood knew very little of the technicalities of Shari'a) revered Shari'a as a sacred bridge to the Almighty God. For example, in a well-known passage, the famous Muslim jurist Ibn al-Qayyim (d. 751/1350–1) conveys a sense of the reverence and adoration with which the Shari'a was held in Islamic history. He states:

> The Sharia is God's justice among His servants, and His mercy among his creatures. It is God's shadow on this earth. It is His wisdom which leads to Him in the most exact way and the most exact affirmation of the truthfulness of His Prophet. It is His light which enlightens the seekers and His guidance for the rightly guided. It is the absolute cure for all ills and the straight path which if followed will lead to righteousness.... It is life and nutrition, the medicine, the light, the cure and the safeguard. Every good in this life is derived from it and achieved through it, and every deficiency in existence results from its dissipation. If it had not been for the fact that some of its rules remain [in this world,] this world would become corrupted and the universe would be dissipated.... If God would wish to destroy the world and dissolve existence, He would void whatever remains of its injunctions. For the Sharia which was sent to His Prophet ... is the pillar of existence and the key to success in this world and the Hereafter.[8]

In this passage, Ibn al-Qayyim is speaking of Shari'a not as a technical legal system, but as a symbol, which despite its remarkable diversity and pluralism represents the unified Muslim identity. Because of Shari'a's symbolic role and its ability to appeal to and mobilize popular Muslim sentiment, activists and the leaders of puritan movements have found it necessary to exploit Shari'a in order to win significant popular support.

In fact, in the 1970s various governments, such as those of Egypt, Jordan, Pakistan, Malaysia, Indonesia, and Sudan, were complicit in supporting various Muslim movements in order to counter the spread of Marxist and leftist organizations. These governments also hoped to bolster their own power base by appearing to support Islamic movements that raised the banner of Shari'a and called upon Muslims to rally around it. However, this honeymoon period between secular governments and puritan movements was short-lived because these governments soon discovered that puritan movements posed a serious threat to the stability of secular governments. For the many despotic Muslim states, the 1979 Iranian Revolution, in particular, came as a rude awakening that drove home the terrifying realization of the power of Shari'a to mobilize the masses and overthrow powerful secular governments. Moreover, the 1981 assassination of Egypt's President Anwar Sadat by a puritan group only added to the apprehension and animosity of the various despotic governments against the puritan movements.

By the early 1980s, in an effort to get rid of the puritan danger, many governments in the Muslim world replaced the short-lived honeymoon with vicious repression. Political repression, however, only succeeded in further radicalizing these puritan movements. It also generated considerable broad-based sympathy for the puritans, who were seen as "victims" of injustice and barbaric cruelty. In the 1970s and early 1980s, most Muslims sympathized with puritan movements as a statement of protest against the repression of the corrupt and despotic governments in power, but they did not necessarily agree with or approve of the puritan interpretation of Islam.

But other than political repression, there were other historical factors that led up to the puritans' exploitation of Shari'a as a powerful symbol of legitimacy in an effort to fill the vacuum of religious authority plaguing contemporary Islam.

In the 1960s and 1970s the Muslim world, especially the Middle East, was flooded by nationalistic ideologies and anti-colonial movements. Ideologies of Arab nationalism and pan-Arabism were staunchly secular; Islam was seen as a hindrance to developmental progress and modernization. Because of the social power of Islam and its ability to mobilize the masses, secular nationalist and pan-Arabist states attempted to strictly regulate religion and then use it to lend support to their cause. For example, Egypt's President Gamal 'Abd al-Nasser tried to do this by making the once prestigious Azhar University entirely dependent on the government, and then had it lend support to all governmental policies (including Nasser's severe repression of Islamic groups such as the Muslim Brotherhood).[9] A more recent example of this phenomenon was when Saddam Hussein, the leader of the zealously secularist Ba'th party, put "God Is Great" on the Iraqi flag and plunged into speeches about the duty of jihad in a failed effort to get Iraqis to fight to defend his regime.

As in the case of Saddam, the effort in the 1950s and 1960s to exploit religion in a shamelessly opportunistic fashion lacked credibility, and only succeeded in exacerbating the crisis in religious authority felt around the Muslim world. The 1967 war, in which Israel defeated several Arab countries, rubbed salt in the wound by underscoring the collective weakness of Muslim countries. The 1967 war also severely undercut the credibility of Arab nationalist and pan-Arabist ideologies. But the loss of Jerusalem to Israel was a blow not just to Arab countries, but to Muslims around the world. This blow to Muslim sentiment had deep historical roots; for instance, in 1187 when Saladin reconquered Jerusalem from the Franks, the Qadi of Damascus stood in the Aqsa Mosque and praised "Saladin by whose deeds the dignity of Islam was restored." So with the loss of the Aqsa Mosque to Israel, many Muslims felt that Islam had lost its former glory, and some even felt that Islam was in danger. The military defeats and resulting devastation to the national pride of many Muslim countries augmented the sense of frustration with prevailing political orders and also made the crisis in religious legitimacy much more acute. After the loss of Jerusalem, and the spread of the sense that secular governments had neither developed their nations nor restored to Muslims their lost sense of pride, the 1970s and 1980s witnessed what some scholars have described as the Islamic revival or the return to Islam. However, the Islamic revival consisted of the emergence of mass movements, which were often led by self-proclaimed experts in Shari'a who took advantage of the existing vacuum in religious authority. In response to the severe blows to the national pride of Muslims, these self-proclaimed experts were not interested in furthering the integrity or development of Islamic law or thought. Increasingly, their central interest became to augment the Islamic tradition's mass appeal by transforming it into a vehicle for displays of power symbolisms. The objective of these power symbolisms was to overcome the pervasive sense of powerlessness and to restore the pride of Muslims by clinging on to Islam as a symbol of resistance and defiance. Furthermore, these power symbolisms became a means of expressing resistance to Western hegemony in the contemporary age, as well as a means of voicing national aspirations for political, social, and cultural independence throughout the Muslim world.

This meant placing the Islamic tradition at the service of political objectives and nationalistic causes, which had two further effects. First, as the Islamic intellectual heritage was persistently made to support shifting and temperamental political causes, the Islamic intellectual tradition and Islamic law suffered increasing degradation and deconstruction. Second, to the non-Muslim world, Islam became wedded to certain political causes, so that it became difficult for Westerners to think about Islam without reference to these political causes.

The most obvious example of this is the Israeli/Palestinian conflict so that, for instance, many people in the West are unable to think of Islam except in terms of how Islam affects that conflict. I often encounter this problem in teaching Islamic law. Many of my students enroll in the class thinking that a course on Islamic jurisprudence will inevitably focus on the Israeli/Palestinian conflict. When I announce that alas the course will not address this conflict at all, a considerable number of students politely withdraw from the course. Another rather typical example: Yale Law School organizes an impressive annual international symposium on Islamic law; and for as long as I have been involved with this symposium, the whole conference has been spent discussing the Arab/Israeli conflict.

Leaving aside the unfortunate but understandable confusion about the relationship of Islam to political issues and causes, as far as Islamic thought was concerned, the highly impoverished intellectual climate was ripe for exploitation by various "evangelical" mass movements, two of which were fated to become particularly influential: the *Salafiyya* (Salafis) and the Saudi Arabia–based *Wahhabiyya* (Wahhabis). It bears emphasis that these two movements were not the only ones to find the impoverished intellectual climate suitable for growth and expansion—indeed, there were many such mass movements around the Muslim world that contributed to the insufferably chaotic conditions plaguing the world of Islam. At the same time, in my view, by the 1980s and afterward there is no doubt that the Salafis and Wahhabis had become the most influential puritan movements throughout most of the Muslim world, and also had the most far-reaching impact upon the contemporary theology of puritan Islam. Eventually, these two, more than any others, became the defining ideological forces for puritan Islam.

THREE

THE RISE OF
THE EARLY PURITANS

THE WAHHABI ORIGINS

The story of puritanical Islam should properly start with the Wahhabis. Even after 9/11 and the world's rude awakening to al-Qa'ida's violence, it is impossible to quantify the impact that the Wahhabis have had on modern Muslim thinking. It is unequivocal, however, that they have influenced every puritanical movement in the Muslim world in the contemporary age. Every single Islamic group that has achieved a degree of international infamy, such as the Taliban and al-Qa'ida, has been heavily influenced by Wahhabi thought.

The foundations of Wahhabi theology were set in place by the eighteenth-century evangelist Muhammad bin 'Abd al-Wahhab (d. 1206/1792). The main theme of 'Abd al-Wahhab was that Muslims had gone wrong by straying from the straight path of Islam, and only by returning to the one true religion could they regain God's pleasure and acceptance. With a puritanical zeal, 'Abd al-Wahhab sought to rid Islam of all the corruptions that he believed had crept into the religion; for 'Abd al-Wahhab these included mysticism, the doctrine of intercession, rationalism, and Shi'ism as well as many practices that he considered heretical innovations.

By 'Abd al-Wahhab's day, modernity had revolutionized human conceptions of reality around the world by introducing the destabilizing awareness of the relativity and subjectivity of all human knowledge, and also by introducing scientific empiricism. Modernism had also added considerably to the complexity of social and economic arrangements, which augmented the sense of alienation in traditional societies struggling to develop and modernize. In the Muslim world, different societies, cultures, and movements responded to the destabilizing impact of modernity in a variety of ways. Some, like the Kemalist movement in Turkey, for example, responded by attempting to Westernize and move as far away from Islam as possible. Others, while rejecting Western culture, attempted to reconcile Islam and modernism by emphasizing that scientific and rational thought is completely consistent with Islamic ethics. Wahhabism responded to modernity's destabilizing forces, and to its overpowering moral and social insecurities, by running for shelter. In this case, the shelter consisted of clinging on to particular Islamic texts for a sense of certitude and comfort. It is as if Wahhabism inoculated itself from the challenges and threats of modernity by forcing religious texts to provide definitive and incontestable answers to practically all individual and social issues.[1]

Wahhabism exhibited extreme hostility to all forms of intellectualism, mysticism, and sectarianism within Islam, considering all of these to be corrupt innovations that had crept into the religion due to un-Islamic influences. The Wahhabis tended to treat everything that did not come out of Arabia proper to be inherently suspect, and they believed that un-Islamic influences came from nations such as Persia, Turkey, and Greece. For example, Wahhabis believed that Sufism was a Persian import; belief in the intercession of saints and the veneration of gravesites, a Turkish import; and rationalism and philosophy, a Greek import.[2] These Wahhabi claims are overly simplistic and inaccurate, but there is no question that Wahhabis have always equated the austere cultural practices of Bedouin life with the one and only true Islam.[3]

According to the Wahhabis, it was imperative to return to a presumed pristine, simple, and straightforward Islam, which was believed to be entirely reclaimable by a literal implementation of the commands and precedents of the Prophet, and by a strict adherence to correct ritual practice. In effect, the Wahhabis treated religious texts—the Qur'an and the Sunna—as an instruction manual to a virtual utopia modeled after the Prophet's city-state in Medina. If only Muslims would return to adopting the correct beliefs and practices mandated by God, the reasons for their backwardness and for their collective sense of humiliation would disappear because Muslims would once again earn God's favor and support. Wahhabism also rejected the long-established Islamic practice of considering a variety of schools of thought to be equally orthodox, and attempted to narrow considerably the range of issues upon which Muslims could legitimately disagree. Orthodoxy was narrowly defined by the Wahhabis, according to whom the historical practice of accepting a plurality of opinions as equally legitimate and valid was one of the reasons for Muslim disunity and also one of the reasons for the backwardness and weakness of Muslims.

'Abd al-Wahhab and his followers often engaged in rhetorical tirades against prominent medieval and contemporaneous jurists, whom they considered heretical, and even ordered the execution or assassination of a large number of jurists with whom they disagreed.[4] In his writings, 'Abd al-Wahhab frequently referred to jurists as "devils" or "the spawn of Satan" (*shayatin* or *a'wan al-shayatin*), and therefore removed any psychological barrier to violating the memories or lives of distinguished scholars.[5] According to 'Abd al-Wahhab and his followers, the juristic tradition—with the exception of a few jurists, such as Ibn Taymiyya (d. 728/1328), whom they held in high esteem—was largely corrupt, and deference to the well-established schools of jurisprudential thought or to contemporaneous jurists was an act of heresy.[6] All jurists who were not strict literalists—or those who were suspected of using reason in legal interpretation or who had integrated rationalist methods of analysis into their interpretive approaches—were considered heretics. Among the medieval jurists that the Wahhabis explicitly condemned as *kuffar* (infidels) were prominent scholars such as Fakhr al-Din al-Razi (d. 606/1210). This is akin to Jews accusing Maimonides or Catholic Christians accusing Thomas Aquinas of being infidels because they relied on rationalist criteria in thinking about God's law. Furthermore, all Shi'is, without exception, and all jurists suspected of harboring Shi'i sympathies were also considered heretics. The significance of calling a Muslim a heretic was enormous: a heretic was to be treated as an apostate, and thus killing or executing him was considered lawful.[7]

'Abd al-Wahhab himself was fond of creating long lists of beliefs and acts which he considered hypocritical and the adoption or commission of which would immediately render a Muslim an unbeliever. For instance, 'Abd al-Wahhab contended that if a Muslim proclaimed that the consumption of bread or meat was unlawful, then such a Muslim had become an infidel, because it is clear that bread and meat are lawful in Islamic law. And as an infidel, such a Muslim could be killed.[8]

In his teachings, 'Abd al-Wahhab consistently emphasized that there was no middle of the road for a Muslim: either a Muslim was a true believer or not. And if a Muslim was not a true believer, according to his standards, 'Abd al-Wahhab had no qualms about declaring that Muslim an infidel and then treating him as such. If a Muslim explicitly or implicitly committed an act that betrayed the impurity of his belief in God or implicitly or explicitly "associated partners with God"[9]—an Islamic expression meaning to fail to believe that there is one and only one God who is immutable and eternal. To associate partners with God is to ascribe to God partners or to believe that God has co-equal partners—then that Muslim must be considered an infidel and killed. For 'Abd al-Wahhab, any indulgence in rationalism or frivolity—such as music, art, or nonreligious poetry—was indeed a form of associating partners with God serious enough to take a Muslim out of the fold of Islam.

'Abd al-Wahhab was rabidly hostile toward non-Muslims as well, insisting that a Muslim should adopt none of the customs of non-Muslims, and should not befriend such people either. It was entirely immaterial what a non-Muslim might think about Muslim practices, and it was equally immaterial whether non-Muslims were impressed by or approved of Muslim behavior. Importantly, 'Abd al-Wahhab saw as unbelievers not only Christians and Jews but also Muslims who, due to their beliefs or actions, had (in his estimate) become apostates.[10] In the balance of things, according to 'Abd al-Wahhab, apostate Muslims were *worse* than Christians and Jews because their heretical beliefs or actions were more damaging to the faith.[11]

Significantly, 'Abd al-Wahhab also insisted that it was a sign of spiritual weakness for Muslims to care for or be interested in non-Muslim beliefs or practices. Pursuant to a doctrine known as *al-wala' wa al-bara'* (literally, the doctrine of loyalty and disassociation), 'Abd al-Wahhab argued that it was imperative for Muslims not to befriend, ally themselves with, or imitate non-Muslims or heretical Muslims. Furthermore, this enmity and hostility of Muslims toward non-Muslims and heretical

Muslims had to be visible and unequivocal.[12] For example, it was forbidden for a Muslim to be the first to greet a non-Muslim; and even if a Muslim returned a greeting, a Muslim should never wish a non-Muslim peace. Likewise, Muslims could convey their condolences to non-Muslims, but they should never pray that God have mercy upon them or ask God to forgive their sins. Muslims were only allowed to say, "May God guide you to the right path" or "May God compensate you for your loss." If a Muslim violated any of these rules, he or she was to be treated as an apostate. The same dire consequences would follow if a Muslim referred to a non-Muslim as "brother" or "sister."

Moreover, Wahhabis prohibited the use of labels of respect intended to honor human beings, such as "master," "doctor," "mister," or "sir." 'Abd al-Wahhab argued that such prefixes were a form of associating partners with God; therefore, using them was enough to make a Muslim an infidel. More importantly, 'Abd al-Wahhab argued, the prefixes and labels constituted an imitation of Western unbelievers and were thus condemnable, because those who imitated unbelievers were themselves unbelievers. Similarly, partaking in celebrations, vacations, festivities, or any other social event originally invented by non-Muslims was sufficient to make a Muslim an infidel.[13]

'Abd al-Wahhab espoused a self-sufficient and closed system of belief that had no reason to engage or interact with any other, except from a position of dominance. This is especially important because 'Abd al-Wahhab's orientation did not materially differ from the approach adopted by later Muslim puritan groups concerning the irrelevance of universal moral values to the Islamic mission. This insularism and moral isolationism, clearly manifested in the writings of 'Abd al-Wahhab, was powerfully reproduced by ideologues of subsequent puritan movements. For instance, Sayyid Qutb, one of the most influential puritan ideologues, argued in the mid-twentieth century that the world, including the Muslim world, was living in *jahiliyya* (the darkness and ignorance associated with the pre-Islamic era). Like 'Abd al-Wahhab, Qutb espoused a closed system of intellectual isolationism and argued that Muslims ought not interact with non-Muslims except from a position of supremacy.[14]

The real irony is that at the heart of 'Abd al-Wahhab's zeal for Islamic purity was a pro-Arab ethnocentrism that was completely at odds with Islam's universal message. As in later puritan movements, there was a strong political and nationalistic cause to 'Abd al-Wahhab's thought—a cause that was promoted and concealed behind a veneer of religious language. 'Abd al-Wahhab's sworn enemies were not Christians or Jews but the Ottoman Turks. 'Abd al-Wahhab accused the Ottoman Turks of corrupting Islam, and he described them as the moral equivalent of the Mongols, who earlier had invaded Muslim territories and then converted to Islam. But like the Mongols, the Turks had converted to Islam in name only, as 'Abd al-Wahhab saw it. Indeed, according to him, the Ottoman Turks were the primary enemies of Islam because they were corrupting the religion from the inside while pretending to be sincere and true Muslims. 'Abd al-Wahhab described the Ottoman caliphate as *al-dawlah al-kufriyya* (a heretical nation) and claimed that supporting or allying oneself with the Ottomans was as grievous a sin as supporting or allying oneself with Christians or Jews.[15]

'Abd al-Wahhab was wrong about the Ottoman Turks: they were nothing like the Mongols that ravished the Muslim world in the twelfth century, massacring hundreds of thousands of people and destroying an untold number of Muslim manuscripts. The Ottomans had established one of the strongest caliphates and had been long-time defenders of the Islamic faith. Even before the Ottoman caliphate, the Turks had become an important ethnicity in the pluralist ethnic mosaic forming the Islamic Empire. It is true that in the late Ottoman period, the Ottomans had adopted an extremely inefficient and corrupt system of taxation based on special concessions and patronage, and at times they were very repressive and exploitative. But in their writings, 'Abd al-Wahhab and his followers do not protest these policies, and so their hostility to the Ottomans does not seem to have been motivated by a principled stand against Ottoman injustice. Rather, 'Abd al-Wahhab was, in part, reacting to the old ethnocentric belief that only Arabs can represent the one true and authentic Islam.[16]

But the other factor that explains 'Abd al-Wahhab's animosity toward the Ottomans was that he was responding to British efforts in the eighteenth century to destroy the Ottoman caliphate by igniting the fires of local ethnicities, including that of Arab nationalism.[17] Interestingly, unlike other nonsecular Arab nationalists, 'Abd al-Wahhab did not advocate the creation of an Arab caliphate instead of the Ottoman caliphate. But 'Abd al-Wahhab was not interested in political theory or political practice as much as he was interested in pure Arab culture, which in 'Abd al-Wahhab's mind was indistinguishable from true Islam. 'Abd al-Wahhab, however, did not realize or did not acknowledge that he was confusing the Arab culture—more precisely, the Bedouin culture of Arabia—and the universal precepts of Islam. Effectively, 'Abd al-Wahhab was declaring the particulars of Bedouin culture to be the one and only true Islam and then universalizing these particulars by making them obligatory upon all Muslims.

This all points to a fact that has been overlooked by many contemporary observers: Wahhabism in the eighteenth century was plagued by ideological inconsistencies that to this day have not been reconciled or resolved.[18] So, for instance, while condemning all cultural practices and insisting on strict submission to Islam, in reality Wahhabism was thoroughly a construct of its own culture—that is, the Bedouin culture of the Najd region of Arabia (part of modern-day Saudi Arabia).[19] While insisting that there was only one true Islam, in reality Wahhabism universalized its own culture and declared *it* to be the one true Islam. While consistently condemning non-Muslim influences and rejecting any form of cooperation with the West, in reality Wahhabis were incited and supported by English colonialists to rebel against the Ottomans, which effectively meant that Wahhabis sided with non-Muslim Englishmen against their Muslim Ottoman enemies. Moreover, while condemning all forms of nationalism as an evil Western invention, in reality Wahhabism was a pro-Arab nationalistic movement that rejected Turkish dominance over Arabs under the guise of defending the one true Islam. Fundamentally, while the Wahhabis of the eighteenth century took the culture of the Bedouins of Najd and universalized it into *the* Islam, the Wahhabis of today take the culture of Saudi Arabia and universalize it into the singularly true Islam.

Wahhabism's cultural dependency belies its claims to textual literalism. The fact that Wahhabism gives expression to a specific and narrow cultural context and understanding is not consistent with its claim that its convictions and laws are based on literal readings of Islamic texts. In fact, 'Abd al-Wahhab and his followers interpreted texts in a selective matter in order to bolster their preconceived notions on a variety of issues. This selective reading of the textual evidence was greatly facilitated by the fact that the Wahhabis had liberated themselves from a considerable part of the Islamic juristic heritage. Not having to contend with the interpretations of the past made it much easier to read Islamic sources in such a way as to support Wahhabi cultural understandings and biases. Legal precedents that did not support Wahhabi positions were simply ignored, and past generations of jurists who did not share 'Abd al-Wahhab's understandings of Islam were treated as heretics.

'Abd al-Wahhab argued, for example, that Muslims who engage in acts of *shirk* (heresy) must be fought and killed, and he interpreted precedents set by the first "Rightly Guided" caliph in Medina,[20] Abu Bakr (d. 13/634), in support of the argument that although people might hold themselves out as Muslims, they could, and should, be killed as hypocrites. 'Abd al-Wahhab claimed that Abu Bakr fought and killed many so-called hypocrites, despite the fact that they practiced the five pillars of Islam. Arguing that his followers were justified in killing their Muslim opponents, he contended that the Ottoman Turks, their allies, and all other heretical and hypocritical Muslims were in truth infidels deserving of the worst death.

'Abd al-Wahhab was also fond of citing a precedent in which Abu Bakr reportedly burned so-called hypocrites to death, and he used this purported precedent to argue that his supporters were justified in torturing their opponents.[21] There is no doubt that this precedent is apocryphal, and nearly all Muslim scholars dismiss it as an invention. 'Abd al-Wahhab's reliance on this bizarre historical report is very telling. It clearly demonstrates his willingness to select precedents from the Islamic tradition that support cruel and inhumane behavior— precedents that jurists and scholars of the past had already expended considerable effort challenging and deconstructing.

For instance, most scholars in the Islamic tradition who studied the purported Abu Bakr precedent concluded that the claim that Abu Bakr accused people of hypocrisy who upheld

the five pillars and fought them is without support or foundation. Furthermore, the use of fire against Muslim or non-
Muslim enemies is severely condemned in classical Islamic
law. Many classical scholars carefully documented that the report of Abu Bakr using fire against Muslim opponents was invented by Abu Bakr's enemies and reported by highly suspect
individuals.[22] Not only did classical scholars challenge the authenticity and historical veracity of these Abu Bakr incidents,
they also argued that precedents of cruelty were contrary to
the ethics of the Qur'an and the Prophet.

'Abd al-Wahhab ignored this considerable body of contra-
vening literature in his effort to justify killing and torturing
those he considered heretical Muslims, and his students em-
braced and legitimated these precedents of cruelty.[23] By dis-
carding and at times demonizing the classical heritage and its
interpretations, 'Abd al-Wahhab gained unfettered access to
the precedents of cruelty, unencumbered by the challenges
posed by past scholars. 'Abd al-Wahhab was able to reinject
these precedents of cruelty into the heart of Muslim theology
and law, thereby reinventing Islam on the basis of a new immorality.

The reason this is extremely significant is that Muslim extremists such as Bin Laden and Omar 'Abd al-Rahman followed in the footsteps of 'Abd al-Wahhab by relying on the
same exact precedents of cruelty as a means of justifying
killing innocent people. In fact, it is very disturbing that the
very precedents that 'Abd al-Wahhab defended were cited in
Web sites set up by groups that butchered hostages in Iraq. It
is not all that surprising that these extremists appear to have
been directly influenced by the writings of 'Abd al-Wahhab
and by his unabashed efforts to defend the credibility of historical reports that justified murder and torture.

Considering the dismissive attitude of the Wahhabis toward Islamic history and law and the whole classical tradition, it is not surprising that the movement came under severe criticism by a considerable number of contemporaneous scholars— most notably, 'Abd al-Wahhab's own brother, Sulayman, and reportedly, 'Abd al-Wahhab's father as well. Sulayman, Muhammad bin 'Abd al-Wahhab's brother, wrote a full treatise dedicated to criticizing the manners, education, and teachings of his puritanical brother. The *mufti* of the Hanbali in Mecca, Ibn Humaydi (d. 1295/1878), a man of considerable note and authority at the time, reported that Muhammad bin 'Abd al-Wahhab's father was upset with his son because Muhammad bin 'Abd al-Wahhab was not a good student of Islamic jurisprudence and was arrogantly defiant toward his teachers. In fact, the younger 'Abd al-Wahhab did not complete his Shari'a studies, and it is not clear whether he dropped out of law school or was expelled. Ibn Humaydi claimed that, fearing the wrath of his father, Muhammad bin 'Abd al-Wahhab did not dare to start preaching his puritan message until after his father's death.[24]

On the whole, the criticisms leveled against 'Abd al-Wahhab and his followers by their contemporaries were not that surprising. The Wahhabis were criticized for showing very little regard for Islamic history, historical monuments, shrines and relics, the Islamic intellectual tradition, or the sanctity of Muslim life.[25] 'Abd al-Wahhab's brother, as well as other critics, claimed that 'Abd al-Wahhab was an ill-educated, intolerant man who was ignorantly and arrogantly dismissive of any thoughts or individuals that disagreed with him.[26] Sulayman complained that except among the most extreme and fringe fanatical elements, his brother's views were without precedent in Islamic history. For instance, Sulayman asserted, the majority of the scholars of Islam refrained from accusing the ratio-

nalists and mystics of heresy, and instead debated them peace-
fully.[27]

'Abd al-Wahhab, according to his brother's treatise, did not
concern himself with reading or understanding the works of
the juristic predecessors. And yet, while 'Abd al-Wahhab was
dismissive toward the works of most jurists, he treated the
words of some, such as Hanbali jurist Ibn Taymiyya (d.
728/1328), as if they were Divinely revealed, not to be questioned or debated. But even then, 'Abd al-Wahhab was very
selective with the works of Ibn Taymiyya, citing only what he
liked and ignoring the rest. Rather tellingly, Ibn Humaydi, a
strong admirer of Ibn Taymiyya as well, repeated the same accusation against 'Abd al-Wahhab.[28]

Sulayman and other scholars noted the irony in the fact
that 'Abd al-Wahhab and his followers, while prohibiting
taqlid (imitating or following the precedents of jurists), ended
up affirming and even mandating it, but in a different form.
They prohibited the practice of *taqlid* as far as it related to jurists whom they did not like, but demanded that Muslims imitate Wahhabi thinking blindly and unthinkingly, a double
standard that Sulayman condemned. Effectively, Sulayman argued, the Wahhabis acted as if the only actual measure of
commitment to Islam was to follow and obey them, since if a
Muslim disagreed with them, they deemed that Muslim a
heretic by definition.[29] Indeed, the Wahhabis used to label
themselves *al-Muslimun* (the Muslims) or *al-Muwahidun* (the
monotheists), intimating that those who did not accept their
creed were neither Muslims nor monotheists.[30]

In short, Sulayman insisted that the Wahhabi methodology
was based on a profound sense of despotism, wherein the
whole of the Islamic intellectual tradition was dismissed
offhandedly and Muslims were given the choice of either accepting the idiosyncratic Wahhabi interpretations of Islam or

being declared *kuffar* (infidels) and killed. And indeed, during their conquest of Arabia in the eighteenth century, every time the Wahhabis conquered a town or city they would demand that the Muslim inhabitants repeat the testament of faith, but this time, the inhabitants must proclaim the testament while vowing to adhere to Wahhabi beliefs and practices. Those inhabitants who would not declare their commitment to Islam as it was understood and interpreted by the Wahhabis were presumed to be infidels and swiftly put to the sword.[31] Historical sources describe horrendous massacres committed by Wahhabi forces in the eighteenth century all across Arabia.[32]

Sulayman argued in his treatise that the Wahhabis in effect pretended as if they alone, after many centuries of Islamic history, had discovered the truth about Islam and considered themselves infallible. Sulayman noted that from a theological point of view, this claim was very dangerous. It was impossible for Muslims to have been deluded and mistaken in understanding and practicing their religion for so many centuries and then to discover the truth only after Muhammad bin 'Abd al-Wahhab was born. Sulayman pointed out that the implications of such a claim were nothing short of disastrous for the Muslim faith.[33] He was careful to note that the act of declaring Muslims to be infidels was a grave sin in Islam, and even Ibn Taymiyya, the jurist 'Abd al-Wahhab was so fond of, prohibited the practice of *takfir* (branding Muslims as infidels).[34] In order to prove his point, Sulayman concluded his treatise by quoting fifty-two traditions, attributed to the Prophet and some to the Companions of the Prophet, on the sin of accusing a Muslim of being an unbeliever or heretic.[35]

I have focused here on Sulayman's treatise in which he criticized his brother and the Wahhabi movement because of the historical importance of that text. Not surprisingly, Sulayman's treatise is banned by Saudi Arabia, and there has been considerable effort expended in that country and elsewhere to bury that text. Presently, this important work is not well known in the Muslim world and is very difficult to find. I was forced to go to considerable lengths to locate it even in Egypt. But it presents a powerful contextual picture of the birth of the puritan movement that would later play such an important role in the twentieth century and beyond. The Wahhabi movement would have a powerful impact upon defining the creed and theology of all subsequent puritan movements, but Sulayman's text demonstrates that many of the beliefs and practices of Wahhabism were considered an aberration and a corruption of mainstream Islam.[36] Puritan Islam was a deviance that was thought of as marginal to the mainstream, and several jurists, including Sulayman, believed that it would be a short-lived phenomenon.

Other jurists also expressed grave concerns about the potential danger that Wahhabism posed to the integrity of Islamic ethics. Sulayman bin Suhaym (d. 1175/1761), a prominent Hanbali jurist from Najd and a former supporter of 'Abd al-Wahhab, wrote what was at the time an influential treatise appealing to Muslim jurists to take the Wahhabi threat seriously and to take active measures to counter it.[37] Several mainstream jurists writing during this period, such as the Hanafi jurist Ibn 'Abidin (d. 1253/1837) and the Maliki jurist al-Sawi (d. 1241/1825), described the Wahhabis as a fanatic fringe group, and because of the Wahhabi's bloody practices, labeled them the "modern-day Khawarij of Islam."[38] The Khawarij was a violent and fanatical sect that appeared in Arabia in early Islam but was eventually weakened and marginalized. Like the Wahhabis, the Khawarij considered all Muslims except themselves to be infidels; and like the Wahhabis, they also massacred untold numbers of Muslims in Arabia. The Khawarij even assassinated 'Ali, who was the

Prophet's revered cousin and the fourth caliph. Eventually, because of the unrelenting hostility and criticism of the classical jurists and the sustained campaigns by various Muslim states, the Khawarij was forced to reform or perish. Today, the only offshoot of the original Khawarij is a sect known as the Ibadiyya, which survives in Oman and parts of Algeria. The law and theology of the Ibadiyya is nothing like that of their fanatic ancestors; in fact, the Ibadiyya were pressured into moderating their views and becoming much closer to the Muslim mainstream. Unfortunately, however, the prediction of many jurists that the Wahhabis would inevitably end up sharing the fate of the Khawarij turned out to be flatly wrong.

The simplicity, decisiveness, and absolutism of the religious thought of 'Abd al-Wahhab made it attractive to the desert tribes, especially in the area of Najd. At the time, Najd was the most tribal and least developed and cosmopolitan area of the Saudi state. Ultimately, however, 'Abd al-Wahhab's ideas were too radical and extreme to have widespread influence on the Arab world, let alone the entire Muslim world. Contemporary scholars have already established the relative marginality of Wahhabi extremist thought in the eighteenth and nineteenth centuries, and have shown that the thought of moderate revivalists such as Muhammad al-Shawkani (d. 1250/1834) and Ali Jalal al-San'ani (d. 1225/1810) were quite dissimilar to Wahhabi thinking, and far more influential at that time.[39]

It is quite likely that 'Abd al-Wahhab's ideas would not have spread even in Arabia had it not been for the fact that in the late eighteenth century the Al Sa'ud family united itself with the Wahhabi movement and rebelled against Ottoman rule in Arabia. Armed with religious zeal and a strong sense of Arab nationalism, the rebellion was considerable, at one point reaching as far as Damascus in the north and Oman in the south. Egyptian forces under the leadership of Muhammad Ali in 1818, after several failed expeditions, quashed the rebellion, and Wahhabism, like other extremist movements in Islamic history, seemed to be on its way to extinction.[40] But that was not to be.

The Al Sa'ud/Wahhabi alliance from 1745 to 1818 is known as the first Saudi state, which ended when the Egyptian and Turkish forces destroyed the city of Dhar'iyya, the hometown of the first Saudi kingdom, and massacred its inhabitants. If anything, this massacre stayed in the Wahhabi memory and further ignited their zeal by becoming a symbol of their suffering and sacrifices.

Wahhabi ideology was resuscitated once again in the early twentieth century under the leadership of 'Abd al-'Aziz bin Al Sa'ud (r. 1319–73/1902–53), the founder of the modern Saudi state, who adopted the puritanical theology of the Wahhabis and allied himself with the tribes of Najd, thereby establishing the nascent beginnings of what would become Saudi Arabia. The first Wahhabi rebellions in Arabia in the eighteenth century aimed to overthrow Ottoman control and enforce 'Abd al-Wahhab's puritanical brand of Islam upon as much of the Arab-speaking world as possible. The Wahhabis also sought to control Mecca and Medina, and by doing so, gain a huge symbolic victory by controlling the spiritual center of the Muslim world.[41]

Although the rebellions of the eighteenth century were quashed, the rebellions of the late nineteenth and early twentieth centuries presented a very different situation. From the seventeenth to the early twentieth centuries, Arabia was a very tribal society with a large number of prominent families vying for dominance over all others. But particularly the Hijaz area of Arabia, as opposed to the Najd area, was very culturally diverse, with all types of customs and theological orientations

forming a very complex mosaic of beliefs and practices. Even
jurisprudentially, in Mecca and Medina, which are in the
Hijaz, there were Shafi'i, Hanafi, Maliki, and Hanbali schools
of law and judges. There were also Sufi orders and Shi'i jurists, leave alone a sizeable Shi'i population in different parts
of the Hijaz. The annual pilgrimage to Mecca looked like a
virtual festival of highly diverse practices and rituals mirroring
the rich diversity of the Muslim world itself, all of which were
accommodated and tolerated by the Ottoman authorities. This
diversity of beliefs, theologies, rituals, and practices was
anathema to the Wahhabis, and one of their stated goals was
to get all pilgrims to the holy sites to abide by a single version
of rituals, which they considered to be the only legitimate
practice of the faith.

A trinity was formed that would forever change the face of
Arabia, and perhaps the Muslim world. This trinity consisted
of the Al Sa'ud family, the Wahhabis, and the British. The Al
Sa'ud family sought to defeat all other contenders and rule
over Arabia; the Wahhabis sought to enforce their puritanical
brand of Islam on all of Arabia; Britain wanted a strong central government in Arabia that would serve British interests by
granting exclusive oil-mining concessions to British compa-
nies, and they also wanted to further weaken the Ottoman
Empire by wrestling Mecca and Medina away from its control. In order to achieve their objectives, rather opportunistically, the British did not put all their eggs in one basket, and
initially supported several strong families simultaneously, like
the Rashidis, the Hashimis, the Banu Khalids, and the Al
Sa'uds, all of whom were fighting for dominance over Arabia.[42]

The relationship between the Al Sa'uds and the Wahhabis
dated back to 1744, when Muhammad Ibn Sa'ud (d. 1762),
the ruler of al-Dir'iyya, a small town in Najd, gave 'Abd al-

Wahhab sanctuary and a territorial base when the jurists of Najd were up in arms against 'Abd al-Wahhab because of his fanatic and unprecedented actions. By allying themselves with the Wahhabis, the Al Sa'ud family gained a zealous fighting force and an ideology that gave them a clear advantage over other families contending for British favor and power. The Al Sa'uds provided the Wahhabis with financial support and, through their British connections, much-needed arms. In turn, after conquering territories and installing the Al Sa'uds as the legitimate political rulers, the Wahhabis expected the Al Sa'ud family to give them free rein over all religious affairs. With this winning combination, in the twentieth century the Al Sa'uds eventually were able to get the full attention of the British, who put their full weight behind the Al Sa'ud family as the legitimate rulers of what would become Saudi Arabia.[43] Although the alliance between the Al Sa'uds and the British, a Muslim/non-Muslim alliance, was not consistent with Wahhabi teachings, it is important to recognize that according to the Al Sa'uds and Wahhabis, their alliance was not motivated by convenience or practical necessity but by a genuine shared ideological motivation and sincere conviction. Pursuant to this view, the Al Sa'uds converted to Wahhabism, and the two forces formed an (un)holy union that continues to this day. Whether out of convenience or conviction, the bond between the Al Sa'uds and the Wahhabis became powerful.[44] In fact, the Wahhabis destroyed all the rich diversity that once existed in the region of Hijaz, especially in Mecca, Medina, and Jeddah, and they forced all of Arabia to submit to the rule of Al Sa'ud.[45]

Importantly, throughout the various stages that led to the creation of the Kingdom of Saudi Arabia in 1932—the failed so-called first Saudi state (1745–1818), the failed second state (roughly from 1824 to 1891), or the third, successful state (commencing in 1902 and continuing until 1932)—the Al Sa'ud family and the Wahhabis had formed a considerable legacy of intolerance, hate, and fanaticism, resulting in atrocities, massacres, and cruelty. This inhumane legacy became part of the past that would forever haunt the Saudi state and would also shape the ethical sensibilities of the type of Islam that the Wahhabis preached and spread around the Muslim world. The list of Saudi-Wahhabi sins of intolerance and cruelty is long indeed. For example, the various Wahhabi rebellions in the nineteenth and twentieth centuries were very bloody, as the Wahhabis indiscriminately slaughtered Muslims, especially those belonging to Sufi orders and the Shi'i sect. In 1802, for example, the Wahhabi forces massacred the Shi'i inhabitants of Karbala,[46] and in 1803, 1804, and 1806, the Wahhabis executed a large number of Sunnis in Mecca and Medina, whom they considered for one reason or another heretical.[47] The number of those executed or massacred by the Saudi-Wahhabi alliance has never been counted, but from historical accounts it is clear that it is in the tens of thousands if not more. In the course of the second conquest of the Arabian Peninsula, for instance, acting under orders from Ibn Sa'ud, the Wahhabis carried out 40,000 public executions and 350,000 amputations.[48]

In 1912, King 'Abd al-'Aziz, from the Al Sa'ud family, formed a fighting force known as the Ikhwan, constituted of Najdi religious zealots strongly committed to the thought of 'Abd al-Wahhab. The Ikhwan fighting force was organized with the explicit purpose of overtaking Arabia, quashing all competing contenders for power, and establishing an Islamic state founded on the religious teachings of 'Abd al-Wahhab. The Ikhwan played an effective role in establishing and expanding the king's control, but they eventually became dissatisfied with what they saw as his liberalism and willingness to cooperate with non-Muslims—the British, in this case. In reality, 'Abd al-'Aziz was forced to learn a lesson that would painfully repeat itself decades later with the Saudi government's experience with al-Qa'ida: the rage of fanaticism cannot be easily controlled or manipulated by any government. 'Abd al-'Aziz had given the Ikhwan a free hand in massacring Muslims within Arabia, especially in Hijaz and Yemen. But rooted in extremism, the Ikhwan were unhappy with 'Abd al-'Aziz's directives allowing for the use of modern inventions such as the telegraph, the telegram, automobiles, and airplanes in territories under Saudi control. Even worse, the Ikhwan started making excursions and committing massacres in Iraq and in territories that are today a part of Jordan. They insisted on their right to continue to spread Wahhabism without regard to territorial borders invented by the British. At the time, these territories were under British occupation, and the massacres committed were deeply embarrassing to the British government because they occurred against populations that the British were legally obligated to protect. Furthermore, during their raids the Ikhwan ended up clashing with and killing British soldiers as well. In 1915, King 'Abd al-'Aziz had signed a treaty of "friendship and cooperation" with the British, and he was receiving an extremely generous monthly annuity from the British government that he could ill afford to lose.

The Ikhwan also got into the habit of attacking and punishing pilgrims coming from all over the Muslim world to Mecca for engaging in what according to the Wahhabis were un-Islamic rituals. In many instances, the Ikhwan flogged and even executed pilgrims for performing rituals that violated the Wahhabi understanding of Islamic law, although according to other schools of thought those rituals were considered perfectly valid. Not surprisingly, since 'Abd al-'Aziz was working hard to forge political alliances that would empower him against his enemies in Arabia, the conduct of Ikhwan caused a diplomatic crisis not only with Britain but also with a number of Muslim states.

King 'Abd al-'Aziz tried to prevent the Ikhwan from raiding the territories under British control, and also tried to restrain the Ikhwan from interfering with pilgrims, but the Ikhwan were offended by what they saw as his willingness to compromise with heretical people and their evil practices. As a result, the Ikhwan rebelled against the king in 1929, but with the assistance of the British, who used their airpower to massacre them, 'Abd al-'Aziz crushed and disbanded the forces of the Ikhwan.[49] The British duly rewarded their loyal subject by increasing King 'Abd al-'Aziz's annuity and conferred upon him a knighthood in 1935[50] (he was made a knight of the Order of the Bath). Although the tribal organization of the Ikhwan had been disbanded, this did not mean that the Sa'ud family had abandoned Wahhabism. That was practically impossible. Wahhabism and the Al Sa'uds had created a codependent relationship in which one could not exist without the other. Most of the time, the Wahhabis served the state or those in power as much as the state or those in power served the Wahhabis.

In the areas that fell under their control, the Wahhabis introduced practices that considerably expanded the intrusive powers of the state into the enforcer of a narrowly defined code of behavior, which, in their view, was the only correct Islam. The relationship between the Al Sa'ud family and the Wahhabis went well beyond a pragmatic relationship of mutual support. Rather, the Saudis and Wahhabis invented a model for how an Islamic state ought to behave in the modern world. According to this model, which became very influential among puritanical Muslims, the newly intrusive powers of the state severely restricted personal liberty and forced its unwilling subjects to abide by a very specific code of conduct, all in the name of enforcing God's law. Instead of the state's embracing and tolerating a wide set of diverse religious and cultural practices, as used to exist in Ottoman Mecca and Medina, for instance, the state abolished all appearances of religious pluralism and enforced a strict orthodoxy. In the Saudi model, the state created and empowered what is in effect a religious police force, and this force played the dual role of enforcing the strict orthodoxy sanctioned by the state and destroying all expressions of religious diversity or dissent. Invariably, Wahhabi conduct was committed in the name of enforcing God's law, but in reality it enforced a very narrow and idiosyncratic view of Islamic law that was strongly at odds with then-prevailing Muslim beliefs and practices. For instance, the Wahhabis regularly flogged the residents of territories under their control for listening to music, shaving their beards, wearing silk or gold (this applied to men only), smoking, playing backgammon, chess, or cards, or failing to observe strict rules of sex segregation; and they destroyed all the shrines and most of the Muslim historical monuments found in Arabia.[51]

The Wahhabi practice of destroying the tombstones of the Prophet's family and his esteemed Companions caused an enormous amount of trauma and controversy around the Muslim world.[52] Like the Taliban's infamous destruction of the Buddha statues in Afghanistan, the destruction of tombstones of the Prophet's family and Companions in Mecca, Medina, and Jubila was unprecedented in Islamic history. These tombstones were preserved and revered by Muslims for well over a thousand years and some of the gravesites were turned into shrines, which were visited by millions of Muslims through the centuries.[53] In another unprecedented action that offended the sensibilities of many Muslims, Muhammad bin 'Abd al-Wahhab cut down a tree (known as Shajarat al-Dhib) in an area known as Wadi Hanifa near Jubila—a tree that was more than a thousand years old and that was of great historical significance.[54] This wanton destruction of historical sites was all done in the name of protecting Islam from the threat of re-adopting pagan practices.

They also introduced the first reported precedent of taking roll call at prayers: they prepared lists of the inhabitants of a city and called off the names during the five daily prayers in the mosque, and anyone absent without a sufficient excuse was flogged.[55]

Being the caretakers of Mecca and Medina, the Wahhabis were uniquely positioned to enforce their version of orthodoxy upon Muslim pilgrims from around the world. As an indication of the limited popularity of the Wahhabi creed at that stage of its development, the uncompromisingly austere practices of the Wahhabis during pilgrimage led to several clashes with pilgrims coming from Africa and Southeast Asia. In 1926, for example, the Wahhabi hostility to all forms of musical instruments led to a crisis between Egypt and Saudi Arabia when Egyptian soldiers carrying the ceremonial palanquin to the sound of bugles during pilgrimage were attacked and beaten, and their musical instruments were destroyed. The crisis was resolved when King 'Abd al-'Aziz made some conciliatory statements toward the Egyptian government, but that was the last year that the Egyptians were able to perform their annual ceremony to the sound of bugles and music. The Wahhabis also criminalized all forms of Sufi chants and dances in Mecca and Medina, and eventually in all of Saudi Arabia.[56] One of the acts that 'Abd al-Wahhab committed in Arabia, which generated a great amount of turmoil and opposition, was the stoning to death of a woman accused of adultery. Historical sources state that no one had been stoned to death in Arabia in a very long time, and that many jurists were horrified by what they considered to be the inhumane execution of this woman.[57] This historical report is intriguing, because today stoning people to death is carried out all the time in Saudi Arabia without raising as much as an eyebrow.

Before they solidified their power base in Arabia, the Wahhabis, with their fanatical and cruel practices, often generated widespread protests from Arab and non-Arab Muslim countries, leading to politically embarrassing situations for the Al Sa'ud family. In order not to lose the much-needed political support of Muslim states, the Saudis (both before and after the modern state of Saudi Arabia was founded) often dealt with these embarrassing situations by issuing conciliatory statements aimed at alleviating Muslim anxieties about what would become of the holy cities of Mecca and Medina.[58] But other than the exceptional circumstances leading to the violent suppression of the Ikhwan in 1929, the Al Sa'ud rulers did little to restrain or moderate the practices of the Wahhabis. Through the 1930s and 1940s the Saudi government overcame all sense of restraint regarding the fanatic practices of Wahhabism, and strengthened its claim over the holy cities of Medina and Mecca. With that claim came the exclusive right to define the rituals that could legitimately be performed in the holy cities. By the 1950s the Saudi government no longer made conciliatory statements toward Muslim countries or apologized for the practices and excesses of the Wahhabis. While the Saudi government continued to rely on the support of the British government (and increasingly the American government as well), it no longer needed the support of other Muslim countries. Wahhabism had become firmly established in Saudi Arabia and also in the nerve center of Islam, Mecca and Medina. Because of the twin factors of non-Muslim support and the discovery of oil, the Saudi government was in a position to withstand the criticism of moderate Muslim countries.

There was no way that those countries could exert effective pressure on the Saudi government and influence the kind of Islam that had become dominant in the holy land, and the Saudi government simply had no incentive to modify or moderate the creed to which it adhered. However, the 1970s became truly transformative for Saudi Arabia and the Muslim world. Before the 1970s, the Saudis acted as if Wahhabism was an internal affair well adapted to native needs of Saudi society and culture. The 1970s became a turning point in that the Saudi government decided to undertake a systematic campaign of aggressively exporting the Wahhabi creed to the rest of the Muslim world.[59]

Initially, this process of dissemination consisted of lending financial support to fundamentalist organizations, but by the 1980s it had become far more sophisticated and comprehensive. For instance, Saudi Arabia created a number of proxy organizations, such as the Muslim World League, which widely distributed Wahhabi literature in all of the major languages of the world, gave out awards and grants, and provided funding for a massive network of publishers, schools, mosques, organizations, and individuals. The net effect of this campaign was that many Islamic movements across the Muslim world became advocates of Wahhabi theology. Furthermore, a wide range of individuals and institutions learned to shape their thought, speech, and behavior in such a way as to incur and benefit from Saudi largesse.

In summary, four main factors contributed to the survival and expansion of Wahhabism in contemporary Islam:

1. By rebelling against the Ottomans, Wahhabism appealed to the emerging ideologies of Arab nationalism in the eighteenth century. By treating Muslim Ottoman rule as a foreign occupying power, Wahhabism set a powerful

precedent for notions of Arab self-determination and autonomy.

2. As noted above, Wahhabism advocated the return to what 'Abd al-Wahhab saw as the pristine and pure origins of Islam. Accordingly, Wahhabism rejected the cumulative weight of historical baggage and insisted upon a return to the precedents of the "Rightly Guided" early generations (*al-salaf al-salih*). The expression "rightly guided early generations" refers to the generation of Companions of the Prophet and the generation after it (the generation of the successors—*al-tabi'in*). These two generations were seen in an idealistic light and they were often cited as an example to be imitated. The Wahhabi idea was intuitively liberating for Muslim reformers since it meant the rebirth of *ijtihad,* or the return to de novo examination and determination of legal issues unencumbered by the accretions of precedents and inherited doctrines. In other words, this idea of throwing away the past with its baggage and starting fresh was liberating. Theoretically, at least, Muslims could use *ijtihad* (independent and new analysis and thinking) to look with a fresh eye at the original sources of the Qur'an and the Sunna and come up with new interpretations and new solutions to the problems of the present without being burdened by the past. According to the Wahhabis, the only relevant and binding past was that which had been created by the Prophet, his Companions, and the Companions' immediate successors.

3. By controlling Mecca and Medina, Saudi Arabia became naturally positioned to exercise a considerable influence on Muslim culture and thinking. The holy cities of Mecca and Medina are the symbolic heart of Islam, and

are the sites where millions of Muslim perform pilgrimage each year. By regulating what might be considered orthodox belief and practice while at pilgrimage, Saudi Arabia became uniquely positioned to greatly influence the belief systems of Islam itself. For instance, for purely symbolic purposes, the king of Saudi Arabia adopted the lowly title of the custodian and servant of the two holy sites to emphasize that he was the servant of all Muslims. In reality the title only underscored the moral position of authority the Saudi king claimed to himself in relation to the Muslim world.

4. Perhaps most importantly, the discovery and exploitation of oil in Saudi Arabia provided that country with high financial liquidity. Especially post-1975, with the sharp rise in oil prices, Saudi Arabia aggressively invested in the promotion of Wahhabi thought around the Muslim world. Even a cursory examination of the predominant ideas and practices prevalent especially in mosques reveals the widespread influence of Wahhabi thought on the Muslim world today.

Part of the reason for Saudi Arabia's aggressive proselytizing of its creed is related to the third element mentioned above. It would have been politically awkward for Saudi Arabia to be the custodian of the two holy sites, but at the same time adopt a system of belief that was at odds with the rest of the Muslim world. To say the least, custodianship of the holy sites is a sensitive position in the Muslim world, and the Saudi exclusive claim to sovereignty over these cities remained problematic from the 1920s throughout the 1960s, especially because of the Wahhabis' intolerant attitude toward ritualistic practices that they deemed unorthodox. In the 1950s and 1960s, Saudi Arabia was coming under considerable pressure from republican and Arab nationalist regimes who tended to consider the Saudi system archaic and reactionary. Arab nationalist regimes, especially the regime of Gamal 'Abd al-Nasser of Egypt, were secular, staunchly socialist, and revolutionary. The dynastic, capitalistic, and theocratic system of government in Saudi Arabia and the other Gulf countries were considered historically retarded, and antirevolutionary. According to revolutionary Arab nationalists, Saudi Arabia was an artificial state invented by colonial forces in order to serve the interests of Western imperialism. Therefore, for instance, Gamal 'Abd al-Nasser not only challenged the custodianship of the Saudis over the holy sites, but he also attempted to overthrow the Saudi Arabian government. In the 1970s, Saudi Arabia finally possessed the financial means to address its legitimacy concerns. The Wahhabis either had to alter their own system of belief to make it more consistent with the convictions of other Muslims, or they had to aggressively spread their convictions to the rest of the Muslim world. The first would have required the Saudi regime to reinvent itself, but in many ways it was easier to attempt to reinvent the Muslim world, and that is the option they chose. Consequently, the Saudi Arabian government launched upon an aggressive campaign aimed at reinventing the Muslim world by disseminating Wahhabi ideology across the globe as the only legitimate form of Islam.[60] Initially, this process of dissemination consisted of lending financial support to fundamentalist organizations, but by the 1980s, this process became far more sophisticated and comprehensive. So, for instance, Saudi Arabia created a number of proxy organizations, such as the Muslim World League (*Rabitat al-'Alam al-Islami*), that widely distributed Wahhabi literature in all of the major languages of the world, gave out awards and grants, and provided funding for a massive network of publishers, schools, mosques, organizations, and individuals. The net effect of this campaign was that many Islamic movements across the Muslim world became advocates of Wahhabi theology. Furthermore, a wide range of institutions, whether schools, book publishers, magazines, newspapers, or even governments, as well as individuals, such as imams, teachers, or writers, learned to shape their behavior, speech, and thought in such a way as to incur and benefit from Saudi largesse. In many parts of the Muslim world, the wrong type of speech or conduct (such as failing to veil or advocate the veil) meant the denial of Saudi largesse or the denial of the possibility of attaining Saudi largesse, and in numerous contexts this meant the difference between enjoying a decent standard of living or living in abject poverty.

Nevertheless, it is important to note that Wahhabism did not spread in the modern Muslim world under its own banner. Considering the marginal origins of the Wahhabi creed, this would have been quite difficult to accomplish. Wahhabism spread in the Muslim world under the banner of Salafism. In fact, the term *Wahhabism* is considered derogatory to the followers of Ibn Abd-al-Wahhab since Wahhabis prefer to see themselves as the representatives of Islamic orthodoxy. According to its adherents, Wahhabism is not a school of thought within Islam, but is Islam itself, and it is the only possible Islam. The fact that Wahhabism rejected the use of a school label gave it a rather diffuse quality and made many of its doctrines and methodologies eminently transferable. Salafism, unlike Wahhabism, was a far more credible paradigm in Islam, and in many ways, an ideal vehicle for Wahhabism. Therefore, in their literature, Wahhabi clerics have consistently described themselves as Salafis (adherents of Salafism), and not Wahhabis.

THE SALAFI ORIGINS

Salafism is a creed founded in the late nineteenth century by Muslim reformers such as Muhammad 'Abduh (d. 1323/1905), Jamal al-Din al-Afghani (d. 1314/1897), Muhammad Rashid Rida (d. 1354/1935), Muhammad al-Shawkani (d. 1250/1834), and Jalal al-San'ani (d. 1225/1810). Some people even attribute the origin of the creed to Ibn Taymiyya (d. 728/1328) and his student Ibn Qayyim al-Jawziyya (d. 751/1350). The word *salaf* means predecessors, and in the Islamic context, it usually refers to the period of the Prophet, his Companions, and their successors. As such, the term *salafi* (someone who follows the *salaf*) has a flexible and malleable meaning and a natural appeal because it connotes authenticity and legitimacy. As a term, it is exploitable by any movement that wants to claim that it is grounded in Islamic authenticity. Although the term was originally adopted by liberal reformers, in the early twentieth century the Wahhabis referred to themselves as Salafis. However, the term did not become associated with the Wahhabi creed until the 1970s.

Salafism appealed to a very basic and fundamental concept in Islam—that Muslims ought to follow the precedents of the Prophet and his Rightly Guided Companions (*al-salaf al-salih*) as well as the pious early generations. Methodologically and in substance, Salafism was nearly identical to Wahhabism, except that Wahhabism was far less tolerant of diversity and differences of opinions. In many ways, Salafism was intuitively undeniable, partly because of its epistemological promise: it offered a worldview that was difficult to deny or challenge. The founders of Salafism maintained that on all issues, Muslims ought to return to the original textual sources of the Qur'an and the Sunna (precedent) of the Prophet. In doing so, Muslims ought to reinterpret the original sources in light of modern needs and demands without being slavishly bound to the interpretive precedents of earlier Muslim generations. But as originally conceived, Salafism was not necessarily anti-intellectual, but like Wahhabism it did tend to be uninterested in history. By emphasizing a presumed "golden age" in Islam, the adherents of Salafism idealized the time of the Prophet and his Companions, and ignored or were uninterested in the balance of Islamic history.

Furthermore, by rejecting juristic precedents and under-valuing tradition as a source of authoritativeness, Salafism adopted a form of egalitarianism that deconstructed tradi-tional notions of established authority within Islam. Accord-ing to Salafism, effectively anyone was considered qualified to return to the original sources and speak for God. The very logic and premise of Salafism was that any commoner or layperson could read the Qur'an and the books containing the traditions of the Prophet and his Companions and then issue legal judgments. Taken to the extreme, this meant that each individual Muslim could fabricate his own version of Is-lamic law.

Effectively, by liberating Muslims from the burdens of the technocratic tradition of the jurists, Salafism contributed to the vacuum of authority in contemporary Islam. However, un-like Wahhabism, Salafism was not actively hostile to the juris-tic tradition or the practice of various competing schools of thought. It is as if Salafism considered the juristic tradition more as optional rather than necessarily dispensable. Further-more, unlike Wahhabism, Salafism was not hostile to mysti-cism or Sufism. Many of the proponents of Salafism were eager to throw off the shackles of tradition and to engage in the rethinking of Islamic solutions in light of modern de-mands. As far as the juristic tradition was concerned, most Salafi scholars were synchronizers; they tended to engage in a practice known as *talfiq,* in which they mixed and matched various opinions from the past in order to emerge with novel approaches to problems.

An important dimension to Salafism was that, for the most part, it was founded by Muslim nationalists who were eager to read the values of modernism into the original sources of Islam. Hence, Salafism was not necessarily anti-Western. In fact, its founders strove to project contemporary institutions such as democracy, constitutionalism, or socialism onto the foundational texts, and to justify the paradigm of the modern nation-state within Islam. In this sense, Salafism, as originally conceived, betrayed a degree of opportunism. Its proponents tended to be more interested in the end results than in maintaining the integrity or coherence of the juristic method. Salafism was marked by an anxiety to reach results that would render Islam compatible with modernity, far more than a desire to critically understand either modernity or the Islamic tradition itself. For instance, the Salafis of the nineteenth and early twentieth centuries heavily emphasized the predominance of the concept of *maslaha* (public interest) in the formulation of Islamic law. Accordingly, it was consistently emphasized that whatever would fulfill the public interest ought to be deemed a part of Islamic law.[61]

This, however, exemplified a problem that came to plague Salafi thought throughout the twentieth century: its political opportunism. Salafism, which initially promised a liberal type of renaissance in the Islamic world, persistently compromised religious and ethical principles to power dynamics and political expedience. Confronted by the challenge of nationalism, Salafis—often invoking the logic of public interest and necessity—consistently transformed Islam into a politically reactive force engaged in a mundane struggle for identity and self-determination. As a result, Salafism became a highly diluted

and unprincipled moral force, constantly restructuring and re-
defining itself to respond to a never-ending, constantly shifting
power dynamic.

   In the end, no one could be entirely sure about the ethical
and moral principles that Salafism represented, other than a
stark form of functionalism that constantly shifted in response
to the political demands of the day. By the mid-twentieth century, it had become clear that Salafism had drifted into stifling
apologetics. These apologetics consisted of an effort to defend
Islam and its tradition against the onslaught of Westernization
and modernity by simultaneously emphasizing both the compatibility and the supremacy of Islam. Apologists responded to
the intellectual challenges of the modern age by adopting
pietistic fictions about the presumed perfection of Islam, es-
chewing any critical evaluation of Islamic doctrines. A common device of apologists was to argue that any meritorious or
worthwhile modern institutions were first invented and realized by Muslims. Therefore, according to the apologists, Islam
liberated women, created a democracy, endorsed pluralism,
and protected human rights, long before these institutions ever
existed in the West.[62] Nonetheless, this was not asserted out of
a critical engagement with the Islamic tradition, or even out
of a genuine ideological commitment or a rigorous understanding of the implications of the ideas and institutions asserted. Rather, these issues were asserted primarily as a means
of affirming self-worth and attaining a measure of emotional
empowerment. The apologists simply raised the issue of Islamic authenticity in relation to issues such as democracy,
human rights, and women's rights, but did not seriously engage them. According to such apologetics, all society needed
to do in order to fully attain the benefits of democracy, human
rights, economic development, or women's rights was to give
full expression to the real and genuine Islam. But what natu-

rally flowed from this was an artificial sense of confidence and an intellectual lethargy that took neither the Islamic tradition nor these modern challenges very seriously.[63] The incipient opportunism in Salafi approaches, which was strongly exemplified in its apologetic literature, had degenerated into an intellectual carelessness and whimsicalness that had all but destroyed any efforts at systematic and rigorous analysis. By the 1960s the initial optimistic liberalism had dissipated, and what remained of this liberal bent had become largely apologetic.

Meanwhile, through a complex sociopolitical process, Wahhabism was able to rid itself of some of its extreme forms of intolerance, and it proceeded to co-opt the language and symbolisms of Salafism in the 1970s until the two had become practically indistinguishable. Both Wahhabism and Salafism imagined a golden age within Islam; this entailed a belief in a near-historical utopia that they thought was entirely retrievable and reproducible in contemporary Islam. Both remained uninterested in critical historical inquiry and responded to the challenges of modernity by escaping to the secure haven of the text. And both advocated a form of egalitarianism and anti-elitism to the point that they came to consider intellectualism and rational moral insight to be inaccessible, and thus corruptions to the purity of the Islamic message. Curiously, this amounted to an attitude that treated whatever was intellectually complex and challenging as somehow contrary to Islam. This stand was quite odd coming from the offspring of a civilization that had produced a remarkably rich tradition of Islamic philosophy.

These similarities between the two facilitated the Wahhabi co-optation of Salafism. Wahhabism from its very inception, and Salafism especially after it entered its apologetic phase, were infested with a kind of supremacist thinking that prevails until today. The level of intellectual sophistication found in the

writings of early Salafists like Muhammad 'Abduh and Rashid
Rida, for example, became increasingly rare, and increasingly
the texts written by Salafis became indistinguishable from
those written by Wahhabis. It is this blend of Salafism and
Wahhabism, which took place in the 1970s, that forms the
theology of the puritanical movements of today.[64] The puritanical approach became best represented in the writings of
people such as Abu al-A'la al-Mawdudi (d. 1979) and Sayyid
Qutb, executed in 1966, who to different extents were both
Salafi and Wahhabi. Mawdudi was an influential Islamic
thinker who wrote over twenty books, and who exercised a
considerable impact upon Indo-Pakistanis as well as Arab
Muslims. Following in the footsteps of 'Abd al-Wahhab,
Mawdudi believed that all Muslim societies have reverted to a
pre-Islamic condition where darkness and ignorance prevails
(a state of *jahiliyya*). Like 'Abd al-Wahhab, Mawdudi believed
that Muslims have lost their true faith and that much of their
beliefs and actions betrayed a lack of understanding of
tawwhid (monotheism). Like 'Abd al-Wahhab, Mawdudi believed in the seclusion of women, and emphasized orthoproxy
or correct ritualistic practice as true proof of the faith. Mawdudi, however, was not willing to go as far as declaring all
Muslims as apostates, and on that basis spill their blood.
Mawdudi did not resort to violence during his lifetime, but he
led a fairly large grass roots movement in Pakistan, which
aimed to amass enough popular support to eventually overthrow the government and take power. Mawdudi did not object to the use of violence as a matter of principle, but he
believed that a premature use of violence would lead to state
suppression and the ultimate defeat of Islamic forces. It is
fair to say that the difference between Mawdudi and 'Abd al-
Wahhab was a difference of circumstance. Tribal feuding, the
existence of a weak state in Arabia, and British support aimed

at weakening the Ottoman Empire were factors that helped 'Abd al-Wahhab in using violence as the primary means of propagating his message. Mawdudi advocated the idea of delayed jihad—the idea that true Muslims should not use violence as long as the balance of powers did not favor their victory, but if the balance of powers changes, resorting to violence becomes justified. In a very significant respect, Mawdudi was quite similar to 'Abd al-Wahhab—both shared the dream of establishing a new and improved alternative society that is genuinely Islamic, and that is nothing like the societies that already existed and in which these two activists lived. According to these two activists, this highly coveted alternative society was an imagined utopian state, which ought to be modeled after the Prophet's city-state in Medina. Ultimately, Mawdudi and his many followers, as well as the Wahhabis, shared in the belief in a dictatorial theocratic state that forces people to comply with their puritanical version of Islamic law. Mawdudi, however, reflected a clear Western influence insisting that an Islamic state is a theo-democracy—a combination between theocracy and democracy. But this was nothing more than apologetic rhetoric aimed at defending his followers against the charge that they were activists working to transform Pakistan into a religious dictatorship.

Sayyid Qutb has often been called the father of all militants, but this accusation is not entirely accurate. Qutb was sentenced to death by Nasser's regime in Egypt for his ideas, not for any violent acts that he committed. But because he was executed for his ideas, even people who do not agree with his thought remember him as a martyr. Not surprisingly, that martyrdom has virtually ensured his survival in the Muslim memory for generations to come.

Moreover, Qutb was a complicated figure because he lived most of his life as a moderate Muslim and, as a result, he left a

legacy of influential studies on the Qur'an and literary criticism. Qutb was highly educated and widely read, familiar
with Mawdudi's and 'Abd al-Wahhab's writings as well as the
writings of several Western philosophers. However, he was
not drawn to the thought of Mawdudi or 'Abd al-Wahhab
until he was arrested and severely tortured by Nasser's
regime; it is this experience that proved to be truly transformative for Qutb. Qutb became an extremist, and he wrote
the treatise titled *Milestones on the Road,* which became his
most influential and famous work. As an extremist, Qutb
truly exemplified the simultaneous influences and contradictions of puritanical Islam, which were Salafism, Wahhabism,
and Western thought. In *Milestones* he attempted to offer a
description of the genuine Islamic society and the true Islamic
faith, but in reality, Qutb's book did nothing more than attempt to add an Islamic veneer to a thoroughly fascist ideological construct.

Qutb was a member of the Muslim Brotherhood organization in Egypt and insisted that like Hasan al-Bana (assassinated in 1949), the founder of that movement, he was a Salafi.
However, like 'Abd al-Wahhab, Qutb divided society into the
true faithful versus those who live in the age of *jahiliyya* (pre-
Islamic ignorance and darkness). In his view, it was obligatory
upon all Muslims to migrate (do *hijra*) to the land of true of
Islam; those who failed to do so were to be considered apostates and infidels. Qutb insisted that the Qur'an was the constitution of all true Muslims, and he also claimed that
sovereignty exclusively belongs to God. This meant that in a
true Islamic society, God is the only legislature, and perfect
justice could be achieved if the ruler faithfully applies God's
commandments. The land of true Islam must be governed in
all its particulars by Islamic law. It is not surprising that neither Qutb nor Mawdudi were trained jurists, and their knowl-

edge of the Islamic jurisprudential tradition was minimal. Nevertheless, like 'Abd al-Wahhab, Mawdudi and Qutb imagined Islamic law to be a set of clear cut, inflexible, and rigid positive commands that covered and regulated every aspect of life. Qutb imagined Islamic law to be a cure-all—its implementation meant that God's justice was being implemented and God's justice was perfect.

Qutb argued that when this land of true Islam is founded, all Muslims must promptly migrate (do *hijra*) and settle in it. If, however, it does not exist, Qutb contended that the true believers must isolate themselves from the rest of society (*i'tizal*), which is Muslim by name only but which is in reality heretical and foul. The true believers must withdraw and isolate themselves from society so that they will not be contaminated by the state of pre-Islamic ignorance that prevails in society (*jahiliyya*). But then after withdrawing and forming their own community, it is incumbent upon Muslims to expend every effort at founding the true Islamic state. Clearly, Qutb's willingness to declare Muslims to be apostates was reminiscent of 'Abd al-Wahhab's rhetoric on true belief and apostasy. Like 'Abd al-Wahhab, Qutb accused the vast majority of Muslims of being hypocrites and heretics. In essence, both 'Abd al-Wahhab and Qutb believed in the idea of the community of the truly saved (*al-firqa al-Najiya*) fighting against other Muslims to establish the true Islamic state and enforce God's law. However, Qutb provided a more detailed vision of the idealistic and utopian Islamic state. In this regard, Qutb, unlike 'Abd al-Wahhab, was influenced by Western thinkers, particularly the German fascist philosopher Carl Schmidt. Although Qutb does not once mention Schmidt in his works, a careful reading of *Milestones on the Road* reveals that many of Qutb's ideas, constructs, and phrases are clearly adapted from the works of Schmidt.[65]

As a true sign of the shifting fate of Salafi Islam, when Qutb
wrote his *Milestones,* the director of the Muslim Brotherhood,
Hasan al-Hudaybi, who described himself as a Salafi, wrote a
book refuting Qutb's claims. Al-Hudaybi criticized the thinking
of 'Abd al-Wahhab and Mawdudi and strenuously protested
the practice of *takfir* (the act of accusing Muslims of being
apostates and heretics). Al-Hudaybi argued that this practice is
inconsistent with the tradition of tolerance in Islam. Al-
Hudaybi also challenged the idea that Muslim societies as a
whole have drifted back into the age of darkness and ignorance
(*jahiliyya*). Muslim societies, according to al-Hudaybi, might
have become too Westernized or they might have drifted away
from some Islamic values, but this does not mean that these societies ceased to be Muslim. The answer to all problems that
might confront Muslims is to advocate, persuade, and seek incremental reform, and not to resort to violence or to try to
force change. In all cases, it is a grave error to assume that all
Muslims deserve to be killed or to consider oneself in a state of
war with society at large, as the Wahhabis have done. Significantly, al-Hudaybi argued that political sovereignty should
properly belong to the people, and therefore a theocratic system of government is inconsistent with Islamic theology, history, and morality. Al-Hudaybi was very critical of the idea of
God's sovereignty, claiming that it is alien to Islam and that it is
being used for the wrong purposes. He contended that the concept of a utopian state in which God alone is sovereign is fac-
tually impossible and politically naive. Al-Hudaybi was a judge
and a jurist and, indeed, in his book he demonstrates a greater
degree of competence and knowledge of Islamic law. Consequently, he does not consider the application of Islamic law to
be a cure-all to whatever problems that might confront Muslims. Islamic law cannot be applied without first developing the
appropriate institutional apparatus and social context.

It is very telling that while most Muslims have at least heard of *Milestones on the Road,* and while Qutb's book is widely available, the same is not true for al-Hudaybi's book. Few have heard of it, and it is long out of print and difficult to locate.[66] Sadly, al-Hudaybi's liberal book was written long after the liberal phase of Salafism had passed. It no longer represented Salafi thought; it represented only the lonely thought of al-Hudaybi.[67] Today, Salafis resoundingly reject al-Hudaybi's thought, as they reject the thought of the liberal Salafis of the early twentieth century.

In the 1970s, the Wahhabi-Salafi assimilation was represented by the thought of the new puritans, such as Salih Saraya (executed 1975), Shukri Mustafa (d. 1978), and Muhammad 'Abd al-Salam Faraj (executed 1982). All three formed militant organizations and were executed for committing terrorist acts in Egypt. Of the three, Faraj was particularly influential because of his famous treatise, titled *Jihad: The Neglected Duty.*[68] In addition, Faraj was the chief ideologue behind Egyptian President Anwar Sadat's assassination in 1981. Faraj's treatise called for the waging of an unrelenting military campaign against the heretical rulers of all Muslim countries. He went further, however: in Faraj's view, it was not just the rulers that deserved to be excommunicated and fought against as infidels, but all Muslims must be treated as if they have reverted to a state of near apostasy.

Faraj and his predecessors, Saraya and Shukri, had come to accept 'Abd al-Wahhab's and Qutb's vision of Muslim society as misguided and foul and dreamed of an alternative society in which the true Islam would be fulfilled. All three activists were severely alienated from their present-day Muslim societies and rejected any level of moral attachment to fellow Muslims.[69] Therefore, in their view, a country such as Egypt was thought to be as un-Islamic as Israel—in their view, Egypt and Israel were equally un-Islamic countries.[70] Although these three activists accepted Qutb's worldview, and even accepted the idea of withdrawing from infidel society, they rejected the idea of deferred military action. Rather, they found 'Abd al-Wahhab's model, which excommunicated, attacked, and punished infidel societies, to be far more compelling. Therefore, militants like Faraj, in terms of their theological outlook, were much closer to 'Abd al-Wahhab than Qutb. This is exactly why this new form of puritanism was rather ambivalent toward Qutb. While they were attracted to Qutb's dichotomous view of Muslim societies and the world, they found Qutb's reluctance to resort to military force most troubling, and so the new puritans often attacked and condemned Qutb, while praising and idealizing 'Abd al-Wahhab.[71]

In the same way that the traditional jurists used to describe the Wahhabis as the modern-day Khawarij of Islam, the same label was used to describe these new puritans. These new puritans, like the Wahhabis, had nothing but contempt for the jurists of Islam. So, for instance, the Shukri Mustafa group in 1977 abducted and executed Muhammad al-Dhahabi, a respected shaykh from Azhar who was a former Minister of Religious Endowments. In many of its particulars, Shukri Mustapha's thought was nearly identical to that of 'Abd al-Wahhab.[72]

By the late 1970s, Wahhabism had co-opted the Salafi creed to the point that Salafism had become a code word for antiliberal values. The puritanism that resulted from this co-optation was invariably intolerant, supremacist, oppressive toward women, opposed to rationalism, hostile toward most forms of creative artistic expression, and rigidly literalistic. But while all Islamic militant groups were puritan, Salafi, and Wahhabi, not all puritan groups were militant. Some puritan groups opted for the Mawdudi or Qutb approaches, following Wahhabism in every respect except that they hoped to establish the true Islamic society through constant activism and proselytism rather than violence.

The majority of Muslim governments tolerated puritan movements as long as they did not turn violent. But in very few countries was there an effective ideological response to these puritan movements. One of the main reasons for this widespread failure was the reluctance of Muslim scholars and intellectuals to confront the Wahhabi origin of puritan movements. Especially by the 1980s and 1990s, other than Sufis and Shi'is, very few scholars dared criticize the Wahhabi influence upon Salafism.[73] Criticism directed at Saudi Arabia or Wahhabism was considered a risky and even dangerous activity. For one, by virtue of their control of the two holy sites of Mecca and Medina, the Saudi government possessed a formidable power—that of granting or denying any Muslim around the world a visa. The power to regulate access to Mecca and Medina effectively meant that the Saudi government could decide whether any individual Muslim will be able to perform pilgrimage to the holy sites. This fact alone allowed the Saudi government the ability to have a very serious impact upon the life of any Muslim in the world. Any Muslim scholar who dared criticize Wahhabism, for instance, was denied a visa to visit the holy sites, and for many pious Muslims this would have constituted a very serious emotional blow.[74] Moreover, starting in the late 1970s and early 1980s, Saudi Arabia had embarked on a systematic campaign of promoting Wahhabi thought among Muslims living in the Muslim and non-Muslim worlds.[75] More importantly, Saudi Arabia had created a complex worldwide system of financial incentives that amply rewarded those who advocated "the right type" of thought or those who simply refrained from criticizing Wahhabism. This system of financial incentives was also employed to control what publishers decided to print or who gets invited to join prestigious associations or conferences. The disparity in wealth between most Muslim countries and Saudi Arabia, and the hegemonic influence of oil money in the Muslim world made it highly impractical for most Muslim scholars to attempt to say anything critical about Wahhabism. Concretely, for instance, a Muslim scholar spending a six-month sabbatical in a Saudi Arabian university would make more money in the course of this sabbatical than he would make in ten years of teaching at the Azhar University in Egypt. Similarly, writers or *imam*s espousing pro-Wahhabi positions would qualify for very lucrative contracts, grants, and awards. And very often the Saudi Arabian government would purchase a sizeable number of copies of books by pro-Wahhabi writers in order to guarantee these authors a high level of profit and to create a strong incentive system for publishers to print particular kinds of books. In fact, the most alarming development in the 1980s and 1990s was that even Muslim scholars who were known for their liberalism and rationalism wrote books defending Muhammad bin 'Abd al-Wahhab and Wahhabism—portraying it as a movement most capable of confronting the challenges of modernity. Whatever one can say about the motives of those writers, they were handsomely rewarded for their contributions, although their books were very selective and full of historical inaccuracies.[76]

In 1989, a prolific and influential Salafi jurist, Muhammad al-Ghazali (d. 1996), did the unthinkable: he wrote a blistering critique of the Wahhabi influence upon the Salafi creed. Al-Ghazali was growing increasingly tired of the antirationalism and immoralism of those who described themselves as Salafis, and of the puritan movement in general. Though cognizant of the influence of Wahhabis on contemporary Islam, al-Ghazali did not dare criticize the Wahhabis explicitly or directly. Instead, he called them the modern-day *Ahl al-Hadith,* and he severely criticized what he called their literalism, anti-rationalism, and anti-interpretive approach to Islamic texts.

Ahl al-Hadith is an amorphous expression that refers to literalist movements in Islamic history that claimed to adhere to the traditions of the Prophet faithfully, and without the "corrupting" influence of human interpretation or reason. The *Ahl al-Hadith* concerned themselves with collecting, documenting, and transmitting traditions attributed to the Prophet and the Companions, and claimed to base their legal judgments on these traditions without the interference of human subjectivities. In the fourth/tenth century, there was a close affinity between the followers of Ahmad Ibn Hanbal (d. 241/855), the founder of the Hanbali school of thought, and the *Ahl al-Hadith*—although the *Ahl al-Hadith* claimed not to follow any of the established schools of thought and to simply be the adherents of the truth. This affinity was sufficiently close that for a period of time the term *Ahl al-Hadith* referred to the literalist and strict constructionist Hanbali scholars. Most importantly, in the jurisprudential tradition, *Ahl al-Hadith* represented closed-mindedness, conservatism, and ignorance.[77]

For al-Ghazali, in his day and age, the approach of Salafi Muslims to Islamic texts had become very reminiscent of the pedantic literalism of the *Ahl al-Hadith* in the premodern period, which opposed every rationalist orientation in Islam.[78] By using the expression *Ahl al-Hadith* to describe the Wahhabis, al-Ghazali was also alluding to an old historical controversy between what some called the "pharmacists" and the "doctors" of Islam. According to some classical scholars, those who collected and transmitted traditions, *Ahl al-Hadith* were like pharmacists who made and preserved the chemicals, but did not know how to diagnose a disease or prescribe the appropriate medicine. The jurists, however, were more akin to doctors, who used the material supplied by the pharmacists, but who also used superior knowledge and training to treat diseases.[79]

Likewise, al-Ghazali believed that the modern-day *Ahl al-Hadith,* whom he also called the traditionists, knew how to collect and memorize the traditions, but did not know how the source material could interact with legal methodology in order to produce jurisprudence. The traditionists (that is, the pharmacists) did not know how to apply the methods of law to the raw or primary materials, to balance between competing and contradictory pieces of evidence, to weigh the objectives of the law against the means, to evaluate private against public interests, to analyze tensions between rules and principles, to balance between deference to precedents and demands for change, to comprehend the reasons for differences of opinion, and to study the many other subtleties that go into the production of a legal judgment. Al-Ghazali argued that traditionists are not trained in legal theory or the technicalities of legal methodology, and therefore are not qualified to issue legal judgments. In fact, according to al-Ghazali, when the traditionists transgress upon jurisprudence and attempt to practice law, they end up acting as *hadith* hurlers—that is, hurling traditions at their opponents to score cheap points. In effect, al-Ghazali accused the Wahhabis of being nothing more than hurlers of Prophetic traditions. Hurlers of Prophetic traditions, because of their ignorance of jurisprudential theory and methodology, treat law in a whimsical and opportunistic fashion. They search through the thousands of statements and sayings attributed to the Prophet in order to find anything that they could use to support their already preconceived and predetermined positions. In effect, they utilize the inherited traditions about the Prophet in an arbitrary and whimsical personalized fashion in order to affirm whatever positions they feel like supporting.[80] As a result, traditionists (or *hadith* hurlers) often end up confusing their cultural habits and preferences and Islamic law. They selectively pick evidence that supports their cultural biases and claim that these cultural practices are the Islamic mandated law. Al-Ghazali asserted that because such people do not abide by any disciplined methodology or principled way in thinking about the Divine Will, they end up corrupting Islamic law.

However, al-Ghazali went beyond accusing *Ahl al-Hadith,* the traditionists—ultimately, the Wahhabis—of corrupting Islamic law. He blamed the modern *Ahl al-Hadith,* or the Wahhabis, for perpetuating acts of fanaticism that defiled the image of Islam in the world. He contended that the modern-day *Ahl al-Hadith* suffered from an isolationist and arrogant attitude that made them uninterested in what the rest of humanity thought about Islam or Muslims. In al-Ghazali's view, this arrogant and intolerant attitude deprecated and impoverished Islamic thinking, and denied Islam its universalism and humanism. Rather tellingly, al-Ghazali claimed that the modern *Ahl al-Hadith,* or Wahhabis, trapped Islam in an arid and harsh environment in which the earmarks of a humanist civilization were clearly absent. In effect, al-Ghazali argued, the contemporary Salafis under the influence of the Wahhabis had created a Bedouin Islam, and this Bedouin Islam had become widespread and influential.

Al-Ghazali strongly defended the juristic tradition in Islam, and decried the ambivalence and dismissiveness by which this tradition was being treated by Bedouin Islam. Aware of the confusion that had come to surround the meaning of the word *Salafism,* al-Ghazali avoided engaging in an argument about who were the real and genuine Salafis, but he did advocate a return to the methodologies of the scholars, such as Muhammad 'Abduh and Rashid Rida, both of whom were pioneers of the Salafi movement. In other words, al-Ghazali tried to bring Salafi thought back to its liberal and enlightened origins as a genuine reform movement. Implicitly, he was once again trying to differentiate and divorce Salafism from Wahhabism, claiming that the latter had corrupted the former.

Not since the 1930s had a major Muslim scholar attempted such a task. Al-Ghazali engaged in an introspective critical assessment of the state of Muslim thought, and concluded that the failures of Muslims were their own. Al-Ghazali insisted that the failure to democratize, respect human rights, modernize, and defend the reputation of Islam around the world was not the product of an anti-Islamic world conspiracy. It is contrary to the ethics of Islam, al-Ghazali argued, for Muslims to fault anyone for these failures but themselves.

The sad reality was that the problems al-Ghazali was trying to address were more endemic and had become more complex than even he recognized. For too long influential Muslims had remained silent about the genocidal practices of the Wahhabis. Even more, the Saudi sphere of influence was far more extensive than al-Ghazali realized. For instance, Rashid Rida, whom Ghazali praised, was probably one of the most liberal and creative jurists of the early twentieth century, but he was also an apologist for the Wahhabis. Rida wrote a large number of articles portraying 'Abd al-Wahhab as a major reformer and as a pioneer of the Salafi movement. But Rida's liberal ideas and writings were fundamentally inconsistent with Wahhabism, and this is why after Rida's death, the Wahhabis regularly condemned and maligned Rida.[81] As demonstrative proof of Wahhabi influence in the Muslim world, the Saudis banned the writings of Rida, successfully prevented the republication of his work even in Egypt, and generally speaking made his books very difficult to locate.[82]

Another liberal thinker whose writings, due to sustained

Saudi pressure, were made to disappear was a Yemeni jurist named Muhammad al-Amir al-Husayni al-San'ani (d. 1182/1768). Al-San'ani died about a century and a half before Rashid Rida, but like Rida he was one of the founding fathers of the liberal Salafi creed. Like Rida, al-San'ani praised 'Abd al-Wahhab as a Salafi reformer and even wrote a celebratory poem in his honor. However, unlike Rida, once al-San'ani learned of the vast atrocities committed by the forces of 'Abd al-Wahhab, he refused to play the role of the apologist for an inhumane form of Islam and condemned 'Abd al-Wahhab in a new strongly worded poem.[83] Perhaps if more Salafi writers had chosen to follow in the footsteps of al-San'ani instead of Rida, Salafism could have retained its liberal orientation, and perhaps it would not have been so easy for the Wahhabi creed to co-opt it. Maybe if Salafism had stayed liberal, it could have been used to resist the spread of Wahhabism. However, with Saudi Arabia bankrolling the Wahhabi creed, it is doubtful that anything could have effectively stemmed the spread of the Wahhabi influence.

Because of Saudi Arabia's extensive influence, it is not surprising that the reaction to al-Ghazali's book was frantic and explosive, with a large number of puritans writing to condemn al-Ghazali and to question his motives and competence. Several major conferences were held in Egypt and Saudi Arabia to criticize the book, and the Saudi newspaper *al-Sharq al-Awsat* published several long articles responding to al-Ghazali in 1989. Notably, perhaps as an indication of Saudi influence and contrary to what one would expect, most of the books written against al-Ghazali were published in Egypt, not Saudi Arabia.[84] Many of al-Ghazali's critics made the highly implausible claim that al-Ghazali was not well educated in Islamic law, while others accused him of being awestruck by the West, or simply of treason. It is difficult to assess whether the virulent response to the book was indicative of any anxiety felt by the puritans over losing their grip over Muslims because of the power of al-Ghazali's arguments. In any case, the response to al-Ghazali's book was, to say the least, intimidating to any other Muslim scholar who would dare to undertake a similarly self-critical approach. It was simply much safer to stick to apologetics or popular political causes and to leave the issue of Wahhabism alone.[85]

Muhammad al-Ghazali died shortly after suffering through the controversy that surrounded his book. I knew al-Ghazali, and I know that he agonized over the future of Islam and the fate of Salafism. But al-Ghazali's book has come to symbolize a cry of protest over the transformation of Salafism—a transformation that ultimately undermined much of the efforts of the liberal reformers writing at the end of the nineteenth and beginning of the twentieth centuries. In the past fifty years, Salafism has regressed from a potentially modernizing force to an apologetic discourse. But wedded to Wahhabism, it gave birth to the vigorous, potent, and at times lethal, puritan movement.

FOUR

THE STORY OF
CONTEMPORARY PURITANS

Puritan movements took things to their logical extreme. The bonding of the theologies of Wahhabism and Salafism produced a contemporary trend that is anchored in profound feelings of defeatism, alienation, and frustration. The product of these two combined theologies is one of pronounced alienation, not only from the institutions of power of the modern world, but also from the Islamic heritage and tradition. Puritanism is not represented by formal institutions; it is a theological orientation, not a structured school of thought. Therefore, one finds a broad range of ideological variations and tendencies within it. But the consistent characteristic of puritanism is a supremacist ideology that compensates for feelings of defeatism, disempowerment, and alienation with a distinct sense of self-righteous arrogance vis-à-vis the nondescript "other"—whether that "other" is the West, nonbelievers in general, so-called heretical Muslims, or even Muslim women. In this sense, it is accurate to describe the puritanical orientation within Islam as supremacist, for it sees the world from the perspective of stations of merit and extreme polarization. Instead of simple apologetics, the puritan orientation responds to feelings of powerlessness and defeat with uncompromising and arrogant symbolic displays of power, not only against non-Muslims, but even more so against fellow Muslims, and women in particular.

Two of the main issues that distinguish puritans from other Muslims are (1) whether the religious text is intended to regulate most aspects of life, and (2) whether aesthetics or an innate human capacity to reflect upon and realize "the good" is possible.

Not surprisingly, puritans exaggerate the role of the text and minimize the role of the human agent who interprets the religious text. The puritan orientation anchors itself in the confident security of texts. It uses religious texts like the Qur'an and books of Prophetic reports and traditions like a shield in order to avoid criticism or to escape challenges that mandate the use of reason and rationality. According to puritans, not only does the text regulate most aspects of human life, but also the Author of the text determines the meaning of the text, while the reader's job in engaging the text is simply to understand and implement, as if the meaning of the text is always clear. In the puritan paradigm, subjectivities of the interpreting agent are irrelevant to the realization and implementation of the Divine command, which is fully and comprehensively contained in the text. Therefore, the aesthetics and moral insights or experiences of the interpreting agent are considered irrelevant and superfluous.

But in my view, far from being respectful toward the integrity of the text, the puritan orientation is abusive toward religious texts. Their approach to religious texts is inconsistent and hypocritical, because it empowers its adherents to project their sociopolitical frustrations and insecurities upon the text. In fact, despite their claims of objectivity, the puritan orientation forces religious texts to validate the social and political frustrations and insecurities of its adherents. If the adherents of this orientation are angry at the West, for example, they read the religious text in such a way as to validate this hostility. Similarly, if the men of this orientation feel the need to compensate for feelings of powerlessness by dominating women, they read the text to validate the subjugation and disempowerment of women. In every situation, we find that the proverbial arm of the text is being bent and twisted to validate whatever the puritan orientation wishes to do. All along the puritans claim to be entirely literal and objective, and to faithfully implement what the texts demand without their personal interference. This claim is simply fraudulent and untrue because in every situation we find that the puritan reading of the text is entirely subjective.

Elsewhere, I have described the dynamics of puritanism vis-à-vis the text as thoroughly despotic and authoritarian. Consistently, religious texts become whips to be exploited by a select class of readers in order to affirm reactionary power dynamics in society.[1] This is why al-Ghazali described the puritans as *hadith* hurlers—they use the inherited tradition and law to silence their opponents and to stunt critical or creative thinking. This is especially the case when it comes to dealing with subjects that the puritans believe are Western inventions, such as human rights or aesthetics.

The adherents of puritanism, unlike Muslim apologists, no longer concern themselves with co-opting or claiming Western institutions as their own. Under the guise of reclaiming the true and real Islam, they proceed to define Islam as the exact antithesis of the West. Apologetic attempts at proving Islam's compatibility with the West are dismissed as inherently defeatist.

The puritans argue that colonialism ingrained Muslims with a lack of self-pride or dignity and convinced Muslims of the inferiority of their religion. This, they maintain, has trapped Muslims in an endless and futile race to appease the West by proving Islam's worthiness. According to the puritan model, in reality there are only two paths in life: the path of

God, or "the straight path"; and the path of Satan, or "the crooked path." By attempting to integrate and co-opt Western ideas such as feminism, democracy, or human rights, Muslims have fallen prey to the temptations of Satan, they argue, by accepting ungodly innovations (*bida'*, sing. *bid'a*).

Puritans believe that Islam is the only straight path in life, and such a way must be pursued regardless of what others think and regardless of how it impacts the rights and well-being of others. Importantly, according to puritans, the straight path (*al-sirat al-mustaqim*) is firmly anchored in a system of Divine laws or specific commandments that trump any considerations of morality or ethical normative values. Put differently, a group of very specific commandments and rules delineate and define the straight path of God, and there is no room in this outlook for reason-based moral or ethical speculative thought. Therefore, in the puritanical outlook, God is manifested through a set of clear and precise legal commands that cover nearly all aspects of life, and the sole purpose of human beings is to realize the Divine manifestation by dutifully and faithfully implementing the Divine law. In the puritan paradigm, God is represented (manifested) in earthly life by a set of laws, and human beings have no choice but to obey. Puritans insist that only the mechanics and technicalities of Islamic law define morality; there are no moral considerations that can be found outside the technical law. This fairly technical and legalistic way of life is considered inherently superior to all others, and the followers of any other way are considered either infidels (*kuffar*), hypocrites (*munafiqun*), or the iniquitous (*fasiqun*). Anchored in the security and assuredness of a clear, precise, and unequivocal law found in the Qur'an and the Sunna, the puritans believe it is easy to differentiate between the rightly guided and the misguided. The rightly guided obey the law; the misguided either deny, attempt to dilute, or argue about the law. Any method of thought or process that would lead to indeterminate results, such as social theory, philosophy, or any speculative thought, is part of the crooked path of Satan. According to the puritans, lives that are lived outside the Divine law are inherently unlawful and are therefore an offense against God that must be actively fought or punished.

There is a real irony in the way puritans approach social and political issues that they believe originated in the West. In fact, the contradictions that plague various aspects of the puritan approach in this regard border on the schizophrenic. As I mentioned earlier, puritans reject inquiries into philosophy, political theory, morality, and beauty as too subjective—and, even worse, as Western inventions that lead to nothing but sophistry. With the majority of the puritan leadership comprised of people who studied the physical sciences, such as medicine, engineering, and computer science, they avowedly anchor themselves in the objectivity and certitude that comes from empiricism. According to puritans, public interests, such as the interest in protecting society from the sexual lures of women, can be empirically verified. However, in contrast, they say, moral or ethical values and aesthetic judgments about what is necessary or compelling cannot be empirically quantified, and therefore must be ignored. So values like human dignity, love, mercy, and compassion are not subject to quantification, and therefore cannot be integrated into Islamic legal judgments.

Because aesthetic judgments are considered anathema and humanism is waved away as a Western corruption, puritans render the humanistic legacy of the Islamic civilization irrelevant as they ignore the accomplishments of past generations of Muslims in fields such as philosophy, the arts and architecture, poetry and music, moral and ethical theory, and even romanticism and love. Puritans ignore the fact that long before there was a Western influence, Muslims wrote volumes upon volumes on love, beauty, and chivalry. If anything, this puritan attitude only augments the sense of disoriented rootlessness keenly felt by many modern Muslims. But even more, puritans conveniently ignore that one can as easily—or even more easily—claim that empiricism itself is a Western invention. (Of course, I am not claiming that empiricism is indeed a Western invention. Rather, I am pointing out that puritans ignore the fact that, like humanism, empiricism is not a Western invention but simply a part of the shared heritage of humanity.)

In the final analysis, whether puritans, with their various approaches and accomplishments, have contributed, or can contribute, to honoring God's Kingdom on this earth is a question I am not prepared to engage here. But in my view, it is clear that the impact of puritans on the Islamic intellectual heritage, and on the humanistic and universalistic orientations within Islam, has been nothing short of devastating.[2]

In light of the recent attention focused on the issue of terrorism, it is important to note that Bin Laden, Ayman al-Zawahiri, and the Taliban, as well as most extremist Muslims, belong to the orientation that I have called puritan. Bin Laden, although raised in a Wahhabi environment, is not, strictly speaking, part of that creed. Wahhabism is distinctively introverted; although focused on power, it primarily asserts power over other Muslims. Militant puritan groups, however, are both introverted and extroverted: they attempt to assert power over and against both Muslims and non-Muslims. As populist movements, they are a reaction to the disempowerment most Muslims have suffered in the modern age at the hands of harshly despotic governments and interventionist foreign powers. In many ways, these militant groups compensate for extreme feelings of disempowerment by extreme and vulgar claims to power. Fueled by the supremacist and puritan creed, these groups' symbolic acts of power become uncompromisingly fanatic and violent.

It would be inaccurate to contend that militant supremacist groups fill the vacuum of authority in contemporary Islam. Militant groups such as al-Qa'ida or the Taliban, despite their ability to commit highly visible acts of violence, are a sociological and intellectual marginality in Islam. However, these groups are in fact extreme manifestations of more prevalent intellectual and theological currents in modern Islam. In my view, they are extreme manifestations of the rather widespread theological orientation of puritanism. While it is true that Bin Laden is the quintessential example of a Muslim that was created, shaped, and motivated by postcolonial experience, he is representative of underlying currents in contemporary Islam. Much of what constitutes Islam today was shaped as a defensive reaction to the postcolonial experience, either as the product of uncritical cheerleading on behalf of what was presumed to be the Islamic tradition, or as an obstinate rejectionism against what was presumed to be the Western tradition. As such, the likes of Bin Laden are the children of a profound dissonance and dysfunctionalism experienced toward both the Islamic heritage and modernity. In my view, Bin Laden, as the whole of the puritan movement, is an orphan of modernity, but their claim to an authentic lineage in the Islamic civilization is tenuous at best. They were produced by the onslaught of modernity—but like illegitimate children, they are an embarrassment to the modern age that produced them, and they are not rooted in the Islamic civilization either.

All religious systems have suffered at one time or another from absolutist extremism, and Islam is not an exception. But the Muslim mainstream has always managed to prevail by forcing extremists to either moderate their views or risk extinction.[3] Other than the Khawarij, there were other extremists, such as the Qaramites and Assassins, whose terror became the raison d'être for their very existence, and who earned unmitigated infamy in the writings of Muslim historians, theologians, and jurists. After centuries of bloodshed these two groups also learned moderation, and they continue to exist in small numbers in North Africa and Iraq. The essential lesson taught by Islamic history is that extremist groups are ejected from the mainstream of Islam; they are marginalized, and they eventually come to be treated as a heretical aberration to the Islamic message.

The problem today, however, is that the traditional institutions of Islam that historically acted to marginalize extremist creeds no longer exist. This is what makes this period of Islamic history far more troublesome than any other, and this is also what makes modern puritan orientations far more threatening to the integrity of the morality and values of Islam than any of the previous extremist movements. This is perhaps the first time in history that the center of the Islamic world, Mecca and Medina, has been under the control of a puritanical state for such a prolonged period of time.

In the course of lecturing and teaching about Islam in different parts of the world, I have been asked by many people whether there is something in Islam itself that encourages extremism, because how else would an extremist marginal faction manage to gain so many adherents and become such a visible reality in the world today? If the puritans are a small percentage of the Muslim world, how could the puritans gain such strength to the point of threatening to fill the vacuum of authority in modern Islam? Although I think it is highly unlikely that this threat will become reality, the existence of the threat is indeed troubling and difficult to understand.

But in response I often answer in the following way: There

is a Jewish sect known as the Karaites that came into being in the eighth century. The Karaites continue to exist today, but in small numbers. The doctrine of the sect was characterized primarily by its rejection of the Talmudic and Rabbinical tradition and its interpretive methods. The Karaites claimed to base all their laws on a literal and strict reading of the Torah, and they also claimed to apply God's law without the interference of human subjectivities. Not surprisingly, the laws of the sect tended to be severe and at times harsh. The Karaites have remained a marginal minority in Judaism, but imagine if they were suddenly sponsored by an extremely wealthy Jewish nation that also happened to be in possession of the most holy of Jewish sites. If this happened, it is reasonable to imagine that the adherents of the Karaites would have significantly increased in numbers and that the sect would have become a serious contender in any effort to define Jewish orthodoxy.

It should not be surprising that, thanks to Saudi largesse, the puritans have become a considerable force in modern Islam. Considering the realities, it was inevitable. But there is another reality to consider: when extremist groups become more successful and thrive, their extremism only increases. This is especially the case when extremist groups are on the one hand supported by some and on the other hand oppressed by others. Their continued ability to spread successfully despite the oppression that confronts them further radicalizes them and strengthens their polarized vision of the world. Therefore, it is not surprising that the puritan movement that Saudi Arabia has for so long supported and nurtured is now turning its zeal against the Saudi state. Al-Qa'ida and several other Wahhabi organizations have sought to overthrow the Saudi government for not being sufficiently Wahhabi. Recently, there has been a wave of terrorist attacks in Saudi Arabia, and also armed clashes between the military and puritanical groups. Like the Ikhwan, who in the early twentieth century rebelled against their Saudi rulers because those rulers failed to meet their puritanical expectations and standards, puritan groups today are exacting from Saudi Arabia the price for nurturing the same type of monster. As in the early twentieth century, the Saudi rulers today find themselves forced to seek the aid of non-Muslims (this time the Americans instead of the British) in trying to contain the puritan monster seeking to overthrow their government.

Although history demonstrates that attempting to sponsor and leverage the zeal of puritanism to serve the state's interest is playing with the proverbial fire—a fire that is likely to burn everything, including those who ignited it in the first place—it is unlikely that the Saudi state will reverse its support of puritanism. If Saudi Arabia were to sponsor a more moderate version of Islam, it would lose its ability to define orthodoxy in the Muslim world. Other Muslim countries are eminently better positioned to authoritatively contribute to the definition of Islamic moderation, and the Saudi state would lose its privileged position in the Muslim world. While it is not impossible for the Saudi state to reinvent itself, other Muslim states, like Indonesia, Egypt, and Malaysia, have had a much longer and better-established tradition of practicing Islamic moderation. The Saudi state has sponsored puritan Islam and derived its legitimacy from that extremist creed for so long that a major political restructuring would be very difficult to achieve.

In my view, the most remarkable fact in this whole narrative is the resilience of the Islamic faith. Despite all the sustained efforts of the Saudis, and all the bombastic criminality of the puritans, the Islamic mainstream lives on. The vast majority of Muslims are not puritans, but they practice a traditional form of Islam based on inherited beliefs and practices that is distinctively different from the puritan creed. For instance, the puritans prohibit all forms of music, and yet there is no Muslim country that is not flooded with all kinds of Western and non-Western music. The puritans prohibit women from seeking employment outside the home, and yet women make up a sizable percentage of the workforce in most Muslim countries. The story of the puritans told in this book is the story of the exception to the mainstream in Islam.

Nevertheless, the Muslim mainstream is targeted by puritans. The puritan creed is strongly evangelical, and through proselytizing, the puritans hope to convert the mainstream to what they consider to be the true Islam. In my view, this is where moderate Muslims must play a critical role. For the reasons discussed, the juristic class will not be able to play its historical role in marginalizing the puritans. The burden must fall on moderate Muslims to articulate the alternative to the puritan menace. Moderate Muslims must be able to tap into the collective inherited memory of Muslims and remind them that the moderate way is indeed the heart and soul of Islam. The moderates should seek to fill the vacuum of authority by standing steadfast, upholding Islam as it was before it was co-opted and forced to alleviate the puritans' sense of social and political alienation. Moderates should seek to recapture the purity of the Islamic message as it was before it was twisted and altered by the puritans and forced to cater to the egoism and opportunism of puritanical causes. Moderates should seek to convince the Muslim world that they are the guardians of the true faith, which existed for centuries—long before the modern puritans came along and decided that the Islamic faith needed fixing.

To accomplish any of that, first it is imperative that moderates start by setting out the tenets of their beliefs. To my knowledge, this book is the first attempt to do just that. In setting out the moderate perspective, I have strived to summarize the fruits of years of involvement and experience with Muslim thinkers and scholars around the Muslim world. Humility and honesty demand that I admit the subjective nature of this task. The theology and law explained below in subsequent chapters are the culmination of the writings, lectures, and conversations by and with individuals that either described themselves as moderate Muslims or that I clearly perceived as moderate. In my view, moderate Muslims are individuals who believe in Islam as the true faith, who practice and believe in the five pillars of Islam (see Chapter 5), and who accept the inherited Islamic tradition, but who modify certain aspects of that tradition in order to fulfill the ultimate moral objectives of the faith in the modern age.

Individuals who accept the inherited tradition but do not modify any aspect of that tradition at all I categorize as conservative. However, for the purposes of this book, for the most part I discount their views. Conservatives accept the inherited tradition without modification because they refuse to admit that the modern age mandates any reforms whatsoever. Practically speaking, the line separating the conservatives from the puritans is so thin that the difference is often blurred. In effect, conservatives end up adopting a literalist method of interpretation and do not believe that any aspect of the Islamic tradition, as they understand it, needs to be reinterpreted in order to better achieve the ethical and moral objectives of the faith in the modern age. Other than the fact that I find the conservative approach unconvincing, I do not believe that conservatism is the creed of most Muslims in the modern age. In any case, this book is not about the belief system of the conservatives, and therefore I address their convictions only for the purposes of contrast and comparison.

Methodologically, I have discounted the views of two other groups as well. There has been a tendency among certain circles, particularly in the West, to accredit Islam-bashers, or former Muslims, as *reformers* and *moderates*. This seems to me offensively incongruous. The category I have in mind here are individuals who write books seeking to explain why they are not Muslims, or claiming that they are clinging to Islam with their fingertips because they were born Muslim but now find nothing about Islam appealing or convincing. Accordingly, this category of people does not believe in or practice the five pillars of Islam, and accepts no part of the Islamic tradition as either desirable or personally binding. It is fair to describe this group of people as critics of Islam, but they are certainly not reformers. What they offer is a deconstruction of the Islamic faith; and regardless of how helpful their views might be, they have chosen to take themselves out of the Muslim fold. They can be considered Muslims only if it is possible to consider Bertrand Russell, who wrote a book explaining why he is not a Christian, a Christian. Nevertheless, remarkable as it might be, some non-Muslim Western writers designate these critics as true and real moderate Muslims. This is akin to saying that the true moderate Muslim is a self-hating Muslim who finds his faith utterly absurd and offensive. This, of course, is their prerogative, but it is silly to call this group of people moderate Muslims. In all cases, this book is not about them, and hence I did not attempt to represent their views.

The other category of people that I have discounted is what may be described as the magic-wand reformers. In the current crisis of authority, the Islamic world has become plagued with armchair pontificators who are self-declared experts and who decree what Islam is because they *will* it to be so. This group of individuals does not bother with annoyances such as methodology, evidence, or alternative views. I do not mean idiosyncratic views: idiosyncratic views that are based on diligence in researching the evidence, and on a fair consideration of the method of analysis, are worthy of consideration. I am referring instead to what has become a well-known phenomenon in contemporary Islam—that of self-declared experts who claim to take on the job of reforming Islamic thought without being minimally qualified to do so. Typically, these magic-wand reformers are by profession engineers, medical doctors, or even social scientists who might be competent as sociologists or political scientists, but their knowledge and command of the Islamic intellectual tradition or its texts is minimal at best. Despite their poor knowledge of Islam, or perhaps because of their lack of familiarity with the Islamic intellectual tradition, these magic-wand reformers write books containing sweeping and unsubstantiated generalizations about what Islam is and what it ought to be. Although invariably lacking any systematic training in Islamic jurisprudence and its methodologies, often such writers designate themselves as *muftis* and call for what they describe as widespread personalized *ijtihad,* which often amounts to nothing more than a call for egotistical self-idolatry. But in attempting to set out the creed of moderate Muslims, I did not give much heed to these egotistical views, which are expressed by individuals who do not show any awareness of the fact that a religion cannot be built on self-idolatry, and whose only evidence that Islam is this or that is that they decided that it is so. People often ask me by what standards they should measure the knowledge and qualifications of someone from whom they should accept counsel on matters of Islamic law. While this is a complex matter, at a minimum such a person should have received at least twenty years of formal training in Islamic law, should be intimately knowledgeable of the local culture, and should have a balanced, humanistic view (since, for example, someone who hates women cannot render fair judgment on issues pertaining to women).

The moderate Muslims I am talking about in this book are those who believe in Islam, honor their obligations toward God, and believe that Islam is fit for every day and age. They do not treat their religion as if it were a fossilized monument, but treat it as a dynamic and active faith. Consequently, moderate Muslims honor the past achievements of their fellow Muslims, but they live in the present. The reforms that they advocate are not intended to ignore or subvert the will of God, but are intended to realize the Divine Will more fully while respecting the integrity and coherence of the faith. Moderate Muslims take seriously the Qur'anic injunctions and Prophetic statements elucidating that balance and moderation are at the heart of all good and at the core of every virtue. They understand, or at least make an effort at understanding, Islamic theology, which maintains that balance and moderation are primary laws upon which God's creation is founded, and they are also the primary attributes necessary for the attainment of personal, social, and political justice. Struggling to discipline oneself to be of a moderate and balanced temperament, even when tempted by anger or rage, is the key that unlocks higher levels of spiritual and moral achievement. It is reported that the Prophet Muhammad once explained that the earmark of the Islamic faith is moderation and that Muslims should set an example to others by being in all matters fairminded, balanced, and moderate. Many Muslims around the globe take this message to heart and try their best to be the kind of people the Prophet described. These are the moderates I describe below.

Before embarking upon the task of describing and defining moderate Muslims, and differentiating between their beliefs and the beliefs of puritan Muslims, we must first undertake the critical step of explaining what they agree on. We must establish the set of theological convictions adhered to by the overwhelming majority of Muslims. These are the tenets that define the Islamic faith, both because Islamic texts describe these beliefs as fundamental and basic to the religion and also because cumulative generations of Muslims have established a consensus that these particular convictions constitute the theological foundations of the religion. In other words, first we need to discuss what all Muslims believe in and agree on.

PART TWO

CHARTING THE MODERATE VERSUS PURITAN DIVIDE

FIVE

WHAT ALL MUSLIMS AGREE UPON

As is the case with all religions, there is a core set of beliefs and practices that define the religion of Islam. These are the least common denominators that distinguish and define the Islamic faith. At a minimum, this core would include what are known as the *five pillars of Islam*. These five pillars are considered the heart and pulse of Islam, and it is often asserted that believing in and accepting them as the foundational articles of the faith differentiates between a Muslim and non-Muslim. The five pillars of the faith are the following:

1. The testament of faith (*shahada*): To believe and profess that there is no God but God and that Muhammad is the messenger of God. The testament of faith is the most fundamental and critical pillar of Islam. Muslim theologians agree that believing in and pronouncing the testament of faith is the defining conviction and act that makes one a Muslim. The converse is also true: denying the testament of faith means that one is not a Muslim. At the most basic level, the testament of faith means a strong and unwavering conviction in one God, who has no partners or equals, and who was not begotten and who begets no other. The testament also means believing that Muhammad is God's prophet and messenger, who

faithfully transmitted what God revealed to him. Believing that Muhammad was but a human being who possessed no Divine powers or attributes is a critical part of the Islamic faith. Muhammad's role was restricted to transmitting the literal Divine revelation, word for word, and to acting faithfully upon God's commands. Muslims do not worship the Prophet Muhammad, but they do honor and respect him as God's messenger, and they treat him as a high moral example to be followed on all matters.

This is considered to be the basic meaning of the testament of faith, but there are various implications and details that follow from it, and those implications are of critical importance to the faith. Some of these Islamic theological tenets, despite their pivotal importance to the faith, are poorly known in the West. In fact, people in the West are often surprised when they learn, for instance, about Islam's relationship to Judaism and Christianity. Therefore, in introducing some of these Islamic tenets, it is best to let the Qur'an speak for itself. Hence, in this particular section I will be quoting extensively from the Qur'an.

As was stated earlier, the Qur'an and the Sunna (the authentic traditions of the Prophet) are the primary sources of Islam, which contain the beliefs and teachings of the Islamic faith. All Muslims accept the Qur'an—the Divine word revealed to the Prophet Muhammad. Therefore, the Qur'an is considered to be the literal, authentic, and unadulterated word of God. It is a tenet of the Islamic faith that the Qur'an is completely authentic; it has not been redacted, altered, revised, or corrupted in any way. However, other than the Qur'an, which was authored by God, there is a body of oral traditions attributed to the Prophet, known as the Sunna.

These Sunna contain descriptions of the Prophet's conduct in different contexts and situations, and also teachings, judgments, instructions, and statements, all attributed to the Prophet. Unlike the case of the Qur'an, the issue with the Sunna is its authenticity—whether the various reports and traditions are accurately attributed to the Prophet. All Muslims understand that some traditions and reports were fabricated and then improperly attributed to the Prophet. However, Muslims accept that Prophetic traditions or reports that are verifiably authentic are to be treated as obligatory and binding.

The God that Muslims believe in is referred to as Allah in Arabic. Christian Arabs refer to Jesus as Allah as well. This point is worth emphasizing, because there is a common misconception in the West that Muslims worship a deity other than the God of Abraham or that the word *Allah* is exclusively used by Muslims. Muslims believe that they worship the same God that Jews and Christians worship. In Qur'anic usage, the phrase "People of the Book" refers to the followers of the Abrahamic faith, mostly Christians and Jews. (The reason I say *mostly* Christians and Jews is that the Qur'an mentions Sabians as well, but Muslim jurists extended the People of the Book status to Zoroastrians, Hindus, and Sikhs, and some jurists even added Confucians to the list.) Addressing the People of the Book, the Qur'an reminds the followers of the three monotheistic religions that they all worship the same God. The Qur'an states: "Tell them [Christians and Jews] that we believe in what has been sent down to us and we believe in what has been sent down to you. Our God and your God is one and to Him we submit."[1]

It is a tenet of faith in Islam that Muhammad is the final prophet in a long line of Abrahamic prophets all conveying the same basic message to humanity. Therefore, a Muslim must necessarily believe in Abraham, Moses, Jesus, and many others as prophets of the same and one God—all bearing the same essential message of submission to God. For example, the Qur'an proclaims the following testament of faith: "The Prophet believes in what has been revealed to him by his Lord. And so do the faithful believe in the same. Each one believes in God and His angels, His Books and the prophets and We make no distinction between the apostles. They all say, 'We hear and obey, and we seek your forgiveness O Lord, for to You we shall journey in the end.'"[2] As this verse emphasizes, God considers all the Abrahamic prophets to be equals, and all the prophets upheld the same core set of beliefs.

The same idea is made even more explicit in the following Qur'anic revelation addressed to Muslims: "Say, we believe in God, and in what has been revealed to us, and in what had been sent down to Abraham and Ishmael and Isaac and Jacob and their offspring, and what has been revealed to Moses and Jesus and to all other prophets by their Lord. We make no distinction between them, and we submit to Him and obey."[3] In this verse, it is Muslims who are commanded to believe in all the Abrahamic prophets equally and without distinction. However, according to Muslim theology, while some of the Abrahamic prophets were sent to a particular tribe or nation, Muhammad carried the final and perfected Divine message to all of humanity. In addition, Muslims believe that aspects or parts of the earlier messages sent by God were altered, deformed, corrupted, or otherwise derailed from their initial purpose, and Islam was sent to reclaim and restore the original message to its pristine form.

One important example of this is the concept of the Trinity in Christianity. Muslims do not believe that Jesus made any claims to being Divine or that he taught the doctrine of the Trinity. The Qur'an affirms the doctrine of the Immaculate Conception, the virginity of Mary, and the miracles of Jesus and asserts that Christ was aided by the Holy Ghost. However, the Qur'an contends that some of the followers of Christ misunderstood or misrepresented his teachings by claiming that he was Divine or that he was God's begotten son. Therefore, in Muslim belief, Jesus was another Abrahamic prophet, just like Moses, preaching the same message of submission to God. In Qur'anic discourses, Jesus is claimed as a Muslim prophet, in the sense that his message to humanity was at its core the same as that of Muhammad. According to the Qur'an, the Torah and the *Injil* (New Testament) are divine books revealed by the same God who authored the Qur'an. However, Muslims believe that various historical forces interceded, leading to a process in which parts of these Divine texts became corrupted by human revisions, alterations, and omissions.

Nevertheless, the Qur'an insists on the essential unity of all the Abrahamic messages; the moral and spiritual path they set out is in a fundamental way of a similar nature. Therefore, for instance, the Qur'an asserts: "God has laid down for you the same way of life and belief that He had set out to Noah, and that We have enjoined for you, and that We had bequeathed to Abraham, Moses, and Jesus so that you will establish the faith, and not divide amongst yourself."[4] The Qur'an states that there is an essential unity not just in revelation and prophetic teachings but in creation. Therefore, the Qur'an often refers to the various prophets as Muslim, and it also describes nature and creation as Muslim as well. According to the Qur'an, revelation and creation attest to God's unity and affirm the moral obligation of recognizing that God is worthy of grateful supplication and submission.[5]

2. Prayer (*salat*): Muslims are required to perform five formal ritual prayers a day. Shi'i Muslims perform the same five prayers, but instead of doing them five separate

times, they perform them three separate times during the day. Muslims are also required to perform a congregational prayer in the mosque once a week, on Fridays, known as *jum'ah* prayers.

Muslims are encouraged to pray in the mosque as much as possible. In fact, each mosque holds a congregational prayer for each of the five prayers daily, which is usually attended by fewer Muslims than those who attend the Friday *jum'ah* prayers. The person leading the congregational prayers is usually called an *imam,* but other terms, such as *shaykh* or *'alim,* have also been used.

The Friday *jum'ah* prayer is designed to bring Muslim communities together to listen to a sermon before performing a prayer together as a congregation. The sermons are supposed to discuss the issues of concern to the whole community, but in current practice often the sermons focus on imparting general moral lessons without discussing any particular problems that might plague the community. Uncensored, Friday sermons often become occasions for mobilizing the masses and for inducing political change. Historically, Friday sermons have sparked many protests, riots, and even full-scale rebellions against one government or another. Today, in some Muslim countries, governments attempt to dictate the topics that may be discussed in the Friday sermon. At the conclusion of the Friday prayer, in order to strengthen the social bond and sense of unity in the Muslim communities, worshippers are encouraged to shake hands and meet and socialize with each other.

Other than the five ritual prayers and the weekly congregational prayers, Muslims are encouraged to perform informal prayers that could be done any time in the day. Muslims may volunteer additional ritual prayers that are performed according to specifically prescribed movements, or they may pray and supplicate to God in any position and in any place. Some non-Muslims are under the misimpression that Muslims may worship God only through prescribed ritualistic movements. This is not true. It is an article of faith in Islam that the relationship between God and the individual is direct and personal. Therefore, other than the prescribed five prayers, a Muslim may communicate with God in any way that meets the requirements of purity and cleanliness as well as respect and dignity.

3. Fasting of Ramadan (*siyam*): During the Muslim month of Ramadan, from sunrise to sundown every day for thirty days, Muslims abstain from eating and drinking, if they are physically able to do so, as well as from sex, violence, and cursing. This is a month in which Muslims focus on all forms of self-discipline, including refraining from anger, backbiting, and all forms of bad habits.

During the month of Ramadan, Muslims are supposed to intensify their efforts of struggling to overcome their base and vile desires and weaknesses. In Islamic sources, this is known as *jihad al-nafs*, or the struggle against oneself. Put differently, during the month of Ramadam, each Muslim is expected to undertake a personal jihad. According to the Prophet's teachings, this struggle for self-purification is the highest possible form of jihad. In addition to self-purification, Muslims are expected to intensify their efforts at building their relationship with God. They are expected to assess the nature of their past relationship with God, and repent and mend whatever breaches exist in this relationship. Moreover, fasting is supposed to remind Muslims of the sufferings of the poor, and therefore Muslims are expected to give generously to the poor.

In fact, part of the communitarian obligations upon Muslims is to arrange for public meals in which the poor are fed, especially during Ramadan. The month of Ramadan is a month of intensified training for individuals and the Muslim community. However, Muslims are encouraged to fast at least a couple times a week throughout the year if their health permits, and to continue their exercises in developing self-control and discipline.

4. Almsgiving (*zakat*): This is a set percentage (ranging from 2.5 percent to 20 percent, depending on the sect) of their wealth to the poor annually. In addition to these alms, Muslims are strongly encouraged to give to charity (*sadaqa*), each according to his or her wealth and ability.

The giving of charity is one of the most repeatedly emphasized obligations in the Qur'an. The Qur'an mentions groups of people particularly deserving of charity: the poor, the orphan, relatives in need, wayfarers and strangers or aliens in the land, and prisoners of war or other people in a state of bondage. The charity in this case is aimed at freeing them from their bondage. It is also considered highly praiseworthy to give charity to seekers of knowledge, scholars, and students in need. Importantly, most Muslim scholars make no distinction between giving charity to Muslims or non-Muslims. This includes giving charity to non-Muslim prisoners of war or others suffering from the oppression of bondage. The puritans, however, insist that charity must be given only to Muslims.

5. Pilgrimage (*Hajj*): A pilgrimage to Mecca once in a lifetime for those Muslims who can afford the trip and whose health allows them to make it.

Much has been written about the justification for the pilgrimage. Most importantly, pilgrimage is a symbol of Muslim unity and of the basic equality of all Muslims. All Muslims go on the pilgrimage wearing the same kind of clothing so that there is no distinction between rich and poor; all stand next to each other before God while clothed in the same white shrouds for men and simple white dresses for women. The rites performed while at pilgrimage are designed to emphasize not just the unity of all Muslims, but also the basic unity of the Abrahamic faiths. The circumambulation performed by Muslims around the *Ka'ba* (the cubic structure in the center of Mecca) symbolizes the circumambulation of the universe and all of existence around God.

These five pillars constitute the backbone of the Islamic faith, and according to traditional Islamic law, all Muslims must at least strive to fulfill the five obligations honestly and with sincerity. Denying one of the five pillars takes one out of the Islamic faith, meaning that a Muslim, in principle, must accept the five pillars as obligatory. Actually *performing* the five pillars is a different matter. As long as one admits that the five pillars are the essence of Islam and pronounces the testament of faith, one is accepted into the fold of Islam. There is no substantial difference between the moderates, conservatives, and puritans on this point. They do disagree, however, as to what, if anything, makes a Muslim an apostate.

The essential objective of the five pillars is to teach people to consistently work at developing a relationship with God; to learn piety, self-restraint, and humility; to emphasize the shared brotherhood of all Muslims; and to underscore the importance of service to others as a means of worshipping God. The five pillars have been described as the foundation upon which the rest of Islam stands, because they open up the potential of realizing the truly sublime—for realizing Godliness in oneself by surrendering oneself to Divinity.

In discussing the main doctrines that unite all Muslims and that form the backbone of Islam, I should mention that centuries ago a considerable number of Muslims used to believe that Islam is founded on six and not five pillars. The sixth pillar is summed up in the proclamation that every Muslim has a duty to enjoin the good and forbid the evil. Today, all Muslims agree that enjoining the good and forbidding the evil is a solemn religious duty upon all Muslims, but few would still count it as the sixth pillar of Islam. In essence, this religious obligation is very similar to what Thomas Aquinas asserted as the first principle of natural law: that all people ought to do good and refrain from doing evil.

The Islamic precept, however, goes beyond an injunction to do or refrain from doing particular acts; it also includes additional social and political obligations. Besides doing good and refraining from evil oneself, wherever and whenever possible, a Muslim is expected to encourage others to seek the good and to try to prevent others from doing evil. This duty is applicable at various levels—at the level of the family, society, and the state. Parents must discharge this religious obligation when dealing with their children, individuals owe both society and the state the same obligation, and the state owes society the same reciprocal obligation. As examples, at the family level parents fulfill this duty by providing proper moral guidance to their children and raising them well; at the social level, a Muslim might advise his friend to stop consuming alcohol or to start praying; at the state level, a Muslim might discharge his duty by speaking truthfully before the ruler and sincerely counseling him regarding state policies that are causing injustice and undue suffering. Emphasizing that in the political sphere the duty of enjoining the good and forbidding the evil often entails serious sacrifice, the Prophet taught that a word of truth spoken before a tyrant is an act of great moral value; and if as a result of doing so a Muslim loses his life, he dies a martyr.

Although all Muslims agree that enjoining the good and forbidding the evil is an Islamic obligation, this basic principle generated an enormous amount of debate and raised some of the most heated controversies among various theological and legal factions in Islamic history. This is not surprising, because this basic principle became implicated in controversies about political legitimacy, the role of law, methods of legal enforcement, and the legality of rebellion or disobedience. Furthermore, this principle raised numerous questions as to the limits of social and political activism and the permissibility of self-help when one encounters behavior that arguably violates Islamic law. The question incessantly raised and debated was: Assuming that the state is weak, absent, or unwilling to enforce Islamic legal injunctions, may Islamic law legitimately be enforced by, for instance, individuals, or the head of a small community, like a village or a tribe?[6]

It is important to emphasize that the five or six pillars of Islam do not represent *all* that Muslims agree upon, and I am certainly not claiming that other than the pillars of Islam Muslims disagree about everything else. The range of edicts and principles that Muslims agree upon is very broad. For instance, all Muslims agree that good Muslims ought to honor their parents, respect the elderly, be decent and caring toward their neighbors, feel for and help the poor, speak the truth, keep their promises, abstain from consuming alcoholic beverages, and refrain from committing adultery, fornicating, cheating, or stealing. All of these and many other ethical commandments are very important to Islam. All Muslims are expected to work hard to observe these commandments and to instill these virtues in themselves and, in the course of doing so, set a good moral example for others. I have focused on the five pillars because they are often identified as the foundation of the faith, and because taken together they are also the distinctive elements that define Islam.

What unites Muslims is substantial indeed. But the ways that any religion manifests itself in practice are always as varied as the personal psychologies and experiences that attempt to understand and absorb the teachings of that religion. People coming from different cultural and social contexts will live out the doctrines of the same faith in very different and varied ways. For instance, those growing up in despotic cultures will tend to understand their religious faith in ways that affirm their authoritarian experience. The same is true for people who grew up within a pluralist and democratic cultural experience; they will tend to understand their religion in ways that affirm tolerance, personal choice, and greater individual freedom.

Having discussed what all Muslims hold in common, we will now turn to areas where there is a substantial amount of ideological variation within the faith. We will focus in particular on the ideological outlooks and fundamental questions that separate moderate Muslims from puritans. It is important to note that on most theological issues, even those of greatest disagreement, there is a certain amount of shared territory between moderates and puritans; there is hardly a theological question upon which they completely diverge without adhering to a set of common assumptions and beliefs. After all, puritans and moderates still belong to the same religion; they believe in the same Holy Book; and they learn the same basic religious precepts. However, despite that degree of overlapping conviction, the beliefs of moderates and puritans often diverge widely because the two groups adhere to worldviews that are fundamentally at odds with each other. Often the differences between puritans and moderates are due to the amount of emphasis that each group assigns to principled moral imperatives as opposed to pragmatic political considerations; other differences are frequently due to the amount of emphasis that each group places on the overall objectives of Islam as opposed to the technical specifics of the law.

In the chapters that follow, I will compare and contrast the moderate and puritan views on key issues that not only represent critical tensions within Islam, but that (as we witness in the media every day) are often at the foundation of the problems that Muslims and the rest of the world must contend with on a daily basis. As we go through this discussion, the point to bear in mind is that although on any given topic moderates and puritans will often start from the same or similar premises or precepts, for various reasons their ways quickly part and the gap between their ways of thinking becomes increasingly wide.

I will start with the most foundational and critical issue in Islamic theology, and also the issue that is at the core and heart of most of the disagreements between moderates and puritans. This is the issue of God and the purpose of creation. The gap between puritans and moderates goes back to variant conceptions of the Divine Being—God's Self. Although puritans and moderates read the same references contained in the Qur'an about God and God's attributes, their respective understandings of key issues related to God's nature, what God wants from human beings, the purpose of creation, and the nature of the relationship between God and human beings diverge very sharply. As we will see, these are not abstract theoretical disagreements without real consequences to the lives of people. Far from it—these elementary and foundational questions end up being at the very core of the problems that plague the lives of Muslims and non-Muslims today.

SIX

GOD AND THE PURPOSE OF CREATION

The relationship of the individual to God is the most significant dynamic in Islam. There is no disagreement that God is immutable, omnipresent, indivisible, and eternal. Belief in the oneness, completeness, and perfection of God is central to the Islamic faith. God has no partners, associates, or equals, and He is neither begotten nor a begetter. God has many attributes, but it is fair to say that the attributes most emphasized in the Qur'an are the mercy and compassion of God. God is the Merciful, the Compassionate, the Kind, the Indulgent, and the Gracious. God is the Forgiver and the Avenger—the Just and the Punisher. God is Serenity and Peace and the Lover and the Beloved. God is purified and unadulterated Light; God is Beautiful and loves beauty. God is the Generous Giver and the Majestic Inventor; God is the Creator and the source of all goodness; the Sustainer, the Protector, the All-Powerful, and the All-Knowing.[1]

The Qur'an emphasizes that human beings must submit to God and yield to God's commands, and it warns that people should not subjugate God to their own whims. In other words, human beings should seek to understand God as God is, and not invent God as they would like God to be and then whimsically follow their own desires. There is no question that in this relationship, God is the Superior and Supreme, and human beings must approach God with submission, humility, and gratitude.

This much is clear, and I believe that conservatives, puritans, and moderates would be in agreement. But what follows from this? What is the nature of the relationship between God and human beings, and what is the potential of that relationship? What does God want from human beings, and what is the ultimate objective behind submitting to God?

Puritans treat the relationship between God and humans as straightforward enough. Humans were created to submit to God through worship, they say. Ritual practice is the demonstrative proof of total submission to God, and so perfection of ritual practice is the ultimate objective. Importantly, since submission to God is hinged on correct ritual practice, submission is not possible unless one accepts Islam. The road to submission is available only through Islam and therefore, only by becoming Muslim does one gain the opportunity to submit to God.

In the puritan conception, the rules of submission are found in the sacred law (the Shari'a). Therefore, it is imperative that the Shari'a be precise and exact on most points. The Shari'a must set out the code for submission in precise and exact terms so that Muslims may obey it, and attain salvation.[2] Through meticulous obedience, Muslims will avoid punishment in the Hereafter and will enter Heaven. On this point, the puritan conception is nearly mathematical. By performing acts of submission, Muslims earn good points, and by disobeying God they earn sins (or bad points). In the Final Day, God will total up the good points and the sins. Heaven or Hell is determined by the balance of points so that a single point can make the difference between Heaven and Hell. Puritans also dwell on Prophetic traditions that claim that in the Final

Day people will be made to walk on a thin rope, and then, losing their balance, people will fall into either Hell or Heaven. Moderates, however, challenge the authenticity of these traditions, which make the fate of human beings in the Hereafter a by-product of mathematical equations or the end result of acrobatics performed on a thin rope. While moderates consider these traditions to be inconsistent with the Qur'an, and no more than historical fabrications, puritans accept the historical veracity of these traditions and read and understand them in a rigid and literal way.

In the puritan paradigm, the relationship with God is formal and distant; it is strictly the relationship between a Superior and an inferior. God is to be feared and obeyed, and it is the fear of God's vengeance that defines true piety. As for God's mercy and compassion, the puritans believe that these two qualities have already been incorporated into the law. And since God's mercy and compassion are already contained in the law decreed by God, by definition the law must be considered compassionate and merciful. In the puritan view, it is not up to humans to reflect upon or think about the nature of God's mercy or compassion or the implications of this Divine mercy and compassion. All humans need to do is study the law, because the law is already the full embodiment of both God's mercy and compassion. It is as if God took whatever mercy and compassion that human beings might need in life, and put it all in the Divine law. Therefore, if one needs to find, experience, or feel this Divine mercy, all one needs to do is to obey and follow the law. By applying the Divine law, human beings attain a full measure of God's mercy and compassion— through obedience to law, humans will necessarily enjoy God's mercy and compassion.

The actual social impact that the law might have upon people is considered irrelevant. Although people might feel that the law is harsh or that its application results in social suffering, this perception is considered delusional. This is why, for instance, the Taliban in Afghanistan were oblivious to the social suffering caused by the laws that they enforced—since they believed that the law was Divine, there was no point to evaluating its actual impact upon the people they governed.

The approach of moderate Muslims to the relationship with God is materially different in several respects. Explaining the moderate approach must begin with the idea of trust between God and humanity. The Qur'an describes the moment of creation as the moment in which humanity was entrusted with a heavy responsibility. God gave humanity the blessing of rationality and the ability to differentiate between right and wrong. God made human beings God's agents or viceroys on the earth and entrusted them with the responsibility to civilize the land.

In the moderate conception, God is inherently and fundamentally moral. Puritans give God a whimsical quality—God is just, but justice is whatever God wills it to be. Similarly, God is merciful, but mercy is whatever God wills it to be. So, for instance, if God in the Final Day decides to damn all women or all Caucasians regardless of their actions, that would be just and good, simply because God willed it.

For moderates, this would be impossible. God is moral and ethical, in the sense that God shares with human beings an objective standard for goodness, morality, and beauty. Civilizing the earth does not mean constructing buildings or paving roads. It means striving to spread on the earth the Divine attributes such as justice, mercy, compassion, goodness, and beauty. In doing so, human beings spread Divinity itself upon the earth. In contrast, corrupting the earth—spreading violence, hatred, vengeance, and ugliness—means failure in discharging one's obligations toward God. The Qur'an teaches that the act of destroying or spreading ruin on this earth is one of the gravest sins possible—*fasad fi al-ard*, which means to corrupt the earth by destroying the beauty of creation, is considered an ultimate act of blasphemy against God.[3] Those who corrupt the earth by destroying lives, property, and nature are designated as *mufsidun* (corrupters and evildoers who, in effect, wage war against God by dismantling the very fabric of existence.[4]

The earth was given to human beings in trust, and humans share the burden of establishing Godliness—in spreading attributes that constitute the essence of Godliness. The more the earth is permeated with justice, mercy, compassion, and beauty, the nearer the earth is to the Divine ideal. The more corruption permeates the earth, the further away the earth is from Godliness.

The purpose of the gift of rationality given to human beings is to investigate the meaning of Godliness and the nature of the opposite of Godliness—evil. God charges Muslims with a sacred and central obligation: the duty to enjoin the good and forbid the evil, and to bear witness upon humanity for God. Conservatives, puritans, and moderates do not dispute that this is a fundamental and basic obligation upon all Muslims. In the puritan interpretation, enjoining the good and forbidding the evil means applying the Divine law and then bearing witness on the Final Day that the majority of humanity refused to submit to God. Moderates believe that the enjoinment of good and forbidding the evil imposes an obligation to investigate the nature of good and evil, and by necessity investigating the nature of Godliness and the absence of it. The enjoinment of good is part and parcel of the duty to civilize the earth and resist the spread of corruption. But the enjoinment of good and avoidance of evil is an ongoing, everlasting obligation to investigate the nature of Godliness and to attempt to make this Godliness, as much as possible, a part of the reality on earth. Human beings will never be able to reach the perfection of Divinity, but they must relentlessly seek to fulfill the attributes of Godliness. To bear witness upon humanity means that Muslims have an added obligation and a greater burden. Muslims must set an example for the rest of humanity in their diligence and persistence in seeking the perfection of Divinity. If Muslims fail in setting an example for humanity in their fidelity to justice, mercy, compassion, and beauty, then Muslims have failed God.

In moderate thought, God is too great to be embodied in a code of law. The law helps Muslims in the *quest* for Godliness, but Godliness cannot be equated to the law. The ultimate objective of the law is to achieve goodness, which includes justice, mercy, and compassion, and the technicalities of the law cannot be allowed to subvert the objectives of the law. Therefore, if the application of the law produces injustice, suffering, and misery, this means that the law is not serving its purposes. In this situation, the law is corrupting the earth instead of civilizing it. In short, if the application of the law results in injustice, suffering, or misery, then the law must be reinterpreted, suspended, or reconstructed, depending on the law in question.

Moderates agree with puritans that submission to God is the pivotal obligation of human beings, individually and collectively. Only by submitting the self to God can a human being liberate himself/herself from his or her base and whimsical desires. Submission to God means refusing to submit to any other person or thing. For a Muslim to be dominated or subjugated by a human oppressor is fundamentally at odds with the duty of submission to God. Human free will cannot be surrendered or submitted to anyone but God, and a Muslim is commanded to accept no master other than God.

However, the moderate conception of submission is different from the puritan notion in very important respects. Moderates differentiate between levels of submission. It is possible
to obey God without submitting to God. It is possible to obey
God's commands while remaining narcissistically self-centered
and selfish. In other words, it is possible to obey God, for
whatever reason, while caring little about God, and while
being entirely motivated by self-interest and without developing any emotional attachment toward God and without both-
ering to invest the time and effort in coming to know God by
reflecting upon God's attributes, which are reflected in God's
wondrous creation. Obeying God out of fear of punishment or
out of a desire for a reward keeps one vested in the paradigm
of self-interest and the artificiality of the mundane physical
world. If this constitutes submission to God, it is formalistic
and superficial because it does not attempt or even seek to internalize the sublime nature of the Divine. To submit to the
Divine in a meaningful and genuine way is to elevate oneself
to the transcendental and the sublime, to overcome the artificial physical world and to seek union with the ultimate
Beauty. As one struggles to purify and cleanse oneself—as one
engages in what is known as the inner jihad (*jihad al-nafs*),
and struggles to know oneself and know God, one is able to
achieve higher levels of submission.

Submission to God through fear and obedience, for moderates, is considered a primitive and even vulgar stage of submission. Submitting to God through fear means that the
worshipper has a tenuous relationship with God—a relationship that is driven by human self-interest or by the primitive
desire to avoid pain or seek pleasure. In the moderate conception, submission to God means to have a relationship with
God that is marked by absolute trust and confidence in God.
Islam means to surrender oneself, but linguistically, *Islam*

means a particular kind of surrender. It is a surrender in which one is in complete tranquility and peace with that who is the object of the surrender. The dynamic of this surrender is to know God and to seek Godliness in oneself. Submission is meaningful only if one strives to internalize and reproduce the qualities that make God deserving of our gratitude. These qualities are the same qualities which a human being is charged with spreading on this earth: justice, mercy, compassion, and beauty.

The ultimate stage in this process is to love God for what God is. First, God consistently sets out in the Qur'an the types of people that God loves—God loves those who are just, fair, equitable, merciful, kind, and forgiving, those who persistently purify themselves, and so on.[5] At the same time, the Qur'an repeats that God does not love those who are aggressors, unjust, corrupters, cruel, unforgiving, treacherous, liars, ungrateful, arrogant, and so on.[6] This addresses the types of people that God loves or does not love because of their actions, regardless of how those people feel about God. In this first instance, what triggers God's love is certain acts and qualities that are appealing to God. God loves those who act in particular ways or possess certain qualities even if some of these people do not love God back.

Second are those who have a reciprocal love relationship with God. Through gratitude one will inevitably love God for God's kindness, generosity, mercifulness, compassion, and beauty. In true gratitude, the only appropriate sentiment would be love. God describes God's self as appreciative for this love, and makes a commitment to those who love God that their love will be reciprocated.[7] To love God, a person must love all that God loves and dislike all that God dislikes. In the terminology of the Islamic tradition, one's desires and whims become consistent with the Divine Will and desire.

Therefore, to love God in an honest and genuine way, a person would necessarily desire and even covet attributes such as fairness, justice, mercy, compassion, equity, forgiveness, and purity. The converse is also true. To love God in a genuine and true fashion, a person would dislike what God finds offensive, such as aggression, injustice, cruelty, treachery, dishonesty, and arrogance, among others.

The highest stage of submission is to love God more than any other, even more than oneself, and for those who achieve this lofty position of loving God absolutely and completely, they become God's beloved, endowed with true perception, wisdom, and compassion.[8] For human beings to love God necessarily means that they must love all that God has created and represents. It would make little sense to love God but hate God's creatures and creation. To truly love God, one must love all human beings, whether Muslim or not, and love all living beings as well as all of God's nature. To truly love God means that one must also detest the destruction of what God has created. For those who reach the lofty stature of being God's beloved, their hearts will be full with love for justice, and full of compassion and love for all. As the classical scholars used to put it, if you find a man full of anger, resentment, hate, and cruelty toward human beings, animals, or nature, then know that the love of God has not entered his heart. In short, it is impossible to love God or be beloved by God and not to exhibit the characteristics of Godliness.

Another important aspect to this relationship with the Divine is the notion of partnership. Puritans place God beyond any emotion such as love. As an absolute master, God rewards the obedient and punishes the disobedient, but this is the extent of the relationship. Moderates emphasize the Qur'anic discourse that reminds human beings of the nearness of God to them. God is ever-present and always interacting with His creation.[9] In fact, the Qur'an explains that God often intercedes to save human beings from the consequences of their follies. Hence, the Qur'an asserts that if it had not been for Divine benevolence, many mosques, churches, synagogues, and homes would have been destroyed because of the ignorance and pettiness of human beings.[10] The Qur'an also states that often God mercifully intervenes to put out the fires of war and save human beings from their follies.[11] The notion that God intercedes to prevent human beings from destroying each other through wars and other acts of violence is of central importance to understanding the nature of Divine benevolence in Islam. God is a savior and caretaker of human beings.

Furthermore, a well-known tradition teaches that if a human being takes one step toward God, God reciprocates with ten steps. Therefore, moderates believe that God's relationship with human beings is not simply the act of judgment. Rather, if people seek God, God reaches out to them as well. Most importantly, for those who strive after Godliness, and through gratitude reach the point of loving God, God reciprocates their love. It is through love that union with the Divine becomes possible, and the manifestation of this union is a partnership between the Creator and the created.

In a well-known tradition the Prophet is reported to have said: "That who knows himself/herself knows his/her God." For moderates, this tradition is of pivotal importance for achieving partnership with God. Only by knowing oneself, which is achieved by self-critical reflection and struggling against one's base and selfish desires, can a person know who or what one honestly and truly worships. A person might believe that he/she worships and has submitted to God, but through critical self-reflection and by engaging in persistent inner jihad such a person will come to realize that in reality he/she worships and has submitted to no one but himself/herself. Critical self-reflection and self-knowledge are necessary to overcome the self-deceptions of the ego that lead to self-idolatry. For moderates, the worst self-deception is for one to slip in the pitfall of self-idolatry while pretending, or while deceiving oneself into believing, that he/she has submitted to God. The ego (al-nafs), if not disciplined by critical introspection, can easily deceive human beings into believing that they worship God, while in truth their real god and genuine source of guidance are self-centered desires such as a sense of self-promotion, the love of material gain, the intoxications of power and dominance over others, or, in extreme cases, it is possible to become enslaved and submit oneself to the unadulterated epitome of evil and true source of ugliness and corruption on the earth, Satan himself. This is why the Qur'an asserts that it is in a state of heedlessness and self-forgetfulness that people come to forget God. Often the converse is also true: forgetting who the true God is causes people to forget themselves by pretending to be who they are not and by demanding to be or have what is not their due or right.[12]

The process of critical introspection and self-knowledge, which enables a person to ascertain the true object of their submission and the real identity of their god, is necessary for building a partnership with God. But it is also a very private and personal undertaking. Unlike puritans, moderates insist that this process of self-edification and purification is a dynamic that is entirely within the purview of one's private relationship with God, to be evaluated and adjudged only by God and the individual involved. In the moderate conception, no person has the right to judge whether any worshipper is honestly and genuinely submitting to the One and Only God or, in the alternative, worshipping some other god. This point is critically important because, as will be recalled, puritans like 'Abd al-Wahhab used to accuse Muslims of associating partners with God, which in effect was another way of saying that Muslims did not worship the One and Only God, but worshipped someone or something else. As a result, engaging in the practice of *takfir*—whether calling a Muslim an idolater, a polytheist, an apostate, or an infidel—'Abd al-Wahhab and other puritans were able to justify murdering many Muslims. According to moderate Muslims, no person or institution is authorized to judge the piety of another or evaluate the closeness of any particular individual to God. In this regard, moderate Muslims rely on the Prophet's teachings, which emphasized that people should not be so arrogant as to presume that they know what is concealed in a person's heart. The Prophet Muhammad did emphasize that ethical individuals ought to behave in a fashion that is consistent with their avowed beliefs, and it is hypocritical for people to claim that they believe in Islam and then act in ways that are fundamentally inconsistent with the teachings of the religion. But in numerous traditions, the Prophet Muhammad also warned Muslims against the immorality of thinking ill of others and the arrogance of presuming to know how or what God thinks about any particular person. Furthermore, in addressing the Prophet Muhammad in the Qur'an, God emphasizes time and time again that he (Muhammad) was sent but to deliver a message and not to subjugate or dominate people. Accordingly, as the Qur'an stresses, even God's Messenger does not have the right to presume to know what is in the hearts of people. Repeatedly, the Qur'an informs the Prophet that it is up to God, not the Prophet, to forgive whom God wishes and punish whom God wishes, and God also draws near and endears whom God wishes. The Prophet's duties end when he truthfully preaches God's message to the best of his ability.[13]

Knowledge of the self is significant for building a relationship with God in one other important regard. Sufi Muslims or mystical orientations within Islam contended that if one truly know himself/herself, one will discover that the only true and genuine inner reality is nothing but the Divine. Through persistent and systematic remembrance of God, and strenuous spiritual exercises, people will uncover the genuine luminous substance within, which then makes union with the Divine truly possible. Moderate Muslims, however, have a different point of emphasis. For moderate Muslims, the issue is not so much whether the Divine is truly within; rather, the point is to maintain the integrity of the individual self and the singularity of the Divine, and in doing so to safeguard the integrity of the partnership between the individual and God.

In the course of building a partnership with God, one of the worst risks is that the individual will invent and construct God in his/her own image by projecting himself/herself onto God. The Qur'an persistently warns Muslims against the danger of transforming God into a source of validation instead of a force for moral elevation. Without critical introspection self-knowledge is not possible, and knowing oneself is necessary if a person is to avoid the risk of, through self-projection, transforming God into simply what validates one's own base desires and whims. Thus, instead of God elevating people to a higher moral existence, God is transformed into a force justifying whatever follies human beings wish to do, all in God's name. Paraphrasing the language of the Qur'an, through the guise of piety, God should not be made to rubberstamp the whimsies of people.[14]

A modern-day example will clarify this point. Take, for instance, the case of honor killings.[15] In the case of an honor killing, the male family member committing the act of murder feels no shame or remorse, because he has convinced himself that killing his sister or daughter is the will of God. That is, he believes that God wants him to kill his sister or daughter for having, for example, fornicated with her lover. Thus the male family member engages in blatant justification—he justifies his heinous act by convincing himself that this is God's will, when in reality, it is the male family member's own anger, vengeance, and shame that are driving his actions. Very often the male family member strongly believes that the death of the woman is satisfactory or even pleasing to God. Assuming that the perpetrator is a devout and religious man, as a necessary prelude to the murder, the perpetrator had in effect projected his own human sentiments onto God, and therefore he was able to assume that what made sense to him, what shamed him and his family, and what vindicated him and his family were identical to what God wants. Rather than thinking of God as merciful, forgiving, and compassionate, he imagines God to be angry, enraged, and vengeful. This imagined view of God was possible only because this supposedly pious and devout man heedlessly projected his own emotions and attributed them to onto God.

Furthermore, if through lack of self-awareness people project themselves onto God and see God through an entirely idiosyncratic and subjective lens, they will in all probability not love God at all. Rather, they have fashioned a god in their own image and then have fallen in love with that image. In this case, God is exploited in an entirely narcissistic process, and the purported partnership with the Divine becomes the means for egotistical empowerment and arrogance.

When it comes to the topic of God and creation, it is not surprising that moderates and puritans have much in common. However, in many ways, the differences between the two focus on their very different understandings of the meaning of submission to God. Their different conceptions of submission revolve around their variant and competing conceptions of

Divine Will or, put differently, what does God want from human beings. In contrast to the puritans, moderates do not believe that the law is a sufficient or complete expression of the Divine Will. God is too grand and majestic to be fully expressed and manifested in a code of law. For moderates, to truly submit means to understand and to love—to understand oneself and understand God and love completely, fully, and without reservation. In the moderate conception, what God wants from human beings is to love—not because God needs human love but because through Divine love human beings are elevated to a higher level of moral existence in which they partake in the attributes of God. In the moderate conception, it is fundamentally inconsistent and even impossible for one to truly love God and fail to reflect, among other attributes, some of God's vast mercy, compassion, forbearance, forgiveness, and beauty. If a person fails to demonstrate the heavenly attributes of God, according to moderate theology, then they have not truly submitted and have not learned to love the Creator of all things.

A further earmark of moderate theology is its anxiety about and even fear of power. More specifically, moderates are mindful of the many historical abuses and atrocities committed by individuals in God's name. Moderates understand God's supremacy and the Divine demand for submission to mean that only God and no other than God is entitled to absolute authority and power. And because authority and power are at the heart of any religious relationship, the often intellectually and practically difficult question is: What are the implications and appropriate parameters to be drawn between the sovereignty of the Divine and the autonomy of the individual?

Nowhere are these parameters more critical and pertinent than in the spheres of law and morality, for it is these two higher sources of governance that have historically reigned over human behavior. Thus the central inquiry becomes: With respect to law and morality, does God's sovereignty eliminate individual autonomy; and if not, what is the appropriate balance to be drawn between God's will as law and individual law-making? Are law and morality solely within the jurisdiction of God, or do human beings have a role to play within these two spheres as well?

Many of the questions raised in this context, whether they relate to the Divine Will, power, supremacy, and the danger of people subjugating or exploiting others in God's name, are inextricably intertwined with the challenging issue of the extent to which the devout followers of Islam are entitled or empowered to act on God's behalf. Indeed, this has been the precise underlying theme in much of the discussion thus far.

SEVEN

THE NATURE OF LAW
AND MORALITY

There is perhaps no issue that sets moderates and puritans apart as much as the subject of the nature and function of law. The law plays a central role in Islam to the point that many Muslims believe that without the law nothing remains of the Islamic religion. Nonetheless, despite its importance, the law is also the least understood aspect of the Islamic faith, by Muslims and non-Muslims alike. In the West, for example, some even go as far as thinking that a Muslim who believes in Shari'a law is by definition a fanatic or fundamentalist. One must admit that in the contemporary age the puritans have given Islamic law a terrible image to the extent that the moment Islamic law is mentioned, what comes to the mind of many are the horrendous abuses committed by the Taliban in Afghanistan, the Wahhabis in Saudi Arabia, or the puritans in Sudan. Yet to accuse every Muslim who believes in Islamic law of fanaticism is akin to accusing every Jew who believes in Rabbinic or Talmudic law of being a fanatic as well. The truth is that so much hinges on the particular conception that one has of Islamic law and the interpretation that one follows.

Islamic law is derived from two distinct sources: the Qur'an and the traditions of the Prophet (known as the *hadith* and Sunna). The Sunna is the orally transmitted record of what the Prophet said or did during his lifetime, as well as various reports about the Prophet's Companions. Traditions purporting to quote the Prophet verbatim on any matter are known as *hadith*. The Sunna, however, is a broader term; it refers to the *hadith* as well as to narratives purporting to describe the conduct of the Prophet and his Companions in a variety of settings and contexts.

In Islam, the Qur'an occupies a unique and singular status as the literal word of God. Whether moderate, conservative, or puritan, all Muslims believe that the Qur'an is the literal word of God as transmitted by the Angel Gabriel to the Prophet Muhammad. When it comes to the Qur'an, the Prophet Muhammad did nothing more than communicate word for word God's revelation, and Muslims preserved the text and transmitted it in its original form and language to subsequent generations. Muslims believe that God warranted and promised to guard the text of the Qur'an from any possible alterations, revisions, deletions, or redactions; therefore, while Muslims may disagree about the meaning and import of the revelation, there is a broad consensus among Muslims on the integrity of the text.

The Muslim belief in the integrity of the text of the Qur'an is well supported historically, but the meaning and context of the text is a far more complicated matter. At times the Qur'an addresses itself to the Prophet specifically, but on other occasions the Qur'an speaks to all Muslims or to humanity at large. In different contexts, the Qur'an will address Jews or Christians or the polytheists. There is a historical dynamic that contextualizes each of these occasions and thereby gives it further meaning and significance. While there is a broad consensus among Muslims on the integrity of the text of the Qur'an, and also on the Qur'an's authoritativeness as God's revealed and divine word, the historical context of the text is far more debated and contested.

After the Qur'an, most Muslims consider the Sunna of the Prophet to be the second most authoritative source of Islam. The Sunna is represented by an amorphous body of literature containing hundreds of reports about the Prophet and his Companions during the various stages of early Islamic history. Although the Qur'an and Sunna are considered the two primary sources of Islamic theology and law, there are material differences between these two sources. Unlike the Qur'an, the Sunna is not represented by a single agreed-upon text. The Sunna is scattered in at least six primary texts (the compilations of Bukhari, Muslim, Nisa'i, Tirmidhi, Ibn Maja, and Abu Dawud), and many other secondary texts (e.g., those of Musnad Ahmad, Ibn Hayyan, and Ibn Khuzayma). In addition, there are several collections of Sunna and *hadith* that are particularly authoritative among Shi'i Muslims (e.g., those of al-Kafi and al-Wasa'il).

Unlike the Qur'an, the Sunna was not recorded and written during the Prophet's lifetime. The Sunna was not systematically collected and documented for at least two centuries after the death of the Prophet. Although some documentation movements commenced in the first century of Islam, the main efforts at systematic collection and documentation did not start until the third century of the Islamic era (the ninth century of the Christian era). The late documentation of the Sunna meant that many of the reports attributed to the Prophet are apocryphal or at least are of dubious historical authenticity. In fact, one of the most complex disciplines in Islamic jurisprudence is that which attempts to differentiate between authentic and inauthentic traditions. Furthermore, reports attributed to the Prophet are not simply adjudged authentic or fabricated—such reports are thought of as having various degrees of authenticity, depending on the extent to which a researcher is confident that the Prophet actually performed a certain act or actually made a particular statement. Therefore, according to Muslim scholars, traditions could range from the highest to the lowest level of authenticity. Although Muslim scholars have tended to believe that they could ascertain whether the Prophet actually authored a particular tradition, the authorship of traditions is historically complicated. Many traditions are the end product of a cumulative development that took place through a protracted historical process, and therefore these traditions often give expression to sociopolitical dynamics that occurred many years after the death of the Prophet.

Aside from the issue of authenticity, there are several other ways that the Sunna is different from the Qur'an. The style and language of the Sunna is very distinct and different— while the Qur'an is poetical, melodic, and lyrical, the Sunna is not. Furthermore, the range of topics and issues addressed by the Sunna are much more sweeping than in the Qur'an. The Qur'an is primarily concerned with ethics and morality; the Sunna, however, contains everything from enunciations of moral principles, to detailed prescriptions on various matters of personal and social conduct, to mythology and historical narratives. Not all of the Sunna can easily translate into a set of straightforward normative commands, and therefore Muslim jurists argued that parts of the Sunna are intended as legislative and binding, while other parts are simply descriptive and, for the most part, not binding. Most importantly, the huge body of literature that embodies the Sunna is complex and generally inaccessible to the layperson. In order to systematically and comprehensively analyze what the Sunna, as a whole, has to say on a particular topic requires a considerable amount of technical knowledge and training. In part, this is due to the fact that the Sunna literature reflects a rather wide array of conflicting and competing ideological orientations and outlooks that exist in tension with each other. Selective and nonsystematic approaches to the Sunna produce determinations that are extremely imbalanced, and that are highly skewed in favor of a particular ideological orientation or another. And yet, such selective and imbalanced treatments of the Sunna of the Prophet are commonplace in the contemporary Muslim world.

Nevertheless, it is important to note that many of the basic rituals of Islam were derived from the Sunna traditions. In addition, the Sunna helps in contextualizing the Qur'anic revelation, and also in understanding the historical framework and role of the Islamic message. Consequently, it is not possible to simply ignore this formidable oral tradition, or focus exclusively on the Qur'an, without doing serious damage to the structure of Islam as a whole.

There is no question that the Qur'an and Sunna occupy a highly authoritative position in the Islamic faith, and that they are boundless and illimitable sources for thinking about ethics, morality, law, and wisdom. But as sources of guidance, they are also multilayered and multifaceted, and when the Qur'an and Sunna are considered together, they tell a complex story. They can be a source of profound intellectual and moral guidance and empowerment. However, the opposite is also true and dangerously so: if approached with the wrong intellectual and moral commitments, or even if approached from within a hedonistic and noncommittal moral framework, they could contribute to a process of ethical and intellectual stagnation, if not deterioration and putrefaction. For instance, the Sunna contains a large number of traditions that could be very empowering to women, but it also contains an equally large number of traditions that are demeaning and deprecating toward women. To engage the Sunna on this subject, analyze it systematically, interpret it consistently with the Qur'an, and read it in such a fashion that would promote and not undermine the ethical objectives of Islam calls for a well-informed and sagaciously balanced intellectual and moral outlook.

Other than the Qur'an and the traditions of the Prophet, there were various methodologies used by jurists for producing legal rulings. Jurists used rule by analogy in which they extended the same ruling from an old case to a new case because the old and new cases were substantially similar. Traditionally, Muslim jurists also used principles such as equity and public interest in order to make the law responsive to changing circumstances and conditions.

Importantly, what is called Islamic law is not contained in a single or a few books. Islamic law is found in an enormous corpus of volumes that document the rulings and opinions of jurists over the span of many centuries. In the Sunni world, there are four surviving schools of thought: the Shafi'i, Hanafi, Maliki, and Hanbali. In the Shi'i world, there are two surviving schools of thought: the Ja'fari (predominant among Shi'is, including those who live in Iraq and Iran) and the Zaydi (widespread primarily in Yemen). Substantively, despite the sectarian differences, the Ja'fari school is very similar to the Shafi'i school and the Zaydi school is very similar to the Hanafi school in terms of their methodologies and rulings. The Isma'ili school of Qadi Nu'man, although Shi'i today, has a very limited following, primarily in India. There is also the Ibadi school of jurisprudence, which is neither Sunni nor Shi'i, but belongs to a third sect known as the Ibadiyya, and its followers live predominately in Oman. Each of these schools generated its own jurisprudential tradition of legal rulings and opinions.

Quite often the sages that belonged to a particular school of law wrote legal treatises that became far more influential than the texts written by the founder of the school. For instance, al-Khiraqi (d. 334/946), author of *al-Mukhtasar,* and Ibn Qudama, (d. 620/1223), author of *al-Mughni,* were both more influential in defining the Hanbali school than the eponym of the school, Ahmad Ibn Hanbal (d. 241/855). Among the many students of the eponym of the Hanafi school Abu Hanifa (d. 150/767), there were three particularly influential sages, the judge Abu Yusuf (d. 182/798), al-Shaybani (d. 189/804), and Zufar (d. 158/774), and each one of them developed his own interpretation of the teachings of the master Abu Hanifa. Yet, although the matter is open to dispute, the Hanafi jurist al-Marghinani's (d. 593/1196) book, *al-Hidaya,* and the Hanafi jurist al-Sarakhsi's (d. 483/1090) huge multivolume book *al-Mabsut* has been more influential than any of the texts written by Abu Hanifa or his three celebrated sages. Al-Shafi'i (d. 204/819), the eponym of his school, wrote several extant texts that continue to be very influential, but the works of many of his followers, such as al-Mawardi (d. 450/1058), the author of the monumental corpus *al-Hawi,* and al-Shirbini (d. 972/1569), the author of the commentary *al-Mughni,* continue to have an impact that is no less important than the works of the founder of the school. The eponym of the Maliki school, Anas bin Malik (d. 179/795), wrote a wildly influential work called *al-Muwatta',* but his disciple, Sahnun (d. 240/854), wrote a more extensive book, titled *al-Mudawwana,* which quickly became an essential reference source for the Maliki school. However, later Maliki jurists, such as Ibn Rusd (d. 520/1122), al-Qarafi (d. 684/1285), and al-Shatibi (d. 790/1388), wrote remarkably creative works that greatly enhanced and developed the field of Maliki law. Similarly, the Ja'fari, Zaydi, and Ibadi schools produced an enormous corpus of jurisprudential works written by different jurists, in different places, and different times, which made each of these schools progressively more sophisticated and mature with the passage of time.

Importantly, the numerous volumes that collectively represent the Islamic legal tradition do not preserve just the rulings and opinions of the living schools of thought, but also record the views of the many extinct schools of law. At one time, there were 130 schools of legal thought in the Islamic civilization, but most of them became extinct for a variety of reasons. In other words, Islamic law is not represented just by the surviving schools, but *all* the schools that at one time or another have thrived in the lands of Islam. Among the jurists who founded schools that ultimately became extinct are the following: Ibn Shubruma (d. 144/761), Ibn Abi Layla (d. 148/765), Sufyan al-Thawri (d. 161/777), al-Layth Ibn Sa'd (d. 175/791), Sharik al-Nakha'i (d. 177/793), Abu Thawr (d. 240/854), al-Awza'i (d. 157/773), Ibn Jarir al-Tabari (d. 310/922), Ishaq bin Rahawayh (d. 238/852), and Dawud bin Khalaf (d. 270/883), who founded what became known as the Zahiri school. Ibn Hazm (d. 456/1064), who was jurist from the Zahiri school, wrote a multivolume work titled *al-Muhalla*. Although the Zahiri school is now long extinct, Ibn Hazm's book continues to be very influential among Islamic legal specialists.

"Islamic law" is a shorthand expression for an amorphous body of legal rulings, judgments, and opinions that have been collected over the course of many centuries. On any point of law, one will find many conflicting opinions about what the law of God requires or mandates. The Islamic legal tradition is expressed in works that deal with jurisprudential theory and legal maxims, legal opinions (*fatawa*), adjudications in actual cases, and encyclopedic volumes that note down the positive rulings of law (*ahkam*). As noted earlier, Islamic law covers a broad array of topics, ranging from ritual practice to criminal law, personal status and family law, commercial and transactional law, international law, and constitutional law.

The question is: How does this substantial body of jurisprudence relate to Divinity or to God's law? In what way can this tradition of juristic disputations, judgments, and opinions claim to be sacred or Divine law?

These questions bring us to a crucial distinction that is central to the very logic of Islamic law. What is customarily referred to as Islamic law is actually separated into two distinct categories: Shari'a and *fiqh*. Shari'a is the eternal, immutable, and unchanging law as it exists in the mind of God. Shari'a is the Way of truth and justice as it exists in God's mind. In essence, Shari'a is the ideal law as it ought to be in the Divine realm, and as such it is by definition unknown to human beings on this earth. Thus human beings must strive and struggle to realize Shari'a law to the best of their abilities. In contrast, *fiqh* is the human law—it is the human attempt to reach and fulfill the eternal law as it exists in God's mind. As such, *fiqh* is not itself Divine, because it is the product of human efforts. *Fiqh*, unlike Shari'a, is not eternal, immutable, or unchanging. By definition, *fiqh* is human and therefore subject to error, alterable, and contingent.

With this background, we can now highlight the fundamental differences between puritans and moderates on the topic of law. The moderates strongly distinguish between the eternal law, as it exists in God's mind, and the human effort to understand and implement the eternal law. In effect, this means that most of what is called Islamic law is a human product subject to error, alteration, development, and nullification. The eternal law as it exists in God's mind is perfect, but it is also inaccessible to human beings. Human beings make a best effort to reach for and understand the eternal law, but it is arrogant and offensive to ever claim that human beings could be certain that they have successfully comprehended the eternal law. Therefore, moderates insist that a jurist must humbly admit the possibility that what is claimed as Islamic law is subject to error. A jurist must expend his best efforts to understand the eternal law, but a jurist must never assume that his opinion is for certain identical to the eternal law.

In principle, puritans do differentiate between the Divine law (the eternal law as it exists in God's mind) and human efforts to understand that law. However, in reality puritans end up obscuring the distinction to the point of rendering it meaningless. Puritans contend the range of *fiqh* or space where *fiqh* may be appropriately applied is limited to cases where God has left matters open to debate and difference, but *fiqh* may not be applied to any question or issue that God has precisely and decisively resolved for Muslims. Put differently, human beings may apply their understanding to all issues that God has left open for debate, but they may not attempt to apply human understanding to any matter that God has decided in an unequivocal and decisive fashion.

Thus far, puritan methodology is uncontroversial—many Muslims would agree that when God speaks decisively and clearly, humans should listen and obey. The problem, however, is that for puritans the range or scope of issues that they believe God has excluded and foreclosed to human understanding is very sweeping. For the puritans, regarding most matters and issues pertinent to human existence, God has revealed a precise and exact law, and all that remains is for Muslims to implement the law. According to the puritans, 90 percent of what they consider the revealed law is not open to debate or discussion, alteration or change. Only 10 percent of the law is open to debate and differences of opinion. Therefore, according to the puritans, *fiqh* is applicable to no more than 10 percent of all legally pertinent issues. Conversely, Shari'a covers 90 percent of all human affairs. Put differently, as to 90 percent of all issues, the Divine Will can be perfectly realized and understood with absolute precision, and only 10 percent of all issues are open to human speculation, debate, and disagreement.

Interestingly, following the example of 'Abd al-Wahhab, puritans have rather arbitrarily picked the Hanbali school of law as providing the only valid and correct legal system. The reality, however, is that puritans are very selective—and opportunistically so—even with the jurists of the Hanbali school. Puritans selectively pick certain Hanbali jurists, such as Ibn Taymiyya and Ibn Qayyim al-Jawziyya, and treat the views of these jurists as immutable and beyond questioning. Moreover, puritans even read jurists like Ibn Taymiyya and Ibn Qayyim al-Jawziyya in an abusively selective manner— they adopt whatever they find in the writings of these jurists that confirms their worldview and ideology, and conveniently ignore the rest.[1] In addition, puritans will never cite or refer to Hanbali jurists such as Ibn 'Aqil or Najm al-Din al-Tufi, who were well known for their rationalist and liberal approaches. As mentioned earlier, this kind of opportunistic selectivity was exactly what 'Abd al-Wahhab did. Perhaps it is not surprising that the Hanbali jurists that puritans select to follow are typically the most hostile to women and to non-Muslims.

In general, the Hanbali school of thought is the strictest and most conservative school in Islamic jurisprudence. Despite some very notable exceptions of Hanbali jurists who were decisively rationalist and liberal, the Hanbali school is known for its literalist, strictly constructionist, and inflexible approaches. Because of its rigidity and inflexibility, by the nineteenth century the Hanbali school was on the verge of becoming extinct. By that time, the only geographic area where the Hanbali school continued to exist was the Arabian Peninsula, but even then several gulf countries, such as Kuwait, had abandoned Hanbalism in favor of the more flexible Maliki school of thought. However, the emergence of Saudi Arabia and its embrace of what may be called selective Hanbalism radically altered the fate of the Hanbali school. Not only did Saudi Arabia save the Hanbali school from extinction, but through the concerted efforts of the Saudi government, selective Hanbalism became the ideology of choice for all puritan movements around the Sunni Muslim world.[2]

The disagreements between puritans and moderates over issues of law and morality are even deeper and more fundamental than discussed thus far. As alluded to earlier, puritans, conservatives, and moderates all believe that the Qur'an is incorruptible. The Qur'an has not been corrupted or changed in any way, and therefore, the revelation was preserved exactly as the Prophet Muhammad received it from God. The Sunna or traditions attributed to the Prophet, however, are a different question altogether. Puritans treat the traditions attributed to the Prophet as if a code of law that must be enforced without question. Although these traditions count in the thousands, puritans will often base a law on a single tradition found in one of the many sources in which these traditions are preserved. The puritans treat certain sources, such as *Sahih al-Bukhari,* as immutable and not open to questioning.[3] Some puritans even go as far as maintaining that if a Muslim questions any of the traditions in *Bukhari,* such a Muslim is an infidel. The problem is that many of these traditions defy reason, or are offensively demeaning toward women and non-Muslims, or are blatantly inconsistent with the ethics and morality set out in the Qur'an. Furthermore, as some researchers have pointed out, puritans are very selective in terms of which particular Prophetic traditions they choose to emphasize or completely ignore. In fact, their approach is very reminiscent of the phenomenon of *"hadith* hurling" that Shaykh al-Ghazali described in his famous work.[4]

The reason that puritans rely on these slipshod methods in dealing with the source materials of Islamic law is partly due to a certain attitude that they adopt toward the Qur'an and Sunna. Despite the complex set of issues raised by these source materials, puritans treat the Qur'an and Sunna as a panacea to all challenges that could confront them in life. Indeed, the Qur'an and Sunna can inspire creative solutions to most problems, but this is a far cry from assuming that they can automatically yield solutions to life's challenges. However, among puritans it has become accepted dogma that the Qur'an and Sunna provide for a complete way of life and contain an antidote to every social and political ailment that confronts Muslims. In this paradigm, one often encounters a simplistic attitude that assumes that the Qur'an and Sunna are full of formulas, and that the only thing missing in the equation is the will and determination to apply the correct formula to the appropriate problem. This attitude induces puritans to treat the tradition as a vending machine of sorts—the puritans make-believe that there is a ready-made solution in the sources for every problem that confronts people. If the lived reality, however, clashes with the puritan pretense, the puritans conclude that the solution is most certainly correct, and it is the people who must be all wrong.

In contrast to the puritans, moderates apply systematic principles of historical criticism to the traditions attributed to the Prophet. Unlike the Qur'an, as mentioned earlier, these traditions were documented and preserved a few centuries after the death of the Prophet. In addition, the traditions clearly reflect historical circumstances, sectarian disputes, and political conflicts that took place years after the Prophet's death. Using modern methods of critical analysis, moderates conclude that many of these traditions are apocryphal or pure inventions. Moreover, many of the Prophetic traditions were reported by single individuals. In other words, an individual told some other individual that he heard the Prophet say such and such. Moderates scrutinize the circumstances to make sure that any given report makes good historical and rational sense; otherwise, the report is dismissed as unreliable. For instance, there is cumulative evidence that when the Prophet wanted to teach Muslims something of importance, the Prophet would have a person call upon the people to gather, and then he would relate the necessary lesson. When moderates find that this procedure was not complied with, despite the significance of the subject matter, they naturally become suspicious and investigate the circumstances. If the report relates to a major aspect of the faith or to a relatively important issue, it would have made little sense for the Prophet to inform a single person about this matter. If the issue was very important or if it would have had a major impact upon Muslims, one would expect that the Prophet would have implemented the above described procedure or would have informed a large number of people about the matter. In certain circumstances and on particular issues, it would have made sense for the Prophet to inform a close confidante, and thus these reports might be treated differently. Without getting lost in the numerous technicalities, it is sufficient to say that moderates seek to make sure that the evidence supporting a ruling is coherent, reasonable, and reliable.

When it comes to the Qur'an, the disputes between moderates and puritans also relate to the validity of using rational methods of analysis in articulating the law. Puritans tend to treat the Qur'an as a code of law—that is, they focus their attention on the specific Qur'anic verses to prescribe detailed rules on marriage, divorce, inheritance, or criminal punishments. They enforce these rulings without regard to the historical circumstances that existed at the time these rulings were revealed to the Prophet Muhammad. The puritans do not pay any attention to the overall guiding principles of the Qur'an or try to analyze the moral or ethical guidelines enunciated in the Qur'an. In effect, the details and specifics take precedence over the ethical and moral objectives of the Qur'an.

Moderates recognize that the Qur'an did express specific rulings on different subjects. But for moderates, the moral and ethical objectives of the Qur'an play a central and pivotal role in the process of legal analysis. The point of the legal analysis is not to unthinkingly and blindly implement a set of technical rules, but to seek after the ultimate objectives of the Qur'an. All Qur'anic laws reinforce and promote moral and ethical objectives, such as racial and ethnic equality, freedom from compulsion in the conduct of human affairs, freedom of conscience, and the right of women to own property, and it is the duty of Muslims to apply themselves intellectually in order to comprehend and fulfill these objectives. These moral objectives are related to the obligation to seek Godliness in oneself and in society.

The specific rulings of the Qur'an came in response to particular problems that confronted the Muslim community at the time of the Prophet. The particular and specific rules set out in the Qur'an are not objectives in themselves. These rulings are contingent on particular historical circumstances that might or might not exist in the modern age. At the time these rulings were revealed, they were sought to achieve particular moral objectives such as justice, equity, equality, mercy, compassion, benevolence, and so on. Therefore, it is imperative that Muslims study the moral objectives of the Qur'an and treat the specific rulings as demonstrative examples of how Muslims should attempt to realize and achieve the Qur'anic morality in their lives. Because puritans do not think of the specific rules as demonstrative examples but as objectives in themselves, they seek to implement the rules *regardless of whether their application will enhance or undermine Qur'anic principles* such as justice, equity, and mercy.

The debate about how the specific rules relate to the ultimate objectives of the Qur'an is closely tied to a far more basic and fundamental issue and that is: What are the ultimate objectives of the Shari'a (the eternal law as it exists in God's mind)? What is the Shari'a for, and what does it aim to do? Historically, legal schools of thought disagreed on many issues, but they agreed on the response to these questions. According to all the jurisprudential schools, the purpose of the Shari'a is to serve the best interests of human beings (*tahqiq masalih al-'ibad*). Perhaps the whole controversy between the puritans and moderates can be summed up in how each interprets this principle. The puritans believe that the best interests of humanity are served by strict application of the law to human conduct and behavior. Using reason is thus absolute anathema—rather, all Muslims need to do is find the law and apply it strictly and faithfully, and that is the end of the process. Puritans believe that not only did God make about 90 percent of the law clear, but they also believe that God has a determinable will as to about 90 percent of human affairs. In the puritan conception, God is a micromanager—God left only about 10 percent of human affairs to human discretion, and this is why God left no more than 10 percent of the law unclear or open to debate.

These presumptions are fundamentally at odds with the moderate approach. Rather, moderates pose the rhetorical question: Why did God grant us reason when in reality God has already resolved most issues in life for us? According to Islamic theology, God declared at the moment of creation that He created a wonder that is worthy of the highest honors—this wonder is the ability to reason (*'aql*). But if one would accept the puritan paradigm, God did not leave much space for

human beings to apply their rational faculties since God un-
equivocally resolved most matters for human beings and all
that is left is for humans to obey.

Furthermore, in Islamic theology, it is believed by moderates that God rewards those who search for the Divine Will,
even if they ultimately reach the wrong conclusions. God, according to this theology, rewards the diligence and the hard
work expended in the effort to find the Divine Will, not the results that one ultimately reaches. Moderates contend that it
would make little sense for God to reward the effort if all God
expects of us on most matters is blind obedience.

Regarding the ultimate objective of Shari'a, moderates contend that serving the interests of humanity means achieving
Godliness on the earth. Put differently, the objective of the law
is not to apply technicalities regardless of their consequences,
but to achieve the ultimate moral and ethical objectives that
represent the essence of Godliness on this earth.

These disputes and debates are not theoretical or pedantic
distinctions without practical consequences. For instance, puritans accept without question the traditional rule mandating
that the punishment for apostasy is death. Moderates do not
accept that traditional position because it is inconsistent with
the Qur'an. First addressing the Prophet, the Qur'an states:
"Remind them for you are but a reminder; you are not a warden over them."[5] This verse emphasizes that even the Prophet
does not have the right to think of himself as a warden who
has the power to coerce people. This is reaffirmed by many of
the historical reports regarding the Qur'anic revelation that
emphasize that belief and conviction cannot be coerced. For
example, it was reported that at the time of the Prophet, a
Muslim man named Husayn bin Salim bin 'Awf had two
daughters who were Christian. This fellow seems to have tried
to persuade his daughters to become Muslim, but they were

persistent in their refusal. Fed up, the father went to the Prophet and asked for permission to compel his daughters to convert to Islam, but the Prophet resolutely refused. Shortly thereafter, the Qur'anic revelation arrived declaring that truth and falsity are clear and distinct, and whoever wishes to believe may do so, and whoever refuses to believe may do so—there can be no coercion in religion.[6] "There is no compulsion in matters of faith," the Qur'an proclaimed.[7] Moderates consider this verse to be enunciating a general, overriding principle that cannot be contradicted by isolated traditions attributed to the Prophet. Therefore, moderates do not believe that there is any punishment that attaches to apostasy.

Other than the issue of apostasy, puritan methodology leads to adopting various positions that moderates cannot accept, including, for instance, that the testimony of women counts as half that of men in court; that the rights of women upon divorce are extremely limited; that men at their absolute discretion may take up to four wives with or without cause; and that shockingly severe criminal penalties can be applied unjustly and without justification. The significant point is that as one observes in Saudi Arabia, Afghanistan (under the Taliban), Nigeria, and Sudan, what is purported to be Islamic law is applied in a fashion that shocks the conscience, and that appears capricious and arbitrary. What one observes is a complete lack of compassion, mercy, equity, or justice.

Even more disturbing is that by relying on the most tangential and tenuous types of evidence, puritans force upon Muslims a kind of austerity that is entirely suffocating. In fact, much of what they advocate is affirmatively designed to remove tenderness and kindness from the human heart. They eradicate art, beauty, and anything else that excites the creative imagination, and demand that Muslims become like mechanized robots. Furthermore, since according to puritans God has an affirmative will as to most matters in life, puritans have rules that regulate how one eats, drinks, dresses, sits, walks, goes to the bathroom, makes love, and undertakes practically every other aspect of life. For every human activity, there are rules that must be observed. Below are examples of common puritan laws as practiced in parts of the Muslim world today:

- Music, singing, and dancing in all forms are forbidden.

- All television programs, unless religious, are forbidden.

- The giving of flowers is forbidden.

- Clapping the hands in applause is forbidden.

- Drawing human or animal figures is forbidden.

- Acting in a play is forbidden, because acting is a form of lying.

- Writing novels is forbidden, because it is a form of lying.

- Wearing shirts with animal or human images is forbidden.

- Shaving one's beard is forbidden.

- Eating or writing with the left hand is forbidden.

- Standing up in honor of someone is forbidden.

- Celebrating anyone's birthday, including the Prophet's, is forbidden.

- Keeping or petting dogs is forbidden.

- Dissecting cadavers even in criminal investigations and for the purposes of medical research is forbidden.

Anyone who has visited Muslim countries, with the exception of Saudi Arabia, would know that these rulings are not followed, much less accepted. Puritans consider this lack of acceptance as a testament to the fact that modern-day Muslims have gone awry and that they must be led to reembrace Islam. In truth, puritans believe that people should be forced to fulfill the strict legal vision which they embrace. Most Muslim societies, however, reject the puritanical social vision and gravitate toward moderation.

Moderates believe that the law should be flexible and dynamic enough to fit the highly complex and ever-changing social conditions of human beings. In essence, then, the moderate view recognizes the temporal and sociocultural changes that have taken place since the time of the Prophet. Indeed, the discussion on law and morality demonstrates the fundamental distinction between what was done in the past, and what must be done now, to conform to the Islamic faith. In short, it is the distinction between history and modernity that further widens the gap between the puritan and moderate viewpoints. We turn to that distinction in the next chapter.

EIGHT

APPROACHES TO HISTORY AND MODERNITY

At the very root of the debates about the nature of God's law and what demands this law places upon believers is the issue of how to think about and deal with history. The problem that confronts all religious legal systems is no less complex than whether history is redundant and static, or progressive and ever-changing. Assuming that history is not static and that as time changes so do people, then the difficult question becomes: How does it make sense that God would intervene at one point in time in history and decree His immutable Will to a people who are constantly evolving and changing? Does it make sense to say that God is ever-present in a historical process that is necessarily fluid and constantly changing? Before long, we are forced to confront the issue of whether God's will is itself constantly evolving and changing; but if so, how can the Divine remain eternal and immutable? Does it make sense to say that the Creator of all things creates history and, in the same breath, claim that the Divine Will changes with history?

These questions and many more have forced moderates and puritans to ask whether there is a specific point in time or a particular historical moment, when the Divine Will was fully and completely expressed. As importantly, both groups had to contend with the extent to which Islamic law ought to change in order to accommodate the changing natures and customs of people in different places of the world. As one struggles with giving effect to the Divine Will and Command, the problem of how to understand and react to history raises one of the most fundamental disputes between puritans and moderates. This issue is far-reaching and pivotal to how one understands Islam's universal and eternal message.

For puritans, it is considered a fundamental premise of the faith that Islam fulfilled its full potential during a particular historical period, which they consider to be "the golden age of Islam." According to puritans, the golden age of Islam consisted of the time that the Prophet ruled Medina and the ages of the four Rightly Guided Caliphs, close Companions and supporters of the Prophet during his lifetime—Abu Bakr (d. 13/634), 'Umar (d. 23/644), 'Uthman (d. 35/656), and 'Ali (d. 40/661). In addition, many Muslims consider the Umayyad Caliph 'Umar bin 'Abd al-'Aziz (d. 101/720) to be the fifth Rightly Guided Caliph, although he was not a Companion of the Prophet. The expression "Rightly Guided Caliphs" (*al-Khulafa' al-Rashidun*) literally means "the wise or sagacious caliphs," and in general reflects the belief of Sunni Muslims that the caliphs who earned this honorific title enjoyed a high degree of piety and religious knowledge and that they were just and fair rulers.[1] While Sunni Muslims in general respect the first four caliphs and admire their achievements, puritans go much further—Puritans highly idealize this time period, which lasted roughly for the first fifty years of Islam, and believe that in the golden age, perfect justice and fairness were fully realized. For puritans it is simply not possible for any polity anywhere, at any time, to accomplish a greater degree of justice and fairness. After the first fifty years, they believe, the balance of Islamic history was one of unmitigated deterioration.

Consequently, puritans believe that Muslims should reclaim the golden age by closely imitating and replicating the institutions and codes of conduct they believe existed at that time. It is as if history had peaked and fulfilled its complete potential during the golden age of Islam. As to what remains of history, puritans imagine that Muslims, and indeed the rest of humanity, must strive to replicate that earlier time when history reached its zenith.

Earlier I explained the profound sense of alienation felt by the puritans in the modern age. It is likely that by clinging to an idealized notion of the past, the puritans only reinforce their own sense of alienation in the modern age. But there are several factors that augment this sense of alienation, which also induce puritans to cling to an idealized past with uncompromising fervor. Prominent among these factors is the suffocating despotism that exists in several Muslim countries.[2]

This despotism results in a feeling of powerlessness and even desperation. People living in these despotic countries are made to feel that their views and opinions are entirely inconsequential and of no relevance vis-à-vis the government. Not only is there an extremely high cost for speaking out, but even thought and creativity are activities full of risk. Generally, the government communicates to its citizenry that to be on the safe side of things, the citizenry ought to occupy itself with personal and private concerns such as earning a living and raising a family. In despotic societies, those who have a sense of social conscience or a desire to be politically involved in their nation's interests are presented with very limited choices: either carefully walk within the strict boundaries set by the government, or risk suffering the considerable punitive powers of the state. The pervasive effect of despotism is that it robs much of the citizenry its sense of dignity and self-worth.

Not surprisingly, the people most affected by this despotism are classes within society that are educated but that also suffer limited economic means and few opportunities for social mobility. Typically, the educated classes develop a higher level of sociopolitical consciousness, and are more aware of their rights as well as their social obligations. Furthermore, educated classes are usually not as complacent about accepting whatever social status they may enjoy and they believe that further education and hard work entitles them to elevate and improve their economic, social, and political status. This is why, for instance, feminist and human rights movements thrive in direct proportion to a rising level of literacy in society. In addition, societies with the highest levels of literacy and education are the most successful in establishing stable democratic states.

In addressing the factors that contribute to this sense of alienation, it is important to take particular note of the consequences of torture, which is a regular staple of despotic governments. State prisons where torture is regularly practiced have given birth to some of the most puritanical and extremist orientations in the Islamic world. Importantly, the very practice of torture generates narratives of torture, tales of horror that are transmitted through society and that become part of the cultural fabric, and that play a significant role in deepening the sense of stress, fear, and lack of self-worth. These narratives help in creating a polarized atmosphere between puritans and the state, empowering the puritans to view the state as part of the hostile environment that is working against them. Furthermore, such narratives bolster and strengthen the puritans' sense of victimhood and their alienation from the societies in which they live. Puritans become convinced that their own societies remained complacently apathetic and noncaring as they were forced to endure savage mistreatment. This, of course, contributes to the process through which puritans end

up excommunicating the societies they live in. Most important
of all, the practice of torture further radicalizes puritans by de-
sensitizing them toward cruelty and humane values in general.
For instance, Salih Saraya (executed 1975), and Shukri
Mustafa (executed 1978), leaders of very extreme puritan organizations, were at one time members of the more moderate
Muslim Brotherhood organization, but became radicalized
after they were severely tortured in Egypt. The Syrian Muslim
Brotherhood became radicalized and resorted to violence in
1982 after enduring years of barbaric treatment by the Syrian
government. In addition, it is not coincidental that the Saudi
government, one of the worse human rights abusers in the
Middle East, is also one of the prime exporters of highly fanatic and violent extremists.

Despotic governments in the Muslim world, which are systematic human rights abusers, tend to fall into one of two categories: either they target and persecute all dissenters,
regardless of their ideological orientation, whether puritan or
not, or they target Islamic, particularly puritanical, movements. In the first category are countries such as Saudi Arabia,
Saddam's Iraq, Syria, Libya, Indonesia, or Sudan, to name just
a few. These countries arrest and torture any real or imagined
opponents of the government, including people who are critical of the state's human rights record or the rampant corruption and nepotism that plagues the institutions of governance
in these nations. They persecute puritan movements to the extent that the policies of these movements are inconsistent with
the policies of the state. In effect, whether puritan movements
end up being persecuted entirely depends on the extent to
which their ideology conflicts with the state. As a result, in
countries such as Saddam's Iraq, Libya, and Syria the vast majority of Islamic movements end up being savagely repressed
because their ideology conflicts with the secular nationalist

ideology of the state. In Saudi Arabia, however, most puritan movements enjoy a high degree of safety, but liberal, Sufi, and secular groups as well as the majority of Shi'i movements are severely repressed. In the second category are countries like Egypt, Pakistan, Kuwait, Algeria, Morocco, Tunisia, and Uzbekistan again, to name just a few. These countries adopted policies of systematically repressing either all Salafi/puritan groups or militant puritanical organizations. In these countries, individuals or groups that fall victim to state repression are given no quarter and are mercilessly obliterated. Whether one deals with the first or second category of states, I think that the net effect is the same. First, the use of severe violence and repression by the state against any particular group has the collateral effect of spreading anxiety and fear in Muslim societies. Second, with some notable exceptions, such as Saudi Arabia, the overall impact of the policies of most Muslim governments, whether they fall in the first or second category, is the repression of puritan movements. This only contributes to the sense of alienation and also to the sense of victimhood felt by puritan movements, and fuels many of the conspiracy theories that have become an essential component of their worldview. Finally, there is no doubt that the fact that puritan movements end up clashing with most of the despotic and unpopular regimes of the Muslim world earns them a certain level of popular sympathy, even from people who would otherwise find their thought most troubling or offensive.

The puritan sense of alienation, however, is more complex than hostility toward the dictatorial governments that control their countries. Puritans believe that the colonial experience of Western governments dominating Muslim nations has not come to an end. Puritans believe that the West continues to dominate and completely control the Muslim world, particularly the Arab heartland in the Middle East. In their understanding, Israel was created as a satellite state to ensure that Arabs remain disunited and weak. Furthermore, they also believe that the rulers of the various Muslim countries are nothing more than subservient peons that serve the interests of colonial powers, and that are kept in power by the West as long as they suppress Islamic institutions and movements. In other words, they believe that the contemporary form of colonialism has figured out that it is less costly to fight Islam by putting in power secularized and Westernized rulers who will do the job for them. This accusation has been made by puritans at one time or another against the governments of most Muslim countries, including Egypt, Jordan, Tunisia, Morocco, Syria, Iraq, Kuwait, Bahrain, United Arab Emirates, Oman, Sudan, Uganda, Pakistan, and Indonesia.

Saudi Arabia presented a very special case for puritan movements. Although the Al Sa'ud family came to power through the help of Britain, as a colonial power, and despite the close relationship between the Saudi and American governments, Saudi Arabia was virtually immune from criticism by puritans throughout the 1970s and 1980s. The situation changed somewhat in the early 1990s, with the first Gulf War. A few puritan movements became critical of the Saudi government because it welcomed and cooperated with American troops in Arabia. Nevertheless, the vast majority of puritan movements remained ideologically aligned with the Saudi government—and also financially dependent on Saudi largesse. Only after the recent American invasions of Afghanistan and Iraq, a sizable number of puritan movements, sympathetic to Bin Laden and the Taliban, started accusing the Saudi government of betraying the Salafi/Wahhabi cause and declared it to be an infidel government. Very recently, this even led to violent clashes between the government and puritan movements in Saudi Arabia. Nevertheless, in my view, even if post-9/11 events force the Saudi government to distance itself from militant puritan movements, it is highly unlikely that Saudi Arabia will cease to be the main sponsor of puritan theology in the Muslim world. However, it is very likely that the Saudi government will try to persuade puritan movements to rechannel their fervor and zeal to fighting heretical Muslims (liberals and feminists) while leaving Western countries alone.

According to puritans, Britain and France were the chief engineers behind the continuing conspiracy against Islam. But as the United States became the dominant superpower in the world, it became the main culprit in this conspiracy. After the Soviet invasion of Afghanistan, and the wars in Bosnia and Chechnya, Russia was added to the list of countries that are hostile to Islam. Until the recent invasions of Afghanistan and Iraq by the United States, puritans used to believe that Russian methods were brutish while American methods were more subtle and behind-the-scenes conspiratorial.

There is another assault upon the Muslim world for which puritans blame the West as a whole, and the United States in particular. According to puritans, military domination is only a small part of the process of asserting domination and hegemony over the Muslim states. More lethal and penetrating are cultural invasions that consist of spreading Western fashions, habits, and values throughout the Muslim world. This cultural invasion takes many shapes and is implemented by a multitude of mechanisms. The rulers, who in reality are agents of the West, allow for the entry of Western shows, music, and art, and establish Western commercial and educational institutions all over the Muslim world. Puritans also believe that Westerners seek to convince Muslims that Western institutions, such as democracy, are fundamentally superior to Islamic institutions, such as the caliphate. Puritans believe that through this process the West will always ensure that the Muslim world remains weak and ineffective on the world scene.

The point of the Western cultural invasion is to deconstruct authentic Islamic values and preempt the possibility of the return of the Islamic Golden Age. In essence, this is the reason for the often-noted puritan hostility to the West.

Puritan hostility to the West is inseparable from the colonial experience and the failed Muslim states in the postcolonial period. Many of the Muslim governments are not only despotic, but they also failed to develop and modernize their states so that these countries could have an industrial and technological infrastructure that is competitive on the world market, and puritans, for the most part, blame the West for that failure. Of course, the ongoing conflict with Israel and its military and technological superiority strongly contributes to this puritanical worldview. One of the reasons the puritans are so opposed to peace with Israel is due to their belief that Israel's very purpose for existence is to defeat and humiliate Muslims as part of the overall Western strategy of containment against the Muslim world. The second main reason has to do with the holy status of the Mosque of the Dome in Jerusalem. There is no question that Jerusalem and especially the Aqsa Mosque occupies a very special place in the hearts of most Muslims; it is considered the third-holiest city in Islam. As an indication of the place of Jerusalem in the Muslim mind, it ought to be remembered that much Muslim blood has been spilled through the centuries trying to defend or liberate Jerusalem from the onslaught of the Crusaders. Therefore, Israel's occupation of Jerusalem and control over the Mosque of the Dome fuels much of the puritans' hostility to peace with Israel.

Puritans are not opposed to modernism, but, somewhat inconsistently, they believe that modernity is a culturally biased concept. For puritans, the culture of modernity, with its concepts of human rights, women's rights, minority rights, religious freedom, civil society, pluralism, and democracy, is largely Western, and therefore both alien and alienating. However, puritans strongly distinguish between the culture of modernity and modernization. Often this amounts to differentiating between modernization and Westernization—the former is acceptable but the latter is not. To become truly modernized, according to the puritans, means to regress back in time and recreate the golden age of Islam. This, however, does not mean that they want to abolish technology and scientific advancements. Rather, their program is deceptively simple—Muslims should learn the technology and science invented by the West, but in order to resist Western culture, Muslims should not seek to study the social sciences or humanities. This is the reason that a large number of puritans come to the West to study, but invariably focus their studies on the physical sciences, including computer science, and entirely ignore the social sciences and humanities. Armed with modern science and technology, puritans believe that they will be better positioned to recreate the golden age of Islam by creating a society modeled after the Prophet's city-state in Medina and Mecca.

Although the puritan position involves a lot of play on words, it ultimately makes little sense. In effect, puritans equate modernity and the progress of history to a point of ultimate human achievement. By claiming that to truly modernize, humanity should regress to the Islamic Golden Age, puritans are simply affirming their belief that history reached its true peak at the time of the Prophet and the Rightly Guided Companions. The difference, however, is that puritans believe that contemporary technology and sciences could be exploited in order to empower themselves sufficiently so that they could pursue their sociopolitical utopian vision.

As noted earlier, the study of certain fields, such as philosophy or democratic theory, are considered sinful by puritans.

Furthermore, puritans warn Muslims against taking courses about Islam in Western universities, because they believe that Western scholars will use the opportunity to confuse Muslims and place doubt in their hearts. Moreover, Western scholars are thought to expose Muslims to heretical Islamic sects such as the Mu'tazila (rationalists) and Shi'ia sects. Being exposed to historical corruptions and forms of heresy, according to the puritans, will only cast doubt in the hearts of Muslims about the straight path of the true Islam. The sad reality is, however, that by rejecting all these fields of study, puritans actually augment their intellectual insularity and isolation in the contemporary age.

Puritans go even further than rejecting particular intellectual fields. It is a basic tenet of the puritan belief system that Muslims must affirmatively adopt cultural practices that are in opposition to the West. But this type of cultural resistance most often takes superficial forms. So, for instance, puritans insist that Muslims should not use toothpaste when cleaning their teeth, but should rather use a little twig known as the *miswak*. The reasoning behind this is that Muslims must do everything possible to distinguish themselves from non-Muslims, and also that the Prophet himself used to clean his teeth with a *miswak*. The Prophet *did* in fact use the *miswak* to clean his teeth, but toothpaste was not invented at the time.

I must admit that I find the selective logic of puritans rather curious. For instance, so far puritans have not prohibited the use of umbrellas, although the Prophet and his Companions did not use umbrellas. However, puritans do prohibit the wearing of neckties, considering them a corrupt Western innovation (*bid'a*). They do not prohibit the wearing of undergarments, although that form of apparel was not available at the time of the Prophet, yet one Saudi puritan jurist has prohibited the use of brassieres if worn to augment the size of the breasts. This, he claimed, would be a type of fraudulent practice.

The premise of puritan thinking is that it is imperative that Muslims be different in substance and form from non-Muslims. Therefore, puritans insist that instead of applauding by clapping hands, Muslims should shout out in unison three *takbir*s (yelling "God is greatest" three times). According to puritans, Muslims must be different—regardless of the usefulness of any given practice. The effect of this puritan stance is quite odd. Whether a lecturer delivers an inspired and brilliant oration or delivers dull, monotonous drivel, in all cases, all lecturers are entitled to the three unspirited *takbir*s. The same logic is behind the prohibitions against celebrating birthdays and also against giving flowers to the ill—all are declared to be Western practices, and therefore Muslims must reject them and do something completely different or opposite. The peculiar thing is that although puritans insist on declaring their rejection of the West by adopting alternative forms of appearance, they have no qualms about using Western weaponry and technologically advanced products such as cell phones and computers.

The puritans' anti-Westernism is a core part of their reaction to modernity as well as a central part of their identity. Having idealized a small portion of Islamic history and declared it the golden age, their developmental compass is set toward the past. However, intellectually they are not rooted in this past—they are too impatient and too absolutist to be able to gain a sophisticated understanding of history, even if it is the history of Islam. So on what basis can they build their sense of identity? I have noticed, for instance, that the way puritans decided to dress themselves has had much more to do with the images invented by Hollywood than with what was actually reported in historical sources about the way

Muslims used to dress at the time of the Prophet. From historical sources, we learn that at the time of the Prophet in the sixth century, men would often be dressed in one piece of clothing that would rarely cover their full bodies, and the cloth was often dusty and full of tears and holes. Wearing several garments and a full turban was a sign of exceptional wealth. Dyed clothing was more expensive and could not be afforded by the majority. But the puritan's image of the authentically dressed Muslim shows that they are more familiar with Hollywood and Egyptian films than with actual historical sources. This is just one illustration of the fact that puritans formed their identity as a reaction to the West, and not as a historically based attempt at achieving Islamic authenticity. In many ways, the puritans locked themselves into a persistent cycle: they alienated themselves from modernity by imagining a perfect and ideal past; but the more alienating modernity became, the more they idealized the past; and more they idealized the past, the more undesirable the modern age became—and so on.

Moderates do not believe that Islam reached the height of its potential at the so-called golden age of Islam or even at the time that the Prophet lived. Islam's potential is everlasting, and the future could bring a greater fulfillment of that potential than the past. Therefore, moderates are interested in history because it contains the record of the successes and failures of the past. Moderates do not believe that history can be made to repeat itself. Rather, each historical period presents its unique set of challenges that must be met by studying and paying careful attention to the demands of the present and the lessons of the past. This means that there is no need to apologetically idealize the past—the mistakes of the past must be admitted and learned from, while the successes must be celebrated but not idolized. Islam, for moderates, is a progressive force that offers never-ending opportunities for greater moral and ethical achievements in every new age.

According to one Prophetic tradition, wisdom and knowledge have no nationality and therefore, regardless of the source, Muslims are free to learn as long as they use this knowledge to serve God and pursue Godliness on this earth. Thus one of the distinguishing attributes of moderates is that they take full advantage of the scientific advancements in the social sciences and humanities. Moderates believe that advancements in these fields improve our awareness of social dynamics, behavioral patterns, political and economic structures, the role of civic society, and the function of institutions. It is not possible to achieve the moral and ethical objectives of the Islamic faith without understanding the particular and specific demands and challenges of each age. It is also not possible to fulfill our obligations as agents of God and discharge the duty to enjoin the good and forbid the evil without understanding the evolving and shifting circumstances and conditions of human beings. As noted earlier, besides enjoining the good and forbidding the evil, the Qur'an instructs Muslims to civilize the earth and avoid corrupting it by shedding blood and spreading strife and fear. Therefore, moderates believe that the human legacy is indivisible, and Islam, through the efforts of Muslims, must contribute to the effort to civilize the earth and avoid its corruption.

Moderates try to strike a balance between the necessary flexibility in dealing with modernity's unique challenges and the need for historical authenticity. The balance is struck differently by different Islamic thinkers, but the essence of the challenge is to reconcile the Islamic historical legacy with the advances made in knowledge and also in the new ways of acquiring knowledge achieved in modernity. The modern age has achieved new realizations about knowledge, memory,

perception, comprehension, point of view, reality, and sociopolitical structures, and the Islamic tradition must be able
to engage the new paradigms of the contemporary age. For instance, in the modern age there have been many studies about
such subjects as the reliability of human memory and the ac-
curacy of human testimony, the meaning and roles of gender
and class, and the social effects of despotism and the function
of civic societies. The question that moderates struggle with is:
How do these new understandings and realizations inform the
Islamic tradition, and how could the Islamic tradition contribute to these new understandings and realizations? In all
cases, moderates do not ignore modernity as irrelevant and
they also do not dismiss Islamic history as an aberration.

The relationship of moderates with the West is multifaceted.
An anecdotal story sheds light upon the various facets of this relationship. At the beginning of the twentieth century, the Egyptian moderate scholar Rafa'a al-Tahtawi visited Paris, and he
was extremely impressed by the city. He noticed that the city
was clean, well-organized, and beautiful, and that Parisians
were hardworking, punctual, well-educated, and productive.
Upon returning to Egypt, Tahtawi made a comment that became well remembered but controversial. Tahtawi said: "In
Paris, I saw Islam but there were no Muslims, but in Egypt, I see
Muslims but there is no Islam." The statement is clearly an exaggeration, but what Tahtawi meant to say is that Parisians unwittingly accomplished the moral values of Islam although they
were not Muslims. In Egypt, on the other hand, people were
Muslim, but the moral values of Islam remained unfulfilled. For
Tahtawi, the ideal Muslims would be hardworking, punctual,
educated, and advanced. To be backward, ill-informed, and
undisciplined is inconsistent with the Islamic ideal.

Tahtawi's statement illustrates a tension in the thought of
moderates. Moderates believe that there are certain values,

such as justice, equity, honesty, diligence, creativity, productivity, and punctuality, that are universally desirable and meritorious. Some have described these as the "civilizing" values—values that lead to social and economic advancement, and to civilization. Moderates believe that when it comes to fulfilling these values, Islam obligates Muslims to be at the forefront and to set a powerful moral example for others. However, many Muslim societies fail to adopt these civilizing values and therefore remain underdeveloped and backward. Meanwhile, the West has managed to adopt these values and be at the forefront of civilization, and so the West is admired and respected by the moderates. The liberal democratic thought of Muslim moderates often leads to their persecution in their homeland and they find refuge and freedom only in the West. It is an unfortunate sociological fact that many moderate scholars, because of the dictatorial governments of their countries of origin, are imprisoned and tortured in their homelands and they escape to the West because of the democratic institutions of these countries.

The prevailing moderate attitude toward the West is one of respect and also one premised upon an insistence that Islam not be defined in reaction to the West or as the antithesis of the West. Guided by the moral and ethical values of Islam, moderates tend to scrutinize Western cultural practices and attempt to adopt the best of these practices and avoid the worst of them. The range of adopted or rejected practices could be very wide. For instance, all moderate scholars object to the Western cultural practice of dating, especially by minors. But this does not mean that moderates believe that the state should be able to interfere to regulate dating practices. The vast majority of moderates also object to beauty contests or the modesty (immodesty) standards that are tolerated in most Western states. A considerable number of moderates find the widespread practice of at-will employment and the ease by which employees lose their jobs Islamically offensive.[3] But so much of Western culture is not only Islamically acceptable, but even desirable; and in their writings moderates often praise Western habits such as punctuality, academic freedom, and the sense of civic duty.

Most moderates, however, strongly disagree with Western, and especially U.S., foreign policies toward the Muslim world, and especially the Middle East. Moderates disagree about the objectives or reasons behind these policies, but most moderates are particularly displeased with the unequivocal support Israel receives from the United States at the expense of the Palestinians. However, one of the distinguishing characteristics of the moderates, as opposed to the puritans, is that they do not believe that the clash between Muslims and the West is inevitable. More significantly, moderates believe that the way for Muslims to progress and for their countries to become more democratic and developed is to engage in self-reflection and self-criticism and to work to address the causes of underdevelopment in Muslim countries. Most moderate Muslims do not deny the historical effects of colonialism and imperialism, but as a matter of principle they refuse to turn them into scapegoats and then use these scapegoats as ways to avoid taking responsibility for the historical failures of Muslims. For instance, unlike puritans, moderate Muslims do not believe that Israel is responsible for the failure of the various Middle Eastern states to develop, modernize, or democraticize.

As far as the issues raised in this chapter are concerned, in the view of the majority of moderate Muslims, the most problematic aspect in the puritans' approach is their practice of defining Islam as whatever the antithesis of the West might be. For moderate Muslims, this is an offensively whimsical way of defining a religion. Puritans rely on Divine commandments ordering Muslims not to follow Jews and Christians blindly, and they also rely on some isolated traditions attributed to the Prophet Muhammad advising Muslims to distinguish themselves in appearance from non-Muslims. But as to the Divine commandments, puritans misunderstand their purpose. The commandments were intended to advise Muslims to be discerning and reflective as they choose their course in life. As to the isolated traditions, they are too historically contingent and too unreliable to serve as a basis for determining what and how God wants Muslims to be. Most importantly, puritans transform Islam into a creed for which the purpose is to negate and even spite others, and this risks transforming Islam into a creed that is so absorbed in superficialities to the point of becoming frivolous. Moderate Muslims take their religion far too seriously to accept the often spiteful and reactionary methodologies of the puritans.

NINE

DEMOCRACY AND HUMAN RIGHTS

In today's world, many Muslims and non-Muslims believe that democracy and human rights are fundamentally at odds with the Islamic faith. In my view, the issue of whether Islam can support and bolster a democratic order that respects individual rights is by far the most important challenge confronting Muslims today. Without doubt there are many different models for successful democratic governance, and it would be deceptive to pretend that all human beings around the world agree on the specific rights that ought to be recognized as fundamental and universal for all human beings. However, the core set of issues confronting moderates and puritans alike is whether, as a matter of principle, people ought to have the collective right to choose or elect their government and to determine the set of laws that govern them. More specifically, the issue is whether devout Muslims can commit to a system that recognizes the sovereignty of human beings over their own affairs. Alternatively, are Muslims duty-bound to recognize that God is the sovereign and that God's sovereignty precludes human beings from being free to conduct their own affairs as they see fit? In short, do Islamic theology and law affirmatively prohibit Muslims from believing in and implementing a democratic system of government?

The issue of human rights raises a similar set of problems, and in fact in many ways the challenge of human rights is inextricably intertwined with the challenge of democracy. It is very doubtful that any system of governance except democracy is capable of supporting the kind of procedural guarantees necessary for the protection and promotion of individual human rights. However, when thinking about the issue of Islam and human rights, it is necessary to distinguish between several pertinent questions, each one raising a different set of problems. One issue is whether Islamic law provides for its own unique set of individual rights that might coincide in certain respects or perhaps conflict with the human rights recognized by the international community. Alternatively, if Islamic law does not already provide for its own list of individual rights, is it possible for contemporary interpreters to delve into the Islamic intellectual tradition and extract and articulate a set of rights that are consistent with the Islamic faith? Put differently, can contemporary readers of Islamic texts interpret them in such a way that supports a regime of individual human rights that is entirely new and novel in Islamic history?

There is, however, another possibility that Muslims cannot but confront, and that is whether the Islamic tradition is fundamentally at odds with the idea of individual rights. In other words, is there something in the Islamic tradition that does not allow Muslims to recognize or believe in individual rights? A somewhat different question is whether certain Islamic laws—for instance, laws regarding the share of women in inheritance, the testimony of women in criminal matters, various matters involving the rules of marriage and divorce, or particular criminal penalties—are inconsistent with current standards of international human rights, and if so, is it possible to change either Islamic law or international human rights standards so that the inconsistency between the two is re-solved?

In part, what makes democracy and individual rights con-troversial, not only in Islam but in many cultures around the world, is that both concepts emerged from the unique histori-cal experiences of the West. Whether it is desirable or even possible to transplant democracy and individual rights out of their historical natural habitat in the West to the non-Western world is a highly contested matter. Although there are many international treaties and declarations that inscribe a fairly long list of rights that purportedly belong to all human beings, many Muslims and non-Muslims have insisted that there is no *particular* set of rights that are recognized by all cultures and people. These writers have argued that any attempt to expli-cate a list of specific rights that are supposed to be transcul-tural and valid for all people is necessarily an indulgence in what they call "false universals."[1] Indeed, rights that are listed in international treaties and declarations tend to vary greatly. For instance, these international documents speak of an indi-vidual right to freedom of conscience and belief, freedom of speech, and a right to privacy, but they also speak of a right to a home or shelter, the right to sufficient nourishment and sustenance, and even the right to a paid vacation or paid ma-ternal leave. Therefore, it is not possible to discuss whether every right found, for instance, in the Universal Declaration of International Human Rights or the Covenant for Political and Civil Rights is compatible with Islam. However, the important point is to focus on whether moderates or puritans accept the very idea of human rights in principle or as a concept, and whether there is a uniquely Islamic scheme of rights.

Most moderate Muslims are very skeptical of the idea that either democracy or human rights are so-called false univer-sals, or that they are uniquely Western practices not suitable or appropriate for any other culture. Such claims often act to conceal a certain degree of ethnocentrism because they amount to saying that non-Westerners are by their very nature incapable of living under a democratic system of government that is bound by the rule of law, and also incapable of understanding or respecting the rights of human beings. While it might be true that the West invented the idea of democracy and also the concept of basic and inalienable individual rights, this, however, does not mean that non-Westerners—because of their supposed cultural boundaries—are doomed to suffer despotism forever. Moderate Muslims believe that it is a matter of fundamental moral principle that respect for human rights, far from being a false universal, should be sought after and pursued as an ethically desirable goal. In fact, many moderate Muslims believe that while it would be disingenuous to pretend that Islamic law offers its own ready-made list of human rights, human rights as a concept and democracy as a system of governance are entirely reconcilable with Islamic theology and law. Some moderates go even further and argue that not only are Islam and democracy and human rights reconcilable, but that Islam *mandates and demands* a democratic system of government.

Building upon the Islamic tradition, moderates argue that at a minimum all human beings have a right to dignity and liberty. The moderates' belief in democracy and human rights begins with the premise that oppression is a great offense against God and human beings. The Qur'an describes oppressors as corrupters of the earth and also describes oppression as an offense against God. In moderate thinking, it is recognized that all human beings are entitled to dignity. The Qur'an clearly states that God has endowed all human beings with dignity.[2]

Liberty and choice are the essential components that constitute human dignity. I think it is all too obvious that when human beings are shackled, imprisoned, suppressed, or denied the means to self-determination, they feel that their sense of self-worth is greatly diminished. The most powerful, over-whelming, and systematic forms of denial of liberty are despotism and oppression by the state. Oppression enables the state to rob people of their dignity without any recourse to individuals against the state. Typically, moderate Muslims observe that the modern nation-state possesses unprecedented capabilities to conduct surveillance and to intrusively interfere with the lives of its citizens. And because of its exclusive right to use force, it has the ability to control the conduct of its citizens through threats and violence simply by hunting dissenters down, arresting them, and torturing them. Importantly, the Qur'an soundly condemns this kind of despotism and whimsical exercise of power and advises Muslims either to resist it, or if they are incapable of doing so, to desert such oppressive lands by migrating to countries that are more just and equitable. In fact, the Qur'an comments that Muslims who acquiesce to living in lands plagued by despotism and become complacent and submissive before oppression are being unjust and iniquitous toward themselves.[3]

In a well-known Islamic tradition, 'Umar, the second caliph and the close Companion of the Prophet, declared that humans are created free. 'Umar instructed one of his governors that injustice could be a form of enslavement and subjugation, and he rhetorically asked his governor: Who has the right to oppress people when God has created them free? Moderates usually cite this tradition and others in arguing that liberty is a natural right for all human beings, and that robbing people of their liberty is equivalent to subjugating and enslaving them. Submission to God can only be meaningful if human beings are free to submit or not to submit. Without freedom of choice, obedience and submission to God become entirely meaningless. Choice (liberty) is a Divine gift, and this gift is part and parcel of the ability to submit to God, and hence, the freedom to pursue Godliness or to refuse to do so.

Being enslaved or subjugated by a human being is fundamentally inconsistent with the duty to submit oneself without reservation to God. In fact, the Qur'an invites Muslims and non-Muslims to reach a consensus between them to worship God alone and not to take one another as lords.[4] For moderates, this verse affirms a basic and crucial principle: human beings should not dominate each other. The only submission that is ethical is submission to God, but the submission of a human being before another is nothing but oppression. This Qur'anic discourse encourages Muslims and non-Muslims to find an arrangement according to which each one of them does not dominate the other.

Another element that makes democracy necessary in moderate thinking is the notion of *haqq* in Islam. This notion also plays a critical role in the efforts expended by moderate Muslims to make the ideas of human rights and democracy well rooted in Islamic law and theology. *Haqq* has two meanings: it means a right or entitlement, and it also means the truth. According to the theory of *haqq* in Islamic law, both God and human beings have their own set of rights. Importantly, if an individual owns a right, the individual possesses such a right against *whoever* violates or threatens that right. As a matter of principle, the right is firmly held and not even the state is allowed to void or cancel out that right. Even God will not void a right held by an individual unless the individual who possess the right decides to forgo it—in other words, unless the individual decides to forgive or waive away his right, no one may legitimately deny an individual his/her right. The meaning of these legal principles is that according to Islamic law an individual's right, whatever that right might be, is sacrosanct, and the possessor of the right enjoys an immunity that cannot be disregarded or violated, even by the state.

These doctrines are critical for building a foundation for the notion of human rights in Islam. Moderates build on the Islamic legal tradition by affirming that God does have rights and individuals have rights, however, they argue that while the rights of God will be vindicated in the Final Day by God, the rights of individuals must be guarded and vindicated by human beings on this earth. In effect, God will take care of God's rights in the Hereafter, but human beings must take care of their rights on this earth, recognizing the human rights of individuals and protecting the sanctity of these rights.

In the classical Islamic tradition, justice is a core and fundamental value. The classical scholars emphasized justice as an Islamic obligation to the point that some of them argued that in the eyes of God, a just non-Muslim society is superior to an unjust Muslim society. Other classical scholars argued that true submission to God is impossible if injustice prevails in society. If injustice is prevalent within a society, moderates like Abd al-Rahman al-Kawakibi and others argued, this leads to the spread of traits and characteristics that are inconsistent with the ability of submission to God. Those traits include fear, apprehension, and lack of tranquility as people live in fear of injury; dishonesty and hypocrisy as people have to lie and dissimulate their true beliefs and convictions in order to survive; insecurity and opportunism as people learn that there is no correlation between acts and results; and suffering as people are ultimately robbed of their rights. In essence, the existence of injustice means the absence of Godliness, while justice means the presence of Godliness. And although only God is capable of perfect justice, humans must work hard and strive to achieve as much justice as possible.

The basis upon which justice revolves is giving each person

his or her due rights. Perfect justice means to achieve a perfect balance between duties/obligations and dues/rights. Moderates reason that the pursuit of justice mandates that Muslims must attempt to construct a political system that is the most capable of creating the right kind of balance between rights and duties in society. Furthermore, the pursuit of justice obligates Muslims to find a system in which people must have access to powers and institutions within society that can redress injustices and protect people from oppression. In moderate thinking, both access to institutions of power and accountability are necessary in any system that could be capable of achieving justice.

Human experience has clearly demonstrated that only a constitutional democratic system of government can fulfill these conditions. In nondemocratic systems, it is very difficult to hold a state accountable for its abuses, and it is also very difficult to guarantee access to venues that could correct or redress social imbalances or injustices. But even more, experience amply demonstrates that only a system of government that is founded upon a constitutionally recognized list of individual duties and rights is capable of respecting the basic dignities of people.

The Qur'an and the Prophet Muhammad's traditions make clear that human beings have a right to certain entitlements and safeguards in life. In the Islamic jurisprudential tradition, the classical scholars constructed a scheme of human rights based on what they called the "protected interests" of human beings. The classical scholars identified five protected interests: life, intellect, lineage, reputation, and property. According to this theory, protected interests are interests that the political and legal systems are duty-bound to safeguard, honor, and promote. Therefore, the Islamic political and legal systems must protect and promote the lives of people (life); the ability of people to think and reflect (intellect); their right to marry, procreate, and raise their children (lineage); their right not to be slandered, defamed, or maligned (reputation); and their right to own property and not to have their property taken without fair and just compensation (property). Some classical scholars argued that lineage and reputation implied a right to privacy. In support, these scholars cited the precedent of the second Caliph Umar who ruled that if the state unlawfully obtains evidence through spying then the illegally obtained evidence must be excluded in a criminal prosecution. Although the classical scholars spoke in terms of the five protected *interests,* most moderates contend that these categories should be called the five basic *rights* instead of interests.

The classical scholars did not believe that the five protected interests (rights) constituted a full and complete list of all that is due to human beings. The five interests or rights represented the basic, but not the exhaustive, entitlements that ought to be recognized as belonging to human beings. Put differently, the five recognized interests are not the end result of thinking about the rights of human beings; they are just the starting point.

In order to enhance the protections afforded the five interests, the classical scholars created a three-part categorization, arguing that issues relating to all of the protected interests can be divided into *necessities, needs,* and *luxuries*:

- *Necessities* consist of the things that are basic and essential for the sustenance and protection of the interests or rights in question. Necessities are the kind of things that if not provided the interest or right in question cannot be protected at all.

- *Needs* are less critical. Needs are the kind of things that are very important for the protection of the interest or right in question, but they are not of pivotal importance. Unlike a necessity, if a need is not supplied, the interest or right can still be protected, but it is greatly undermined.

- *Luxuries* are things that are neither critical nor very important for the protection of an interest or right. Rather, a luxury, if supplied, would perfect the enjoyment of an interest or right.

An example will help clarify this three-part categorization. As noted above, life is one of the protected interests or rights in Islamic law. A prohibition against killing is a *necessity* in order to protect the right to life. Furthermore, welfare laws that ensure that a human being has enough to eat and drink, and also has shelter or a place to live is a *necessity* for the preservation of life. Providing adequate health care, primary and college education, clothing, or employment could be considered a *need*. Providing a means for graduate education, transportation, personal psychological counseling, or paid vacations could be considered *luxuries*.

The classical scholars did not define what exactly qualifies as a necessity, need, or luxury. However, in principle, they sought to differentiate between things that must be guaranteed to people because they are essential for a healthy, respectable, and dignified life, and things that are less important or essential. The classical scholars contended that it falls upon each generation of Muslims to explore and define *in accordance with the shifting demands of the circumstances and changing times* what ought to be defined as the necessities, needs, and luxuries. Therefore, it was considered unwise to set out a specific list of inflexible necessities, needs, and luxuries that are constant and unchanging.

According to the classical theory, an equitable and just society would treat the necessities as sacrosanct and not subject to compromise. A society that could protect the needs of people in addition to the necessities would be considered even more just and equitable. Finally, a society that could provide people with the luxuries of life, in addition to protecting the necessities and needs, would be the most just and equitable of all.

In the classical sources, there were exhaustive debates about what ought to be required to best protect the five protected interests—life, intellect, lineage, reputation, and property. Unfortunately, all of these classical debates have been forgotten in the modern age. In fact, a large number of governments in Muslim countries today neglect both the necessities and the needs of the people they govern. For example, there are countless arbitrary executions at the hands of the Saudi government, which is a clear violation of the first human interest—namely, the interest of life. Furthermore, the very widespread use of arbitrary detention and torture in Muslim countries arguably constitutes violations against life and mind and perhaps reputation.

Moderates wish to build upon this valuable tradition that tried to figure out what is necessary for human beings to thrive, and that also tried to explore what might not be a necessity for existence but would still be considered important enough to count as a need or a luxury. Moderates argue that, at a minimum, these classical debates over necessities and needs ought to be translated in the modern age to rights that can safeguard the interests of individuals. The values that emerge from the classical tradition, such as dignity, liberty, the five protected interests, and the discourse against subjugation and oppression, can be translated into a coherent set of human rights for the modern age that emerge as natural extensions of the Islamic heritage. These rights would bolster the principle of democracy in Islam.

Moderates believe that there are several other concepts and practices in the Islamic heritage that support the principle of

democracy. The Qur'an clearly commands Muslims to conduct all their affairs through consultation (*shura*). Moderates
read this as a Divine command that reemphasizes the unde-
sirability of oppression and authoritarianism. The decision-
making process must not be usurped by a despotic individual
or a despotic elite. Rather, Muslims must find a way to make
decisions as the outcome of a democratic interaction among
the many.

In addition to the principle of consultation, when the
Prophet first entered the city of Medina, he drafted a constitution that clearly set out the obligations, duties, and rights of
each tribal group (as well as the non-Muslims of Medina).

The Prophet Muhammad grew up and began preaching his
message in the city of Mecca (in today's Saudi Arabia). The
Prohpet preached his message for about ten years in Mecca,
but he suffered increasing persecution from the nobility and
elite of the city, who refused to accept his message. Finally,
the Prophet decided to migrate to a city that was willing to
embrace him, his message, and his followers. This city was
Medina, but at that time Medina was divided into several
Arab and Jewish tribes. In addition, there were those in Medina who converted to Islam and joined the Prophet's religious community, and there were those who remained
polytheists, and did not convert to Islam. After negotiating
with the elders of the city, the Prophet Muhammad led a migration of the Muslim community from Mecca to Medina (a
migration known as the *hijra*), and the Prophet was chosen
as the ruler of that city. Shortly after the Prophet became the
ruler of Medina, he carefully worked with the elders of the
city on drafting what became known as the Constitution of
Medina. This historical precedent supports the idea that the
legitimate political system in Islam must be a constitutional
government.

Another precedent that moderates frequently cite and rely upon is the establishment in early Islamic history of a representative body known as the People Who Loosen and Bind (*ahl al-hal wa al-aqd*). Before he died, the second caliph 'Umar appointed a body of the most notable elders representing the various communities in the Islamic state and charged them with temporarily governing the state after his death and also with selecting the third caliph who would rule the Muslim state. The reason they were called the People Who Loosen and Bind was to signify that as representatives of the community, they had the power to bind and unbind the community with their decisions. In later stages of Islamic history, this body gained a largely consultative function. When it existed, this body rendered advice to various caliphs but no longer possessed the power to decide matters.

Finally, many moderates also rely on the concept of consensus (*'ijma'*), or the general agreement of a group of people that a particular issue is wrong or right. The classical scholars utilized consensus in the jurisprudential context, and they often disagreed about the requisites and conditions for a valid consensus. The classical scholars debated a wide variety of matters, including, for the purposes of assessing the existence of a valid consensus, whether only the opinions of jurists should count or whether the views of laypeople should be considered. Some argued that only proof of consensus of the Companions of the Prophet could decisively settle any contentious theological or legal dispute. The classical scholars also debated the appropriate subject matter for consensus. For instance, they disagreed on whether the concept of consensus ought to be utilized to resolve theological disputes alone or whether it should be used to resolve legal disputes as well. Furthermore, the classical scholars debated the appropriate effect of consensus, asking: Should any purported consensus forever close a matter for debate? What happens if a consensus exists at one time but eventually breaks down and disappears? One of the most hotly debated issues was: Assuming that a consensus in fact exists, is it sinful or in any way wrongful to break ranks and disagree with the purported consensus? Many classical jurists were skeptical that consensus could ever be achieved, or that even if it were achieved, its existence could be verified.

Moderate Muslims have tried to reinterpret the concept of consensus to support the idea of democracy that is governed by the will of the majority. Moderates contend that for the purposes of governing a country, the will of the people represents the will of the political sovereign, and this will is binding and obligatory. Moderates argue that *'ijma'* should not mean consensus or unanimity, but that it should mean the existence of a simple majority. In addition, they assert that the views or vote of any citizen, Muslim or not, should count for the purposes of ascertaining the will of the majority, and thus, the will of the people. However, most moderates argue that in order to avoid the tyranny of the majority—or the oppression of the minority by the majority—it is imperative to have a constitutional system that guarantees the basic rights of all individuals. Therefore, the will of the majority is honored, but within certain constitutional parameters; if the will of the majority trumps these constitutional boundaries, it will not be honored. In other words, the will of the majority will be declared unconstitutional. Some moderates argue that the constitutional parameters should not be limited to individual rights, but should include ethical and moral Islamic principles as well. Consequently, if the majority desires a law that runs afoul of Islamic ethical and moral principles, the law would be voided as unconstitutional.

Typically, when speaking about democracy, one of the most central, if not *the* most central, questions is the issue of sovereignty. Who is the sovereign in a democracy? This is connected to the question of who is the possessor of the ultimate and final authority? Moderates have given various responses to this question, but they all seem to have the same effect.

Some moderates have argued that final authority rests with God, and so God is the sovereign. However, God has delegated total authority to human beings to conduct their affairs according to their free will. God retains the right to reward or punish whomever God wishes in the Hereafter. Others have argued that people are sovereign as far as human law is concerned. God is sovereign as far as the eternal law is concerned. Since the duty of human beings is to manage human law, and not eternal law, human beings are free to legislate as long as the legislation attempts to achieve Godliness on earth (that is, attempts to fulfill the eternal law). If the legislation fails the test of trying to achieve Godliness on earth, such a law must be declared unconstitutional. Another view offered by moderates is that the people are sovereign because the affairs of God are left to God, and the affairs of the state are left to the people. This last approach comes the closest to being an outright secular position.

Another topic that has been the subject of considerable debate among moderates has been the expected role of Shari'a law or religious law in a Muslim democracy. This issue has proven to be particularly challenging, and therefore there is a considerable range of views. I have categorized the views on this issue into four main positions:

Some moderates have argued that most of the laws should be in the hands of the people, except for a core group of laws known as the *hudud*. The *hudud* are a particular set of laws that were explicitly set out in the Qur'an. They include, for instance, the punishment for fornication and theft. Although the *hudud* laws include harsh criminal penalties, they are mitigated by the fact that the evidentiary requirements for the enforcement of these penalties are very technical and demanding. This makes the application of the penalties difficult and even rare. For instance, in order to prove a case of fornication, which is punished by one hundred lashes, four witnesses must be able to testify that they saw the penis fully inserted in the vagina. This is already a demanding evidentiary standard, but what makes it even more demanding is that if some of the four witnesses testify they saw the full insertion while one or more witnesses testify they did not see the full insertion those who claimed to have seen the full act (the former group) are punished for slander. Thus, if anyone comes forward with an allegation that is not substantiated by others, he/she does so at his/her own risk. Naturally, this acts as a deterrent against making unsubstantiated accusations of sexual misconduct. In any case, according to this approach, people are free to get rid of the *hudud* laws by voting for a non-Islamic government but an Islamic government, if elected, must apply the *hudud* laws.

Some moderate thinkers have rejected this position and argued that a Muslim democracy should not attempt to apply any part of the Shari'a law, and that the only relevant law is the law of the legislature. In this approach, the Shari'a serves as a moral and ethical guide, but the citizenry should be the sole source of legislation. A third group of moderate thinkers have argued that in a Muslim democracy, the legislature should pass whatever law it deems appropriate, but that there should be a supreme court that strikes down any law inconsistent with the Qur'an. The final view holds that the law belongs to the people, and so legislatures must be free to pass whatever laws they deem appropriate. However, the law must meet certain basic moral standards that are inspired from the Shari'a. Immoral laws, even if willed by a legislature, should be declared unconstitutional and void.

What unites these various approaches is that they all reject theocratic forms of government, and to various extents, they reject a model in which the state exists to enforce a Divine code of laws that is beyond human accountability or change. It is not that moderate Muslims believe that Divine guidance is not necessary or helpful for human beings. They do. But they believe that God speaks to the *hearts* of people, not to their *institutions*. Once institutions pretend to represent God, they offend God and abuse human beings. Divinity is too awesome and immutable to be represented by human institutions or a single individual.

In addition, moderate Muslims argue that the jurists who study and search the Divine law should continue to play their historical role as advisers and teachers of the people. In Islamic history, jurists never assumed power directly but were always a part of civic society. Their real power base was not the position given to them by the state, but their popularity and ability to appeal to the hearts and minds of the people through reason and knowledge, and a solid grounding in jurisprudence. In a Muslim country, jurists may be able to convince the majority of the citizens to pass one law or another. But when a law is passed by the legislature, it is a human law and not a Divine law. It is passed as law because the representatives of the people believe the law to be good, desirable, and in the best interests of their constituency. Those representatives are also free to change the law if that is the will of their constituency. Importantly, moderates believe that Godliness cannot be achieved by a state commanding it to be so. Thus, when the state plays the role of an enforcer for God, the state ends up replacing God altogether, and in this is an absolute absence of Godliness.

Practically everything mentioned above is heretical for puritans. As far as the puritans are concerned, democracy is a

Western invention, and this is reason enough to reject it. In addition, puritans insist on the re-creation of the caliphate as a cornerstone of the Islamic system of governance. By this, they have in mind the model set by the first four Rightly Guided Caliphs, who ruled in succession after the death of the Prophet. Puritans attempt to create what they imagine to be a replica of the system of government created by these caliphs.

The problem that the puritans fail to acknowledge is that the caliphs did not adopt a single form of government; rather, each caliph implemented different policies and adopted various institutions. In reality, the caliphate did not represent any particular theory of governance, but was a historical institution that managed to unite most Muslims at different times in the past. In essence, the caliphate became a symbol of Muslim unity without necessarily embodying a particular form of government. Therefore, most moderates, in principle, do not oppose the reemergence of the caliphate but only in the sense of a government that unites all Muslim countries in a federalism or confederacy of states. Most moderates endorse the caliphate as a symbol that could unite Muslim nations under a single flag without compromising the democratic principles of governance. Puritans, however, do not adopt the caliphate as a symbol of unity—what they have in mind is the return of a purported ideal system of government that existed in the golden age of Islam.

According to puritans, the system of government that existed in the purported golden age of the caliphate called is the "*shura* system," which the puritans insist is superior to the Western democratic system. As mentioned earlier, *shura* is a Qur'anic concept that means governance by consultation. Curiously, however, puritans speak as if there is a full-fledged and complete theory of governance called the *shura*. When one carefully examines the writings of puritans, one discovers that what is meant by a *shura* system is a just, benevolent, and pious despot who applies Islamic law and who governs by regularly referring to a standing consultative body. In the puritan view, a just ruler is a ruler who applies the law of God. The ruler must meet strict requirements related to his character, piety, and religious knowledge, and thus, the ruler will be able to know God's law. The ruler must implement the Qur'anic command of taking consultation, and after consulting with people of knowledge and piety, the ruler will choose the correct course of action.

Interestingly, in their writings puritans say very little about what procedural guarantees they would put into place to ensure that the chosen leader remains just, benevolent, or even pious. Similarly, little is said about the measures that could be taken to ensure that the ruler will actually abide by the laws of Islamic jurisprudence and not flagrantly abuse his mandate. Puritans, however, assume that as long as the consultative body appoints a ruler who is exceedingly pious, his piety will constitute a sufficient restraint.

Puritans would give the state powers that, in reality, are unprecedented in Islamic history. The state in the modern age is capable of mobilizing enormous powers and intruding upon people's lives in ways that were unimaginable in the premodern period. Puritans use these exceptional powers to enforce what they believe to be the Divine Will. For instance, puritans believe that the state should force men to go to the mosque for prayers, and also force women to wear the veil. By enforcing the Divine law, justice will be achieved because, puritans believe, by definition God's law is just. In this imagined order, there is no need for individual rights. In fact, puritans believe that the very concept of human rights is yet another component of the Western intellectual invasion. By applying the Divine law, puritans believe, the rights of God and the rights of people will be fully fulfilled and served.

Interestingly, puritans believe that at the present time, there is no genuine Islamic state. All the current Muslim governments are illegitimate because, among other things, they implement laws that are French or British in origin. Therefore, puritans believe that the current governments should be overthrown, once the means for doing so are available. This is one of the few clear differences and distinctions between puritans and conservatives. Although conservatives do believe that an Islamic state must apply God's law, they do not believe that rebellion against governments that fail to apply the Divine law are justified. Conservatives, in general, reject the use of violence in order to achieve their aims, whereas puritans embrace the ideology of violence.

In terms of contemporary realities, for puritans the states that best approached their political ideal were Saudi Arabia and Afghanistan under the Taliban. Puritans believe that the United States purposely destroyed the Taliban because they came close to establishing a genuine caliphate, and the United States is dead set on not allowing Islam to return to its golden era. As to Saudi Arabia, as I noted earlier, in recent times puritans have increasingly turned against the Saudi government because of the invasions of Iraq and the close ties between the Saudi and American governments. Most puritans believe that the collaboration of the Saudi government with the United States during the invasions of Afghanistan and Iraq exposed the true loyalties of the Saudi ruling family and also revealed that the Saudi state is not truly committed to Islam and therefore deserves to be overthrown.

I must say that in my opinion the truly sad reality is that the puritan ideology of the state will only lead to considerable bloodshed without the puritans ever finding their utopia with its just despot. As some of the classical jurists used to say, justice and despotism are two opposites, and the two will never meet without one killing the other. After much suffering, the puritans are bound to wake up and realize that while they dreamed in clouds of their utopia, on this earth they only managed to create a nightmare.

We turn, in the next chapter, to the treatment of non-Muslims in an Islamic state. For a democracy to work, all its citizens must be treated equally; they must be able to enjoy equal rights and be offered equal opportunities before the law. The question of whether an Islamic democracy is possible is invariably necessarily linked to the status of non-Muslims in such a state. The challenge, however, is not limited to the formal legal or constitutional rights afforded to non-Muslims in an Islamic state. In part, the challenge is the prevalence of a well-established ethic of tolerance that is thoroughly disseminated in the very fabric of civil society. Beyond the protections of the law, this ethic of tolerance would permit the various religious and ideological orientations within a society to coexist without one seeking to dominate or exterminate the other. This is exactly why the issue of interacting with non-Muslims or the relationship between Muslims and non-Muslims is of critical importance for contemporary Islam.

One of the significant issues that could affect the interreligious dynamics within a pluralist and democratic state is what might be called the perception of the ultimate moral worth of individuals. Most religions tend to assert that its own followers are going to be saved in the Hereafter, while all others are doomed to suffer God's wrath. Certainly, it is hardly surprising for a religion to claim that it exclusively possesses the true way for salvation. The question, however, is whether religious exclusivity is inconsistent with the ethic of tolerance, which is necessary for promoting the kind of civil society that could support a democracy. More explicitly, if a religious faith points the proverbial finger at others declaring that they are doomed to Hellfire, does this undermine the moral worth of those who reject that religion as a false faith?

A considerable number of theorists have argued that in essence tolerance means nothing more than putting up with someone; tolerating the other demands no more than accepting their mere existence, perhaps as a necessary evil. These theorists argued that for the purposes of finding a civil society that would support a pluralist democracy an ethic of tolerance is simply not enough. What is needed is an ethic of active embracement, empathy, and cooperation in which diverse groups, including religious groups, come together in a joint venture to promote human rights and equal moral worth of all human beings. According to these theorists, the notion that some people because of their beliefs are entitled to salvation and others deserve to be damned is inconsistent with the civic ethics of human rights and equal human worth. The conclusion adopted by such theorists is not that all religious convictions regarding salvation and damnation ought to be abandoned. Rather, they contend that because of the exclusivist, alienating, and inaccessible nature of religious convictions, religions should be kept strictly private and should not play any role in the public sphere.

The question of the exclusivist and inaccessible nature of religious convictions, and whether religious convictions, language, and symbols must be kept out of the public realm, has been the subject of controversy for a long time. Although this is not the place to engage in an exhaustive discussion on this topic, I think that all strongly held ideological convictions pose the same kind of challenge to cooperative civic ethics in a democracy. But this does not mean that only systems of beliefs that are accessible to all should be admitted to the public realm. I do believe that religion can legitimately play a role in the public sphere as long as it is not dismissive or oppressive toward others. In the case of Islam, whether religion is indeed dismissive or oppressive toward others depends on how one reads the Qur'anic discourse regarding non-Muslims, their moral worth, and even the possibility of their attaining salvation.

TEN

INTERACTING WITH NON-MUSLIMS AND SALVATION

When it comes to thinking about issues such as how to deal with non-Muslims, salvation, and damnation, sometimes it is difficult to imagine that puritans and moderates are reading and interpreting the same religious sources. This is because the conclusions these two groups reach are so diametrically inconsistent that their highly disparate positions raise fundamental questions about the extent to which methods of interpretation make all the difference in deciphering the Divine Will. The meanings of religious texts are heavily affected by the moral and ethical predispositions and commitments of the readers of those texts, but they are also affected by the technical tools that people use to understand the text. But this is not the place to get into the heuristic devices of puritans and moderates and the methods that they use to unpack the meanings and implications of texts. In this chapter, I will focus on the theological and jurisprudential conclusions reached by puritans and moderates without delving into their hyper-technical debates about how one ought to read the Qur'an and other religious sources.

As far as puritans are concerned, the question of salvation is a straightforward one: only Muslims will have any chance of salvation in the Hereafter. Not only that, but Muslims who do not adopt the correct beliefs and practices, as the puritans define them, will not attain salvation either. The basic difference between heretical or sinful Muslims and non-Muslims, according to puritans, is the gradation of Hell to which they are destined. Non-Muslims will occupy lower rungs of Hell than heretical or sinful Muslims. Puritans disagree on whether non-Muslims will ever be released from Hell; heretical and sinful Muslims will last in Hell as long as is required to atone for their sins.

Perhaps this is not surprising. Most religions proclaim that those who refuse to believe in their message will be condemned in one way or another. But the puritans' rejectionist stance extends to life on this earth. Puritans accept without reservation or revision the traditional practice of what was known as the *dhimma* status for non-Muslims living in Muslim territories. According the *dhimma* status system, non-Muslims must pay a poll tax in return for Muslim protection and the privilege of living in Muslim territory. Per this system, non-Muslims are exempt from military service, but they are excluded from occupying high positions that involve dealing with high state interests, like being the president or prime minister of the country. In Islamic history, non-Muslims did occupy high positions, especially in matters that related to fiscal policies or tax collection. It is not clear if puritans would deem this historical practice acceptable or if they would consider it yet another indication of how the earlier generations of Muslims had strayed from the straight path.

Within the basic framework of the *dhimma* system, the way puritans deal with non-Muslims is marked by a remarkable degree of literalism. For instance, the puritans readily accept the Qur'anic command that Muslims must deal with non-Muslims with justice, and they also accept the well-known Prophetic tradition asserting that whoever injures or abuses a non-Muslim in *dhimmi* status, the Prophet will personally bear witness against him in the Final Day. Nevertheless, at the same time, puritans insist that in a Muslim state, non-Muslims must be degraded sufficiently so that their lower status vis-à-vis Muslims is clear. For example, non-Muslims must wear distinctive insignia so that they are easily identifiable. Furthermore, non-Muslims may not build a church or synagogue higher than a mosque, and they must be second to Muslims in practically all social engagements. For instance, puritans insist that Muslims should not initiate greetings of peace with non-Muslims, and if non-Muslims initiate the greeting, the puritans set out a list of expressions that Muslims may use in response.

Muslims may not use an expression other than those on the list. Most of these offensive and immoral laws emerged from various apocryphal traditions attributed to the Prophet in the ninth and tenth centuries. Most classical jurists rightly declared these traditions to be pure fabrications that are inconsistent with the historical practices of the Prophet. Some classical jurists, such as Ibn Taymiyya, did advocate the demeaning treatment of non-Muslims; however, his hostility to non-Muslims was largely due to the fact that he lived at a time when the Islamic civilization was in a real state of crisis because Muslim territories and populations were under siege by several outside invaders. Nevertheless, jurists such as Ibn Taymiyya have had a great deal of influence upon the Wahhabis and other puritans. Consequently, these demeaning laws were implemented by the Taliban in Afghanistan and are partially in force in Saudi Arabia. Today, though the vast majority of Muslim countries do not recognize the legitimacy of these offensive laws and refuse to enforce them.

One of the ambiguities in puritan thought is what to do about unbelievers who are not Christian or Jewish. Traditionally, only Christians and Jews, known as the People of the

Book, could occupy *dhimmi* status. So the question is what to do about individuals who are neither Christian nor Jewish. As Islam entered countries like India, China, and sub-Saharan Africa, the classical jurisprudential tradition was forced to modify its position and grant *dhimmi* status to Hindus, Buddhists, and Zoroastrians. But it is not clear whether puritans would be willing to accept this classical compromise; if they do not accept the classical compromise then they would not extend *dhimmi* status beyond the People of the Book, which would necessarily mean that people who are not Muslim, Christian, or Jewish would have to be banished or killed.

The motivating premise for the puritans is that Islam must prevail and dominate. Consequently, non-Muslims living in Muslim territories must be made to feel inferior so that they will grow tired with their status. This will be an inducement for them to see the truth and convert to Islam, and by doing so abandon their lowly status.

The puritan worldview is bipolar—on the one end is Islam, which represents the unadulterated good, and on the other end are the non-Muslims, who represent evil. Relying on the writings of some classical jurists, the puritans strongly advocate a theology known as *al-wala' wa al-bara'* (the doctrine of loyalty and disassociation), which states it is imperative that Muslims care for, ally themselves with, and befriend only Muslims. Accordingly, Muslims may ally themselves with or seek the assistance of non-Muslims only for limited and identifiable purposes. Muslims should do so only if they are weak and in need, but as soon as Muslims are able to regain their power, they must reclaim their superior status. Muslims must not befriend non-Muslims or allow themselves to care for or love non-Muslims. The fact that non-Muslims are not Muslim is seen as a *moral* fault, and if Muslims care for non-Muslims, it is an indication that these Muslims are putting their emotions before their religious commitments, a clear sign of weakness of faith. Muslims may show kindness toward non-Muslims to set a good example, and Muslims may ally themselves with non-Muslims if it is necessary. But in all cases, Muslims cannot love non-Muslims because this is equal to loving what is immoral, and Muslims must strive to assert their superiority as soon as they are able to do so. The ultimate and final objective is to bring the whole world under the fold of Islam, either as lowly *dhimmi*s or as converts to Islam. In other words, the camp of good (Islam) must not love the camp of evil. The camp of good must either dominate the camp of evil or turn evil to goodness.

Moderates start from very different premises. The moderate position is a product of their understanding of the very purpose of creation and the role of Islam. While puritans believe that the existence of non-Muslims is a temporary situation that Muslims should work hard to remedy, and that the world eventually should be converted to Islam, moderates reject this logic as fundamentally at odds with the Divine Will. Moderates argue that the Qur'an not only accepts, but even *expects,* the reality of difference and diversity within human society. Therefore, the Qur'an says: "O humankind, God has created you from male and female and made you into diverse nations and tribes so that you may come to know each other. Verily, the most honored of you in the sight of God is he who is the most righteous."[1] Elsewhere, the Qur'an reaffirms that diversity is part of the Divine intent and purpose in creation, and so it states: "If thy Lord had willed, He would have made humankind into a single nation, but they will not cease to be diverse . . . And, for this God created them [humankind]."[2]

Moderates argue that not only does the Qur'an endorse a principle of diversity, but it also presents human beings with a formidable challenge, and that is "to know each other." In the

Qur'anic framework, diversity is not an ailment or evil. Diversity is part of the purpose of creation, and it reaffirms the richness of the Divine. The stated Divine goal of getting to know one another places an obligation upon Muslims to cooperate and work toward specified goals with Muslims and non-Muslims alike. As Baqir Muhammad al-Hakim, the fifth Shi'i *imam,* said: "The well-being of people can only be achieved through coexistence."

For example, the Qur'an emphasizes time and again that if God would have so willed, He would have created people all the same, and all of humanity would have believed as well.[3] In fact, emphasizing the inevitability of difference, the Qur'an informs the Prophet that even if he shows some people the most compelling evidence, they will not follow him, and he, in turn, will not follow them.[4] The fact that God has willed that people remain different, the moderates argue, illustrates God's respect for human free will and also mandates that human beings recognize the virtue of tolerance. Since diversity is part of the Divine Will, moderates contend that human beings should not seek to undo what God has willfully done.

In addition to the obligation of tolerance, the Qur'an obligates people to work together in pursuit of goodness. Because of the critical importance of this point, and because this part of the Qur'anic discourse is unfamiliar to most people in the West, I will be quoting extensively from the Qur'an. In one passage, for example, the Qur'an asserts: "To each of you God has prescribed a Law and a Way. If God would have willed, He would have made you a single people. But God's purpose is to test you in what He has given each of you, *so strive in the pursuit of virtue,* and know that you will all return to God [in the Hereafter], and He will resolve all the matters in which you disagree" (emphasis mine).[5] Emphasizing the same reconciliatory point, addressing itself to Muslims, the Qur'an states:

"Do not argue with the People of the Book unless in a kind and fair way, apart from those who have been oppressive toward you. Tell them that we believe in what has been sent down to us and we believe in what has been sent down to you. Our God and your God is one and to Him we submit."[6] Elsewhere, the Qur'an asserts: "Call to the path of your Lord with wisdom and kind advice, and discourse with them in kindness and patience, for your Lord surely knows who has strayed from the path and also knows the rightly guided."[7]

I have already referred to the Qur'anic verse that states: "O People of the Book, let us come to a common and just word between us and you, that we worship none but God and that we associate no partners with God. And that none of us take the others as lords besides God. I will eventually judge between you regarding the issues in which you used to dispute."[8] The first part of the verse reminds Muslims, Christians, and Jews that they all worship the same God. The second part of the verse states a principle applicable to living together on this earth—accepting the reality of God means that one faction should not seek to dominate the other.

The same theme is emphasized in what might be called the *salam* verses—*salam* is the same term from which the word *Islam* is derived, which means peace, tranquility, repose, or serenity. The *salam* verses refer to Qur'anic passages that emphasize the need not just for interreligious tolerance, but for cooperative moral ventures that seek to achieve Godliness on earth. In the *salam* verses, the Qur'an stresses that in dealing with their opponents, Muslims should seek to remind them of their moral obligations toward God, but if the opponents stubbornly reject the truth, Muslims should turn away while wishing their opponents *salam*. In this dynamic, Muslims should act to assure their opponents that their disagreements are not personal, and that Muslims do not bear a grudge or enmity toward their opponents. Even as the opponents refuse the message and turn away, the Qur'an instructs Muslims that the only appropriate response to this rejection is to wish their opponents the bliss of peace.[9]

Even if the call to Islam is rejected, something remains. What remains is that Muslims and non-Muslims search for and create mechanisms not just for tolerating each other, but for uniting in the pursuit of virtue. As the Qur'an succinctly puts it, "Work with one another in promoting goodness and piety, and do not work to promote crime and aggression, and fear God for God is severe in punishment."[10] This injunction cannot be separated from the general command to achieve Godliness on the earth and thus to establish moral virtues such as justice, mercy, compassion, benevolence, and beauty on this earth. The fact that Muslims and non-Muslims ought to cooperate in pursuit of goodness does not mean assimilation or even diluting the differences. It means finding the commonalities so that goodness can be served on this earth. In fact, the Qur'an insists that various groups can have their own laws and rules but this should not prevent them from cooperating. To convey an authentic and meaningful sense of what inspires moderate Muslims, I will quote the Qur'an at length on this issue. As part of a long chapter titled "The Feast," addressing itself to the Prophet, the Qur'an states:

> But why should they make you a judge [between them] when the Torah is in their midst and it contains the Law of God? . . .
>
> We sent down the Torah containing guidance and light, and in accordance with [the Torah] the prophets who were obedient [to God] gave instructions to the Jews, as did the rabbis and priests, for they were the custodians and witnesses of God's writ. So, therefore, do not

fear men, fear Me, and barter not My messages away for
a paltry gain. Those who do not judge by God's revelations are indeed unbelievers. . . .

After that We sent Jesus, son of Mary, confirming the
Torah, which had been [sent down] before him, and We
gave him the Gospel containing guidance and light, as an
affirmation of what We revealed in the Torah, and as a
guidance and warning for those who are pious. Let the
people of the Gospel judge by what God has revealed in
it. And those who do not judge in accordance with what
God has revealed are transgressors.

And to you We have revealed the Book containing the
truth, confirming the earlier revelations, and preserving
them. So judge between them [Muslims] by what God
has revealed to you, and do not ignore the truth that has
been revealed to you by following people's whims. *To
each of you We have given a law and a way of life. If
God would have desired He could surely have made you
into a single people—professing one faith [and following
one law]. But He wished to try and test you by that
which He has given each of you. So excel in good deeds.*
To Him will you all return in the end, when He will resolve that upon which you disagreed.[11] (emphasis mine)

Particularly the followers of the Abrahamic message are ex-
horted to work and excel in serving the good. While clearly
there is a certain moral affinity and spiritual closeness between
Muslims and the followers of the Abrahamic tradition, nothing in the Qur'an precludes cooperation with *all* others in
order to create an earth that is morally more pleasing to God.

Moderates argue that at the same time that humans ought
to cooperate in the pursuit of goodness the Qur'an clearly em-
braces the idea of multiplicity and pluralism of laws. In fact, it

is a part of the Divine objective that people remain different in some significant and important ways. From that perspective, any universalism that would ignore all differences and impose a unitary and single law upon human beings would be challenged by the text of the Qur'an. People may have different laws, creeds, and rituals, but there are moral principles that unite all human beings. While laws pertaining to religious rituals and rites and organizational laws relating to the administration of justice are expected, or even encouraged, to be different, there ought to be considerable space for collective moral pursuits between Muslims and non-Muslims.

In response to this moderate position, puritans refer to Qur'anic verses that address the issue of *wala'* (seeking an alliance with non-Muslims) in an attempt to prove that Islam forbids any friendship, let alone any active cooperation, between Muslims and non-Muslims. Typically, such verses call upon Muslims not to ally themselves with the enemies of Islam. Significantly, however, the very same chapters in the Qur'an that speak about the basic unity of all Abrahamic religions or that command respect for difference and diversity will also contain passages that instruct Muslims not to ally themselves with non-Muslims. This fact led some Western scholars to conclude that the two types of passages are fundamentally inconsistent and irreconcilable. Puritans, however, deal with this same apparent inconsistency by arguing that the conciliatory verses have been abrogated and voided by the nonalliance verses. Moderates, on the other hand, insist that if the Qur'anic text is read from a contextual perspective, it becomes clear that the different passages are a part of a complex and layered discourse responding to various historical situations.

The verses that call upon Muslims to support the newly established Muslim community in Medina do not issue a blanket condemnation against Jews and Christians (who "shall have their reward with their Lord").[12] Instead, they accept the distinctiveness of the Jewish and Christian communities and their laws, while also insisting that *in the case of conflict,* Muslims should not ally themselves against their fellow Muslims. At the background of every single Qur'anic revelation warning Muslims not to ally themselves with non-Muslims is a historical context in which it was necessary to choose sides. But even then the Qur'an addresses itself to situations in which during active hostilities between Muslims and non-Muslims a Muslim party is commanded to refrain from giving active support to non-Muslims against Muslims—the operative word here being *against.* In other words, the nonalliance verses were all revealed while there were ongoing hostilities between Muslims and non-Muslims, and the Qur'an quite reasonably commands Muslims not to assist the enemy inflicting damage against Muslims. But this does not mean that the Qur'an mandates that Muslims create polarized and conflict-filled situations in the first place. In the absence of exceptional circumstances, the Qur'an calls upon all human beings to work to achieve goodness on the earth. This will become clearer when I address the positions of the moderates and puritans on the subject of warfare.

The net effect of the moderates' Qur'anic analysis is that, contrary to the puritans, they do not believe that God intends or desires that Muslims dominate non-Muslims. Muslims are urged to call people to their faith in kindness, but it must be understood that people will never all follow one faith. Most importantly, it is critical that people come to know one another. But it would be entirely futile for people to know one another if the ultimate purpose was not to work together to achieve what is moral and good. From this perspective, moderate Muslims reject the vindictive and hateful doctrines that call for the degradation of non-Muslims living in Muslim lands. Moderates believe that practices such as mandating that non-Muslims wear distinctive insignia or placing restrictions on the building of churches are fundamentally inconsistent with the teachings of the Qur'an and are therefore reprehensible. Depriving non-Muslims of their dignity constitutes a betrayal of the Divine trust to achieve what is morally good on the earth.

In addition, the overwhelming majority of moderate Muslims reject the *dhimma* system as ahistorical, in the sense that it is inappropriate for the age of nation-states and democracies. The system of requiring religious and sometimes ethnic minorities to pay poll taxes in return for self-administration, which included applying the minorities' own customs and laws, was widespread in the medieval age. It was a form of administration used by Muslims and against Muslims in different contexts and situations. But the circumstances of modernity mandate its abolition, primarily because if applied in the contemporary age, it would defeat the objectives of justice and dignity. What justified the poll tax system in the medieval age was the existence of reciprocity; in the medieval world, even in the context of concluding peace treaties, the weaker party was expected to pay a tribute to the stronger party. On many occasions, for instance, Muslims were forced to pay the Crusader states a poll tax. But in the modern age, the unilateral application of the poll tax system by Muslims would result in humiliation and alienation in ways that would seriously obstruct cooperative ventures aimed at furthering goodness and justice in the world.

The poll tax system could be justified today only if Muslims adopted a supremacist attitude toward non-Muslims. While the puritan attitude toward non-Muslims is indeed supremacist, moderates believe that the supremacist attitude is fundamentally inconsistent with Islamic theology, particularly the theology of salvation. What contributes to the puritan supremacist attitude is their belief that they alone possess the exclusive truth and that all others are damned. The belief that God is exclusively on the side of one group and that all others are damned could lead to an arrogant conviction that those others are not of equal worth or value. There is no question that in the case of Muslim puritanical groups, their ideas about salvation and damnation contributed to supremacist thinking that has been used to justify inhumane and even cruel behavior.

The issue of salvation in moderate thought is nuanced, largely in response to the nuanced treatment this issue receives in the Qur'an. The first principle is that God and God alone is the King of the Hereafter, and therefore God's discretion is unlimited. God's discretion in deciding when or who is to be forgiven is unfettered. Therefore, God speaking to the Prophet Muhammad in the Qur'an says: "You [Prophet Muhammad] have no say in the matter; it is up to God to pardon them or punish them for they have been unjust. To God belongs all that is in the Heavens and earth. God may pardon whom God pleases and punish whom God pleases. And God is most forgiving and merciful."[13]

Beyond establishing the principle of God's discretion, God makes commitments to human beings regarding the consequences of their beliefs and actions. The Qur'an clearly states that Islam is the Divine Truth, and demands belief in Muhammad as the final messenger in a long line of Abrahamic prophets. For instance, the Qur'an states: "God has made for each nation a way and method that they follow. So they should not contend with you in this matter. Call to your Lord for you are surely on the right path. If they argue with you, tell them: God knows all that we do, and God will judge between you on the Final Day as to what you disagreed upon."[14]

Importantly, however, the Qur'an does not completely exclude the possibility that there might be other paths to salvation. One component of this issue has to do with who might be entitled to God's mercy. On this, the Qur'an again insists on God's unfettered discretion to accept in His mercy whomever He wishes. In fact, the Qur'an expresses indignation at those who attempt to limit or apportion God's mercy according to their wills or desires. First, the Qur'an asserts that the Prophet was sent but as a mercy to humanity.[15] And second, only God decides who shall receive the Divine mercy either on this earth or in the Hereafter, and it is considered a great act of transgression for human beings to attempt to speculate as to who shall deserve God's mercy and who will not.[16]

Beyond the fact that in principle *anyone* might be entitled to God's mercy, and that this is simply a topic not appropriate for human speculation, the Qur'an goes on to give what it describes as good tidings to some people who are not necessarily Muslim. It states: "For each nation We have ordained a way and path so that they will mention the name of God for the blessings He has given them. Your God is a single God so submit to God and give good tidings to those who bow down before God."[17] This verse implies that, as different as the pathways may be, they may still be directed toward God. Interestingly, the Qur'an acknowledges that those who worship God deserve to receive good tidings and that the core issue, regardless of the path, is submission to God.

Another intriguing aspect of the Qur'anic discourse is that it recognizes that plural religious convictions and laws might be legitimate. The Qur'an states: "Those who believe, those who follow Jewish scriptures, the Christians, the Sabians, and any who believe in God and the Final Day, and do good, all shall have their reward with their Lord and they will not come to fear or grief."[18] Along the same lines, the Qur'an contains the following verse: "Among the People of the Book, there are those who believe in God. They believe in what has been revealed to you, and also in what has been revealed to them. They bow in humility before God, and they do not trade for paltry gain God's messages. Verily, those have their reward with God for God is swift in reckoning."[19] As noted earlier, People of the Book refers mostly to Jews and Christians.

Moderates see in the Qur'anic discourse a subtle but important point. There is no question that Muslims who believe and do good deeds will attain salvation and receive an ample reward in the Hereafter. But, as discussed, the Qur'an is quite adamant about the impermissibility of speculating about who might be the recipient of God's mercy, and the Qur'an leaves open the possibility that non-Muslims might receive God's grace as well. Significantly, the Qur'an repeats this point on many occasions and in many circumstances, stressing that in dealing with others, Muslims cannot preclude the possibility that non-Muslims may be entitled to salvation. Moderates believe that this goes to addressing the basic attitude that Muslims ought to hold toward others. Muslims are simply not privy to how God will decide to deal with non-Muslims, and therefore, Muslims ought to deal with others on this earth in terms of their potential for beauty and goodness that God has deposited into *every* human being. Muslims should not dismissively and arrogantly believe that all non-Muslims are damned, lest this affect their behavior toward non-Muslims. God is stressing that no one, not even Muslims, should commit the idolatry of behaving as if they are the sanctimonious voice of God. Human beings should always know their place, and this humility might make all the difference between acting decent or not.

The puritan response to the moderate position can be summed up in one word: *abrogation*. Abrogation means that all the verses that speak about tolerance or cooperation with non-Muslims are null and void. According to the puritans, it was God that decided to invalidate all the Qur'anic passages that admonished Muslims to be forgiving or to seek peaceful coexistence with non-Muslims. According to puritans, God encouraged Muslims to be forgiving and tolerant when Muslims were weak and could not afford to pursue a confrontational policy with non-Muslims. But once Muslims became strong, God commanded Muslims to seek the destruction of all non-Muslims—or, at a minimum, to be hostile toward them.

For moderates, the puritan position simply does not make sense. In the moderate view, this opportunistic logic is unbecoming of a God who is just, ethical, and merciful. It defies logic that God at one point would instruct human beings to act in a moral fashion, only to completely reverse Himself at a later point for purely opportunistic reasons. Simply put, this is not the God that moderates worship, and moderates have too much respect for the Qur'an to read it in this unethically opportunistic fashion.

Unfortunately, however, puritans habitually declare any part of the Qur'an that is inconsistent with their worldview to have been abrogated. In this case, puritans claim that what they call the jihad verses have abrogated and nullified all of the Qur'anic teachings on tolerance and forgiveness. I will discuss the topic of jihad and the so-called jihad verses in the next chapter. The real issue, however, is that whether puritans invoke the doctrine of jihad or some other jurisprudential doctrine, the fundamental problem is their intolerant and confrontational worldview, which acts like a prism through which they see God and God's text. Unfailingly, puritans seek to find whatever doctrine or mechanism that will enable them to project their worldview onto the Islamic faith. Significantly, it is exactly because their worldview is not supported by the Qur'an that they have to resort to dubious methods such as declaring that parts of the Qur'an have been abrogated, not by human beings interpreting the text, but by God. This way they can avoid taking responsibility for ignoring parts of the Divine book, and instead attribute the responsibility directly to God.

ELEVEN

JIHAD, WARFARE, AND TERRORISM

No aspect of the Islamic religion is in the public eye and all over the media on a daily basis as much as the issue of jihad and terrorism. In fact, the subject of jihad in Islam stands at the foundation of most claims about the ability of Islam to coexist or cooperate with non-Muslims. Despite all the writings on the topic, what seems puzzling is how so many Muslims understand the doctrine so differently. There is no question that much of what is written about jihad is ill-informed or worse. But it is also undeniable that especially in the modern age, Muslim statements and conduct have made the concept of jihad confusing and even chaotic. Jihad, especially as portrayed in the Western media and as exploited by terrorists, is often associated with the idea of a holy war that is propagated in the name of God against unbelievers, and is often equated with the most vulgar images of religious intolerance. Worst of all, the issue of terrorism has defiled the reputation of the world's second-largest religion.

It won't come as a surprise that the positions of moderates and puritans on this issue are worlds apart. The problem is that the puritans speak much louder than the moderates. Puritans speak with guns; what weapons do the moderates possess?

It will be much easier to explain the modern debates with the classical heritage in the foreground. I do not agree with scholars who think that the past determines the future, but on the particular issues of jihad and warfare, the classical tradition has played a strong role.

Jihad is a core principle in Islamic theology; the word itself literally means "to strive, to apply oneself, to struggle, to persevere." In many ways, jihad connotes a strong spiritual and material work ethic in Islam. Piety, knowledge, health, beauty, truth, and justice are not possible without jihad—that is, without sustained and diligent hard work. Therefore, cleansing oneself from vanity and pettiness, pursuing knowledge, curing the ill, feeding the poor, and standing up for truth and justice, even at great personal risk, are all forms of jihad.

The Qur'an uses the term *jihad* to refer to the act of striving to serve the purposes of God on this earth, which includes all the acts mentioned above. The Prophet Muhammad repeatedly taught that the greatest form of jihad is to struggle against one's own base desires or to speak the truth before an oppressive power and to suffer as a consequence of speaking out. By the same logic, striving or working hard in war, provided that the war is just and good, is also jihad. It bears emphasis that as long as the objective or cause is good, struggling to achieve it is jihad. Similarly, resisting an unjust ruler even if by force could be jihad.

Jihad became a powerful symbol for perseverance, hard work, and success in Islamic history. As a symbol, it was used to rally enthusiasm and excitement for a variety of causes, including warfare. In warfare, if the fight was between Muslims and non-Muslims, then the ruler would be the one calling for jihad. If, however, the cause was an internal matter, such as a civic protest, a rebellion, the marshaling of support to build a seminary, or the collecting of funds to build a library or a sanctuary for street dogs and cats (which used to be a common practice in the classical age), the call for jihad would usually be issued by the most honored and respected scholar who happened to be championing the particular cause. Would people heed the call for jihad? It depended on the moral authority and persuasive weight that the scholar or ruler carried in the community. Unless a particular ruler had implemented forcible military conscription, there was no choice but to hope that the call for jihad would persuade enough people to join the fight—whatever the cause might be.

Was there a theology of "holy war" in the sense of "Onward, Christian soldiers" in the Catholic faith? The answer has to be no, as the Islamic theological tradition did not have a notion of holy war. Islam lacked anything like the institution of papal authority that could make determinations on the divine status of a war. The main difference is that in Christianity there was an institution that could decisively and conclusively award a military force the status of being Crusaders or pilgrims in God's army and guarantee redemption to these soldiers. In Islam no one, not even the caliph or a high-ranking jurist, had the formidable power of guaranteeing redemption or rendering a military campaign holy or divine. Jihad simply meant to strive hard or struggle in pursuit of a just cause.

"Holy war" (in Arabic *al-harb al-muqaddasa*) is not an expression used by the Qur'anic text or Muslim theologians. In Islamic theology, war is never *holy;* it is either justified or not—and if it is justified, those killed in battle are considered martyrs. However, martyrdom is within God's exclusive province; only God can assess the intentions of individuals and the justness of their cause, and ultimately, whether they deserve the status of being a martyr. The Qur'anic text does not recognize the idea of unlimited warfare, and it does not consider the simple fact that one of the belligerents is Muslim to be sufficient to establish the justness of a war. In other words, the Qur'an entertains the possibility that a Muslim combatant might be acting unjustly, and if so, then that Muslim is not engaging in jihad. According to the Qur'an, war might be necessary, and might even become binding and obligatory, but it is never a moral and ethical good.

The Qur'an does not use the word *jihad* to refer to warfare or fighting; such acts are referred to as *qital*. While the Qur'an's call to jihad is unconditional and unrestricted, such is not the case for *qital*. Jihad is a good in and of itself, while *qital* is not. Jihad is good because it is like the Protestant work ethic: hard work toward a good cause. *Qital*—war—however, is a different matter altogether. Every reference in the Qur'an to *qital* is restricted and limited by particular conditions; but exhortations to jihad, like the references to justice or truth, are absolute and unconditional. On every single occasion that the Qur'an exhorts Muslims to fight, it hastens to qualify the exhortation by a command to believers to not transgress, to forgive, or to seek peace. Although this fact is recognizable by simply reading the text of the Qur'an, this textual reality has strangely eluded a large number of Muslim and non-Muslim scholars of the Qur'an. Nevertheless, it is beyond dispute that the Qur'an never endorses the military option without conditioning that choice in some significant way.

Although the Qur'an does not condone the notion of unlimited warfare or the concept of holy war, the historical circumstances of medieval Muslim jurists, writing especially in the ninth and tenth centuries, deeply influenced how these jurists read and interpreted the Qur'anic text. During this historical period, nations and empires, in the absence of a peace treaty, considered themselves in a state of perpetual warfare with all others. In the medieval age, conquering and vanquishing the weak was an accepted part of the customs and practices of nations and empires. As is evidenced by numerous historical examples, including the law of the Greeks, the Romans, the

Byzantiums, the Lombards, the Frankish Kingdom, the Kingdom of the Visigoths, the Kingdom of the Ostrogoths, the Mongol tribes, the Crusader states, and many others, throughout the medieval period states and nations regularly invaded each other in a relentless competition for dominance. If nations sought to avoid the danger of invasion, the accepted practice was that the weaker nation, pursuant to an agreement, paid a monetary tribute to the stronger nation. While nations or empires of roughly equal strength often concluded treaties of nonbelligerence and developed trade interests between them, the fact remained, however, that any ambitious ruler could easily abrogate any existing treaty and return to war. This is why any reader of medieval history would notice the seemingly endless saga of invasions and counterinvasions, as well as the constant rise and decline or fall of nations and empires.

This was the prevailing context during the formative years of Islamic law, roughly from the eighth through the tenth centuries. Writing on the topic of international law, Muslim jurists incorporated the practices of their day and age in their interpretations of the Qur'an and the Sunna of the Prophet. Discussing the interpretations and conceptions of medieval jurists is not indulging in mere historical trivia; rather, these medieval determinations have been at the forefront of some of the worst Western misconceptions about Islam, and also have had a substantial impact upon the puritanical worldview in the contemporary age.

Many Muslim jurists divided the world into what they called the two abodes: the abode of Islam (*dar al-Islam*) and the abode of war (*dar al-harb* or at times called *dar al-kufr*, the abode of infidels). Historically, the concept of the abode of Islam was very similar to the papal concept of the lands of Christendom in the twelfth century.[1] Although the word *abode* is a literal translation of the word *dar*, the intended meaning was the territories and jurisdictions of Muslim authorities versus the territories and jurisdictions of non-Muslims. Therefore, in essence, a substantial number of jurists thought of the world as divided between the territories or lands of Muslims and the territories or lands of non-Muslims.

According to this dichotomous view, Muslims and non-Muslims were presumed to be in a perpetual state of war until Muslims were able to defeat non-Muslims once and for all. According to a considerable number of jurists writing during this formative period in Islamic law, Muslims must give non-Muslims one of three options: convert to Islam, pay the poll tax, or fight.[2] It was not deemed necessary that all of humanity convert to Islam, but it was believed to be imperative that Muslims seek to become the supreme masters of the world. Therefore, according to the advocates of the dichotomous view, religious differences and diversity were tolerated as long as the existence of these differences did not challenge Muslim political supremacy and dominance. Consequently, war was always necessary to ensure the supremacy of Muslims over non-Muslims. Advocates of the dichotomous view contended that in the harshly competitive medieval world, it was imperative that Muslims ensure that they be the dominators and not the dominated. Proponents of this view presumed any non-Muslim nation to be in a hostile relationship with Muslims unless there was an agreement providing otherwise, and expressed their opposition to peace treaties that did not have an expiration date—in most cases, they advocated a term of ten years. This view was not exceptional in medieval times. Treaties at that time did not exist in perpetuity—treaties could be dated to expire in ninety-nine years, but some expiration date had to exist. Although dating treaties was common in the law of nations, as far as the jurists of the dichotomous view were concerned, a nonbelligerence treaty was considered an unfortunate concession to political realities. The normal state of affairs and usual condition was that the two abodes, of Islam and war, would be in everlasting conflict—fighting it out until one managed to dominate the other.

It bears emphasis that the presumed permanent state of war between Muslims and non-Muslims more than anything was a function of the historical context many of the early jurists lived in. This permanent state of war had little to do with religious beliefs or convictions. Rather, the reason for this position was that many jurists created a legal presumption that unless proven otherwise, non-Muslims pose a threat to Muslims. According to the prevailing norms of international relations at the time, unless there was an affirmative agreement to the contrary, every nation or empire in existence assumed itself to be in a belligerent relationship with the rest of the world. Accepting this context as a given, many Muslim jurists presumed any non-Muslim nation to be in a hostile relationship with Muslims, and therefore, Muslims to be in a perpetual state of self-defense unless there was a peace treaty or agreement or customary practice providing otherwise. Therefore, for instance, according to many jurists, the Byzantium Empire and the Venetian states were presumed to pose a threat to the Islamic Empire unless they concluded a peace agreement with Muslims. And in fact both the Byzantiums and Venetians in different historical periods signed peace treaties with the Muslim states in Egypt and Syria. The same presumption existed vis-à-vis the so-called Frankish nations, but in this case, the Crusader invasions proved that the presumption was justified.

Although the idea that the world is divided between the territories of Muslims and the territories of non-Muslims had a substantial impact upon Islamic jurisprudence, it is not supported by either the Qur'an or the Sunna. Both sources do mention that all Muslims should think of themselves as a single people belonging to one nation, but they do not divide the world into two abodes, and they do not say that Muslims should be in a perpetual state of war with non-Muslims. The only abodes that the Qur'an speaks of are the abode of the Hereafter and the abode of earthly life, with the former described as clearly superior to the latter. The Qur'anic and Prophetic teachings proclaiming that all Muslims belong to a single nation were meant to emphasize the moral bond that unites all Muslims and the fact that Muslims should empathize with each other as brothers and sisters. The idea that the world ought to be divided into two camps constantly at war with each other finds very scant support in Islamic primary sources.

The dichotomous view of the two abodes, however, was not the only dominant perspective throughout Islamic history. Most jurists writing around the same time, especially after the tenth century, argued that instead of a two-part division of the world, there was a third category—the abode of nonbelligerence or neutrality (*dar al-sulh* or *al-'ahd*)—an abode that was not Muslim, but that had a peaceful relationship with the Muslim world, either through a formal peace treaty or through established customary practice. In relation to this abode, violent jihad had no role to play. In fact, if a group of Muslims attacked or committed violence against a neutral abode, this would not only be considered a sin but this group must also be punished and forced to compensate the government of the neutral territory for any damage caused. In the very first centuries of Islam, for instance, non-Muslim Nubia and Abyssinia enjoyed a friendly status with the Islamic Empire and were considered neutral states. Throughout Islamic history various non-Muslim states concluded peace treaties with either the Abbasid Empire or, after its disintegration, with one of the Islamic dynasties. Treaties of nonbelligerence providing for trade relations were concluded even with Crusader states in the twelfth and thirteenth centuries. Therefore, reading the historical practice, the opponents of the dichotomous view argued that a tripartite or three-abode division of the world more accurately described the reality of interstate relations and conduct.

It is important to note, however, that as to this third abode, what was required was a treaty or customary practice preserving reciprocal nonbelligerence and nonviolence. Friendly or amicable relations were not required. Therefore, a group of Muslims could not use the lack of friendly relations as an excuse to violate a treaty or status of nonbelligerence and attack a non-Muslim state. Therefore, for instance, today the United States has treaties of nonbelligerence with many Muslim countries, including Saudi Arabia. According to classical law, a group of Saudi citizens could not use a set of claimed grievances to attack the United States as long as the treaty of nonbelligerence existed.

As Muslim history progressed, the dichotomous and the tripartite views of the world became increasingly untenable and unrealistic. Many jurists from all over the Islamic world writing especially after the twelfth century, rejected the two- or three-abode division and started theorizing that the world was divided into many kinds and types of abodes. So, for example, many classical jurists argued that regardless of the political affiliation of a particular territory, the real or true abode of Islam was wherever justice existed (*dar al-'adl*), or wherever Muslims could freely and openly practice their religion. Accordingly, if Muslims could live safely and openly practice their religion in the United States, for example, then the United States would be considered a part of the Muslim abode. Therefore, it is possible for a territory to be ruled by non-Muslims with Muslims a small minority, and yet the territory be treated as part of the Muslim world. This would mean that this territory could not be fought and violent jihad against such a territory would not be legitimate.

Some classical jurists even argued that there was an abode of formal Islam and an abode of true Islam. In other words, if the territory was governed by an unjust Muslim ruler, it would be considered the abode of formal Islam. However, the territory that is free from the control of an unjust ruler and where Islam is practiced correctly would be considered the abode of true Islam. Put simply, a large number of classical scholars theorized that the categorization of two or three abodes was too simplistic, and that instead there should be many types of abodes—each abode describing the moral and ethical quality of the particular land and polity in question. Some jurists even went as far as saying that when injustice and corruption fill the lands, the abode of true Islam is to be found in the hearts of the pious.[3]

As classical Muslim jurists debated the complicated issue of abodes, they also debated what would constitute a sufficient and just cause for fighting non-Muslims. The classical debates focused on the question of whether non-Muslims were fought because of their act of disbelief or only because they posed a physical threat to Muslims. Most classical jurists concluded that the justification for fighting non-Muslims was directly proportional to the physical threat they posed to Muslims. If non-Muslims did not threaten or seek to harm Muslims, then there was no justification for acts of belligerence or warfare against them. According to most Muslim jurists, the act of disbelief or the failure to believe (*kufr*) was not a sufficient cause for war because by itself, it did not justify the termination of life.

This is why, according to the classical tradition, the lives of noncombatants are sacrosanct. Although noncombatants might be unbelievers, they do not inherently pose a threat and therefore they may not be targeted. Relying on a precedent set by the Prophet, classical Muslim jurists held that noncombatants like children, women, people of advanced age, monks, hermits, priests, or anyone else who does not seek to or cannot fight Muslims, is inviolable and may not be targeted even during ongoing hostilities. Before any military campaign, the Prophet used to instruct his armies not to hurt noncombatants or needlessly destroy property or vegetation, but to treat the wounded and feed the needy, including prisoners of war. In a well-known report, it was widely recorded that after a battle, upon finding the corpse of a woman, the Prophet became very upset and reproached his army for killing a noncombatant.[4]

This is the basic legacy that modern-day Muslims inherited, and the one that puritans and moderates have had to accept, reject, or modify. As can be observed, the legacy is not straightforward or simple; there are various voices and trends in this legacy, and what remains for Muslims to decide is how they want to handle the novel conditions and new challenges of the modern age. Some of this legacy came directly from the Qur'an—for instance, the prohibition against harming prisoners of war or against violating treaties and pacts. Some of the past legacy had a very tenuous connection with the Qur'an, like the division of the world into two abodes. As noted earlier, the Qur'an speaks about Muslims as a single nation before God, but does not bifurcate the world into two or more abodes.

Despite its tenuous connection to Islamic theology, the dichotomous view has played a major role in shaping contemporary Western stereotypes of Islam. Many of the books written by non-Muslim scholars in the West perpetuate the myth that Islamic law invariably dictates that the world should be divided into two abodes forever locked in conflict.

Often the same books falsely assume that most Muslims today adhere to the same bipolar view of the world. This, of course, is not an accurate description of Islamic legal doctrine; moreover, it does not accurately describe the beliefs of the overwhelming majority of Muslims today. It does, however, accurately describe the convictions and ideology of contemporary puritan thinkers and activists. The puritans latched onto the idea of the two-abode division, with its state of permanent conflict, because it served their bipolar view of the world quite well. Although the whole idea of the lands of Islamdom—or Christendom, for that matter, versus any other territory—was thoroughly a product of historical circumstance, all puritans treated this idea as if it were a tenet of the Islamic faith. Whether a particular puritan group believes that the abode of Islam is currently engaged in a state of active hostilities with the abode of war or believes that, for one reason or another, there is a temporary respite in the hostilities, the end result is the same.

The idea of battling abodes might have served a purpose at a certain point in history, but if applied today it leads to disastrous consequences. As far as the puritans are concerned, this medieval paradigm is particularly convenient because it permits puritans to attack their enemies without giving them notice or a declaration of war. If all non-Muslim countries may be presumed to be the enemies of Islam and Muslims, puritans contend that they are not legally obligated to give notice to non-Muslim states of this ongoing state of war, and therefore, puritans feel justified in attacking non-Muslims anytime and anywhere. The presumption of ongoing hostilities, according to puritans, permits them to attack at will either non-Muslims in their own countries or non-Muslim interests in Muslim countries. In their writings, puritans also adopt the opportunistic logic that Muslims might need to enter into peace treaties with non-Muslim countries for a while, but only if Muslims are weak and need to build up their power. But in principle as soon as Muslims possess the requisite power, Muslims would need to reassert their supremacy over unbelievers by giving them the draconian three choices: convert to Islam, pay the poll tax, or fight.

Does this explain the puritan violence being committed against the West today? Well, not quite. Puritans believe that they are engaging in a defensive war at the current time, not an offensive war. This has a rather odd result, because if it were an aggressive war (or what is called, in Islamic law, a preemptive war), at least the puritans could not commit violence unless they first gave Westerners the option of becoming Muslim. Since, however, puritans believe that they are waging a defensive war, the need for such notice does not exist nor restrain them.

As was noted in an earlier chapter, puritans believe that the vast majority of Muslim lands are still colonized by the West, but by proxy. The current rulers in most of the Muslim world act in proxy for their Western masters, and therefore, when Western forces arrive in the Middle East by invitation from the domestic governments in power, the invitation is immaterial. The Westerners are still the aggressors, because through their local agents (the rulers) they got themselves invited to occupy Muslim lands. This is why militant puritan groups since the 1980s and to this day continue attacking Americans and other Westerners in Saudi Arabia, Yemen, Egypt, and other Muslim countries. In every one of these instances, the puritan militant groups in each of these countries firmly believed that the Muslim local rulers were nothing more than stooges of the West. Therefore, the guarantee of safe conduct offered by these Muslim governments to nationals of non-Muslim countries is considered invalid and void, and since these nationals are "unlawfully" present in Muslim territory, they can enjoy no immunity.

But if puritans believe that Muslims continue to be colonized by proxy, and that the West occupies Muslim countries by manipulating their stooges (Muslim rulers), the real question is: Why don't puritan militants simply wage attacks against the military forces found in their countries instead of waging terrorist attacks against Westerners all over the globe? The answer is entirely functional and opportunistic. For all their talk about literalism when interpreting God's law, puritans rely on a blatant logic of necessity. Puritans reason that the West is strong and has armies with which to wage its destructive wars. Muslims, puritans argue, are weak and would invariably be defeated in a conventional war. Thus, Muslims need to find an alternative method of fighting—they have to strike wherever they can and inflict enough damage on the enemy until the enemy gets the point and retreats from all Muslim lands. The logic of puritans is that they are justified in violating Islamic moral and legal prescriptions against the targeting of civilians because there is no other way to defeat their enemy. Since they are not strong enough to take on the Western armed military, they must achieve victory by any means necessary. And, according to puritans, waging attacks against the civilian nationals of countries that occupy Muslim lands will eventually bring these countries to their knees and teach them not to violate the sanctity of or attempt to dominate Muslim nations.

The disagreements between puritans and moderates are very deep and profound in all matters related to warfare, jihad, and terrorism. The disagreements relate to the sanctity and value placed on life and to what kind of example God wants Muslims to set before humanity. They relate to whether there is an open, never-ending state of war between Islam and non-Muslims, and at what cost this war may be fought. Here, we get to basic and fundamental differences about how to read the text of the Qur'an about war. The issue in this case is one of moral attitude—the attitude about the desirability of violence and the price of war.

Moderates and puritans will recognize that *salam* (peace and tranquility) is a core moral condition that is repeatedly emphasized both in ritualistic practices, such as prayer, and in virtually all Islamic social practices, such as greetings exchanged between people. But the Qur'an is not talking about ritualistic expressions of wishes that are proclaimed as a polite way of ignoring and avoiding the other. The Qur'an associates the prayer of peace with forgiveness and mercy—it counsels Muslims to forgive and say, "Peace," or it instructs Muslims to say, "Peace," and then explains that God has decreed mercy upon God's Self.[5] Both forgiveness and the merciful treatment of others—whether the others are non-Muslims or Muslims belonging to different sects—are necessary for the coexistence of human beings in a state of peace. Significantly, in Qur'anic discourses and Islamic theology, *salam,* or the ability to exist in a condition of peace and tranquility, is considered a profound Divine blessing to be cherished and vigilantly pursued by every Muslim. Classical theological treatises that summarize the quintessential nature of Islam often state that Islam is not only the faith of submission, but also the faith of peace.

But according to the Qur'an, for a state of peace to exist, Muslims must therefore actively cultivate forgiveness and mercy. Therefore, the Qur'an is keen on warning Muslims against allowing the circumstances of rancor and hostility with one party or another from penetrating and corrupting their hearts. This is why the Qur'an instructs Muslims that the injustice committed by others should not be allowed to alter the attitude of Muslims toward their moral obligations to promote forgiveness and mercy. This point is emphasized time and again in the Qur'an. For instance, it states: "O you who believe, stand up as witnesses for God in justice, and do not let your hatred of a people lead you away from justice. Be just! This is closest to piety and be mindful of God in all you do for God is aware of all you do."[6] Even when the collective Muslim ego had suffered a severe blow, it became particularly imperative for Muslims to be extra vigilant in holding steadfast to their moral principles. The Qur'an is specific on this point and instructs Muslims in the following way: "And do not let your anger at those who barred you from the Holy Mosque [in Mecca] lead you to commit aggression. Help one another in goodness and piety and do not assist each other in committing sin and aggression, and be mindful of God for God is severe in retribution."[7]

The Qur'an repeatedly emphasizes that God does not like aggression and does not love aggressors, and it warns Muslims that they must critically reflect upon the way they deal with others so that they do not find that they have unwittingly fallen into the position of the unjust.[8] It is clear that the Qur'an recognizes the law of retribution, and acknowledges that at times it might be necessary to act in a punitive fashion. If attacked, Muslims can respond in kind, but if the enemy desists, Muslims must refrain from further acts of violence. In this context, the Qur'an states: "So if you are transgressed against, deal with them as you have been dealt with and fear God, and know that God is with those who are pious."[9] In this context, the Qur'an is referring to the right of self-defense—particularly to a situation in which the failure to respond effectively would constitute Muslims as "casting themselves onto ruin" by failing to protect themselves.[10] In other words, at times the failure to defend oneself is effectively like allowing oneself to be destroyed or like committing suicide. But it should also be noted that, at times, insisting on committing aggression and picking fights with others also constitutes "casting one's self into ruin."

Obviously, being forced to use force is not an ideal situation. The Qur'an is talking about situations when Muslims must resort to force because there is no other choice. The ideal and better situation is for Muslims to try to cultivate forgiveness and mercy. Therefore, the Qur'an states: "Good and evil are not equal [in status] to each other. Repel evil with goodness and then you will find that your erstwhile enemy has become like an affectionate close companion. This will not be attained except by those who forbear, and those who have been greatly blessed [by wisdom]. And if the Devil incites you to evil, seek refuge in God for God hears all and knows all."[11] It is worth emphasizing that in the Qur'anic discourse, the higher moral existence—the way of those endowed with forbearance, fortitude, and wisdom—is to repel evil with goodness.

The ideal and better condition is to spread forgiveness, not rancor and hate. This is why the Qur'an instructs Muslims to "Cultivate forgiveness, enjoin goodness, and turn away from the ignorant."[12] This means that Muslims ought to cultivate and nurture an attitude of tolerance and forgiveness, and not seek confrontations with those who do not understand the moral worth of either value. Part of this process is to avoid escalating conflict or intentionally inciting hatred and ill will. Thus the Qur'an explicitly commands Muslims not to use foul language or curse their opponents, even if these opponents initiate the verbal abuse. The Qur'an justifies this prohibition by explaining that attempting to reciprocate verbal abuse leads to a dynamic that is essentially uncontrollable and that is bound to result in much ugliness.[13]

The idea that the more virtuous position is to cultivate forgiveness and mercy is entirely alien to puritans. This is why the problem is one of fundamental attitudes. The attitude of the puritans is that real Islamic virtue is to fight and conquer. Puritans are interested in focusing on and inflating what separates Muslims from non-Muslims instead of trying to find common ground in forgiveness and mercy. The attitude adopted by puritans is entirely inconsistent with the Qur'anic advice to seek to make the worst of enemies into affectionate close companions through good deeds.

Perhaps the biggest problem of all is that puritans fail to recognize that the absence of peace is identified in the Qur'an as a negative and undesirable condition. The absence of peace is described throughout the Qur'an as a trial and tribulation, as a curse or punishment, or, sometimes, as a necessarily evil. But the absence of peace is never in and of itself a positive or desirable condition—it is not a moral condition that ought to be desired or preferred by Muslims. War (*qital*) is portrayed in the Qur'an as a product of human follies or weaknesses—it is often cast as a product of humans succumbing to their whims or as a state induced by Satanic temptations. Therefore, as mentioned earlier, the Qur'an asserts that if it had not been for Divine benevolence, many mosques, churches, synagogues, and homes would have been destroyed because of wars caused by the ignorance and pettiness of human beings.[14] Often, God mercifully intervenes to put out the fires of war, and saves human beings from follies that would have resulted in further violence.[15] This moral orientation that the Qur'an strives to instill in Muslims of war as a folly, an evil, and a corruption is curiously absent in the puritans' consciousness.

Puritans entirely ignore the Qur'anic teaching that the act of destroying or spreading ruin on this earth is one of the gravest sins possible—*fasad fi al-ard*, which means to corrupt the earth by destroying the beauty of creation. This is considered an ultimate act of blasphemy against God.[16] Those who corrupt the earth by destroying lives, property, and nature are designated as *mufsidun* (corruptors and evildoers), who, in effect, wage war against God by dismantling the very fabric of existence.[17] Corrupting the earth entails the act of undoing and breaking down the ties and relationships that God has established through creation by disrupting the process of human intercourse and by destroying the very possibility of human beings coming "to know one another" through interactive social dynamics.[18]

Most importantly, according to the Qur'an, war by its very nature is the primary contributor to this process of corruption that plagues and ultimately destroys human beings. This is exactly why Islamic theology teaches that an integral part of the Divine covenant given to human beings is to occupy themselves with building and creating, not ruining and destroying life. This is why the Islamic civilization excelled in the sciences, arts, philosophy, law, architecture, and trade, and this is also why the Islamic historical experience was primarily concerned not with war-making, but with civilization-building.

In order to better understand the Qur'anic principles surrounding the issue of war, there are several significant precedents to consider. The early Muslims living in Mecca as a minority were not allowed to respond to Meccan oppression by taking military action until God gave Muslims specific permission to do so. Muslims in Mecca had endured oppression for many years, and despite the impatient urgings of Muslims, the Prophet would not allow them to respond with violence. At one point the Prophet allowed a group of his most oppressed and powerless followers to migrate and seek sanctuary with al-Najashi, the Christian king of Abyssinia.

God's authorization to Muslims to migrate from Mecca and use force in self-defense came in the form of a Qur'anic revelation addressing the Prophet and his Muslim community. The Qur'an was careful to note that Muslims were given permission to fight (to engage in *qital*) only because they had become the victims of aggression.[19] Furthermore, the Qur'an instructed Muslims to fight only those who fought them and not to transgress by fighting those who sought to make peace with Muslims.[20] According to the Qur'anic revelation, if the enemy ceased hostilities and sought peace, Muslims were to seek peace as well. The Qur'an explained that God never prohibits Muslims from making peace with those who do not fight Muslims, but God does prohibit Muslims from making peace with those who have expelled Muslims from their homes and who continue to persecute them.[21]

Elsewhere, the Qur'an pronounced a stronger mandate in stating: "If your enemy inclines toward peace, then you should seek peace and trust in God."[22] Moreover, the Qur'an instructs Muslims not to haughtily turn away unbelievers who seek to make peace with Muslims, and reminds Muslims that, "If God would have willed, He would have given the unbelievers power over you [Muslims], and they would have fought you [Muslims]. Therefore, if they [the unbelievers] withdraw from you and refuse to fight you, and instead, send you guarantees of peace, know that God has not given you a license [to fight them]."[23] Furthermore, the Qur'an warned Muslims against adopting a belligerent attitude in which excuses are made to pursue war. If a people offer Muslims peace, according to the Qur'an, it is arrogant and immoral for Muslims to cite the fact that such a people are not Muslims as an excuse to continue fighting them.

In other words, Muslims should not invent impediments to making peace. Doing so is an indication that Muslims have succumbed to the temptations of the mundane instead of staying focused on the temporal and Divine. In other words, the rejection of a just peace could be an indication that Muslims have lost sight of the Divine objectives with which they are charged, and that they have become distracted by earthly temptations of power and dominance.[24] In this Qur'anic discourse, failure to seek peace without just cause is considered arrogant and sinful because the desire or willingness to engage in peace is a Divine blessing. God has the power, if God so wills, to inspire in the hearts of non-Muslims a desire for peace, and Muslims must treat this as a blessing and respond with gratitude and appreciation, not defiance and arrogance.[25]

These Qur'anic discourses on peace would hardly make sense if Muslims were ordered to be in a permanent state of war with nonbelievers, and if nonbelievers were expected to be a permanent enemy and perpetual legitimate target. From the moderate perspective, puritans fail to understand that it is peace, not war, that is favored in the Qur'an. Puritans fail to exploit opportunities for peace and fail to understand that peace is a gift from God, not to be wasted except for compelling reasons. Moderates maintain that the idea of two abodes constantly at war with each other, even if it was a historical reality for a period of time, is clearly inconsistent with Qur'anic morality.

It is not surprising that to all of this puritans respond that the "peace verses" in the Qur'an have been abrogated by a command to wage war against the unbelievers.[26] Per this logic, a single verse, 3:85, commanding Muslims to wage war against unbelievers has canceled out and voided all the verses in the Qur'an that speak about making or seeking after peace. This amounts to saying that a single verse abrogated at least thirty verses that call for peace. But even more, puritans ignore that even the so-called war verses in the Qur'an always add the qualification not to transgress and not to become unjust. In fact, there is not a single verse in the Qur'an that calls for an unmitigated, unqualified, or unreserved obligation to fight the unbelievers. As I noted earlier, this abrogation claim is a very whimsical way of dealing with Qur'anic teachings.

When the Qur'an says that God does not like aggressors, this must be taken seriously and interpreted reasonably. We should keep in mind that every hostile and belligerent individual can twist the facts sufficiently until he comes to believe that he is the victim and not the aggressor. But the Qur'anic command must be dealt with in good faith, and the onus is always on the one using violence to scrutinize his conscience and make sure that he has not fallen prey to the mythology of victimization, by which one always sees himself as the aggrieved party. This is one of the most problematic aspects of the puritan creed—they read history in such a way that Muslims are always made to be the victims and non-Muslims are always made to be the aggressors. As a result, they render all the Qur'anic commands on nonaggression simply irrelevant—after all, according to the puritans, Muslims are always the aggrieved party.

I think it is important to note that most moderates are not pacifists. They do recognize that at times it becomes necessary to fight in self-defense, but they read this narrowly. Fighting to wrong historical grievances and avenge injustices that occurred centuries ago is often not self-defense at all, but thinly veiled aggression. Fighting in self-defense has to be proportional and restrained, in the sense that it should repel the impending danger without inflicting more damage than is necessary to terminate the threat. For instance, if an assailant aggressively fires a bullet, responding to the assailant by firing off a volley of missiles would not be a restrained or proportional response. Self-defense must be limited to fighting the group of people who invaded and robbed Muslims of their rights or land. In Islamic law, self-defense is not an excuse for open warfare all around the globe without any restraints or limitations. Of course, the teachings and restrictions of Islamic law are of direct relevance to many conflicts in which Muslims are involved, including Chechnya and Kashmir, among many others.

Moderates take the Prophet's instructions about not killing noncombatants and other limitations on the conduct of warfare very seriously. Therefore, moderates recognize that even if the cause is just, if the limits and restraints are not observed, while the case might remain just the war could become unjust because of the aggressions committed. In other words, aggression is not simply an issue of *why* the war is being fought, but also of *how* the war is being fought. So, for instance, if noncombatants and places of worship are intentionally targeted, the war becomes unjust.

But there is a further dimension to consider here—one related to acts of corrupting the earth, as the Qur'an refers to it. The classical jurists, nearly without exception, argued that those who attack by stealth, while targeting noncombatants in order to terrorize the resident and wayfarer. are corrupters of the earth. "Resident and wayfarer" was a legal expression that meant that whether the attackers terrorize people in their urban centers or terrorize travelers, the result was the same: all such attacks constitute a corruption of the earth. The legal term given to people who act this way was *muharibun* (those who wage war against society), and the crime is called the crime of *hiraba* (waging war against society). The crime of *hiraba* was so serious and repugnant that, according to Islamic law, those guilty of this crime were considered enemies of humankind and were not to be given quarter or sanctuary anywhere.

The classical jurists repeatedly noted that it is simply beneath a Muslim to attack the defenseless, and that when attacks are carried out by stealth and without warning, the inescapable effect will be the spread of terror, the destruction of peace and tranquility, and the undoing of God's will. The result will be the corruption of God's earth because people will not be able to cultivate goodness or work together to establish mercy. This crime was considered to be particularly repulsive because people who commit it observe no sanctity and honor no right. As a crime, it severely threatens all forms of peaceful intercourse and completely undermines the ethical obligation that people strive to know one another. As the classical jurists put it, this crime dismantles the fabric of life and, by spreading terror, leads to the complete corruption of God's earth.

In the modern age, it would seem that terrorism is the quintessential crime of corrupting the earth. When violence is committed against the defenseless, by stealth and without warning, the net effect is to spread fear and horror among God's people. Whether one calls the crime *hiraba* or terrorism, it is fundamentally the same thing. Those who are familiar with the classical tradition will find the parallels between what were described as crimes of *hiraba* and what is often called terrorism today nothing short of remarkable. The classical jurists considered crimes such as assassinations, setting fires, or poisoning water wells—that could indiscriminately kill the innocent—as offenses of *hiraba*. Furthermore, hijacking methods of transportation or crucifying people in order to spread fear and terror are also crimes of *hiraba*. Importantly, Islamic law strictly prohibited the taking of hostages, the mutilation of corpses, and torture.

Islamic law was unusually benevolent toward rebels against the government who had an ideology or cause. Such individuals were not considered common criminals deserving of harsh or severe penalties. However, rebels who committed atrocities such as those described above, regardless of their ideological cause or justification, were treated as the worst criminals. Frankly, in light of this Islamic legal tradition, the commission by puritans of terrorist acts that are explicitly and specifically prohibited by Islamic law defies comprehension. For instance, Islamic law not only prohibits the taking of hostages, but even prohibits the killing of enemy prisoners of war in retaliation if the enemy murders Muslims hostages or prisoners. This position emerged from the fact that the Qur'an repeatedly reminds Muslims that no one should be made to suffer for the sins of another.[27]

One of the most famous stories taught even to Muslim children is the anecdote about a Companion of the Prophet who was captured by the unbelievers of Mecca. The Companion was informed that he would be executed the next day. In the course of the night, this Companion had an opportunity to save himself when he found an unattended child of one of the leaders holding a big knife. The Companion could have taken the child hostage and saved himself. The next day, before he was executed, he was asked why he had not exploited the opportunity by taking the child hostage. His response was unequivocal: "What sin did she commit? The Qur'an does not permit us to punish a person for the sins of others." Sadly, the unbelievers of Mecca killed the man anyway.

Despite these uncompromising traditions, we notice that in the recent conflict in Iraq, for instance, several groups kidnapped Muslim and non-Muslim hostages while parading all types of Islamic-looking banners. Even worse, these groups mutilated and tortured their victims while claiming that this behavior is somehow Islamic. What is most unsettling and inexplicable for moderates is that all matters of *hiraba,* including kidnapping, hostage-taking, mutilation, and torture, are all cited in the Qur'an and in the Prophetic traditions as clear examples of the type of conduct that corrupts the earth and defiles God's creation.

The issue of terrorism and corrupting the earth highlights one of the basic differences between the moderates and puritans: the moderates would rather preserve the earth as God's creation uncorrupted, even if non-Muslims dominate it. Puritans would rather corrupt the earth than see it dominated by non-Muslims. Basically, the difference in attitude between moderates and puritans has to do with the relationship of Islam to power. Puritans believe that for Islam to be victorious, Muslims need to conquer and subjugate others. Only then will God's sovereignty be established, and only then can the Word of God stand supreme. The gap between Muslims and non-Muslims is so vast because in puritan thinking one side possesses the incontrovertible and incorruptible truth and the other side is lost in absolute darkness. In puritan thought, non-Muslims, regardless of what they do, cannot step even partially into the light; while Muslims, if *real* Muslims according to the puritan definition, possess the unadulterated light and truth. For puritans, truth and virtue cannot be shared or even investigated; they are simply possessed by those who accept them. Therefore, there is nothing that Muslims and non-Muslims can cooperate on or collaborate on achieving. The relationship between Muslims and non-Muslims may be non-belligerent at times, but the hostility should always be there, and it can be expected to flare up into war whenever there is a chance to dominate, defeat, or inflict damage upon the other.

Moderates invite non-Muslims to love God, and through submissions permit God to cleanse them of all that is ugly and vile. But if the invitation is refused, that is not the end of the engagement. According to moderates, God's light is not owned by anyone, and so Muslims and non-Muslims can step into the light together. They can share a partnership in which they come to know one another. In the process, they can cooperate to establish virtue and mercy on this earth—they can cooperate to prevent the corruption of the earth through the ugliness of ignorance, hate, war, and destruction. Moderates believe that supremacy belongs only to God. Therefore, when they come to invite the other to step into the light, they do so with utter humility—the humility of knowing that it is impossible to avoid corrupting the earth, and also impossible to achieve any degree of Godliness on this earth, unless they can come to know the other. It is this, the knowledge of the other, that is the requisite for the Divine gift of peace.

Having said all of this, the puritans still find much consolation in their belief that they are not aggressors but are simply exercising their basic right to self-defense. Typically, the discussion on this point will go something like this: "Everything you've said about the moderate position is idealistic and naive. The reality is that the West, and the United States and Israel in particular, use sophisticated weapons to kill civilian Muslims, and we have no way to defend ourselves or to strike back at them. Therefore, what we have is a situation in which dire necessity justifies violating the sacred law. We commit acts of what you would call terrorism, not because we like it, but because this is the only way we can prevent the West, the United States and Israel, from massacring Muslims at will."

There is a pragmatic issue that I will not get into here, and that is whether terrorism actually defends Muslims or whether it simply provides an excuse for people to kill more Muslims. More important is the fact that the logic of necessity is limitless and often immoral. Under the guise of necessity, the whole fabric of Islamic morality could become undone. Importantly, in all cases, relying on the logic of necessity means compromising the ethics and moral virtues of the Islamic faith. Assuming that terrorism does somehow allow Muslims to fight back, and even become victorious, the question is: At what price this victory? If the price of a political victory is moral defeat and also the violation of the ethics of Islam and the teachings of the Qur'an, how is it a victory at all? Often the response to this question is what will distinguish a moderate from a puritan.

As persuasive as the logic of military necessity might be for some Muslims, it is woefully inadequate in explaining some of the dynamics between the use of terrorism and the reliance on the Islamic tradition in justifying terrorism. It is possible for terrorists to openly cite the logic of necessity while publicly disavowing any reliance on the Islamic tradition. A terrorist group could say, for example, "We do what we have to do without regard to what Islam has to say about anything." Necessity does not sufficiently address some of the behavioral patterns of terrorists, especially in terms of how they treat or exploit Islam in the process.

For instance, there is one particularly troubling practice that raises baffling and even peculiar questions about the interaction of violent puritans with the Islamic ethical tradition. I am referring to the practice of beheading hostages in Iraq, a practice that is enforced with much pride, as if the perpetrators are executing Islamic justice. Similarly, beheading is the chosen method for enforcing the death penalty in Saudi Arabia, which the Saudis claim is an Islamic mandate. For many people in the modern age, beheadings are nothing short of shockingly repulsive, and we have a right to ask, What about beheadings is Islamic? In premodern times, beheading was the swiftest way to kill a person, and in many ways, it was the most merciful. Today, we have other ways of killing human beings that are less cruel.

As noted above, Islamic law forbade mutilation. It also forbade methods of execution that are unduly painful and cruel, such as death by stabbing, fire, poisoning, drowning, quartering, or any of the other gruesome methods that were used in medieval times. Hence, it is hardly surprising that beheadings were the most tolerated form of execution. The irony is that the only reliable and authentic report from the Prophet related to the subject is one in which he advised that even if slaughtering an animal, it is imperative to file and hone the knife or sword to a razor-sharp edge so as to minimize the suffering of the slain. Of course, at that time knights trained at swordsmanship for most of their lives, so it was not rare to find men who were capable of chopping off a head with one swift strike. Today, however, those who have had the misfortune of witnessing executions in Saudi Arabia will attest to the fact that it is an ugly and shocking mess, with the inept swordsman striking the poor victim several times before succeeding in his goal.

The most important point, however, is that there is nothing Islamic about executing a person with a sword. Considering the points discussed above, how can all of this become transformed into a conviction that the Islamic thing to do is to chop off heads, even if it is in the most grotesque and torturous fashion? The only thing that can be truly described as an Islamic mandate is that, if a killing is necessary at all, it is imperative to choose the method of execution that is the most merciful and compassionate; and modern science has invented more humane ways of terminating life than beheading. Even the purported penalty of death by stoning, which is prescribed by puritans for adultery, is not mentioned in the Qur'an. It was adapted from the Old Testament, and its acceptability in Islam is highly debated by moderates.[28]

Nevertheless, it is undeniable that in puritan lore, beheadings have become unabashedly claimed as an integral part of Islamic justice. This serves as a reminder of the complexity of the puritans' system of producing meaning and symbols. As is often the case, puritans do not interact with Islamic ethics or reflect on the substance of Islam. More often than not, they are interested in the form, in the external appearance, and in symbolic associations. So, why the sword and beheadings? It is an unabashed exploitation of the fears and prejudices that people have about Islam. Puritans are well aware that in the minds of many, there is a stereotypical prejudice that associates between Islam and the sword, and also the chopping off of body parts. Instead of working to fight the stereotype and deconstruct it, they build upon it and exploit it. In doing so, they gain power—the power that comes from constructing a bogeymen and then reminding people of that bogeyman whenever the puritan sense of insecurity makes them feel that they are losing power. This, for instance, was keenly felt when in 1977 the puritan organization al-Takfir wa'l Hijrah kidnapped and decapitated Shaykh Muhammad al-Dhahabi, the minister of religious endowments and the rector of the Azhar Seminary in Egypt.

In its essence, terrorism is the act of gaining power through the spread of fear. Whether that power is being asserted by a puritan government over its citizenry or whether it is being asserted by puritan groups over governments, the method and effect are the same. But as is often the case with puritans and their power dynamics, the victims are not only the innocent human beings killed, but also Islam and the integrity of its ethical tradition.

TWELVE

THE NATURE AND
ROLE OF WOMEN

It might be surprising to realize that today the question of the role of women in Islam and the issue of jihad are intricately connected. Jihad and the treatment of women in Islam are probably the two most controversial and misunderstood topics about the Islamic faith in the world today. Indeed, the issue of women in Islam, like the issue of jihad, invokes images of oppression, cruelty, and brutality in the eyes of the world. In both cases, puritans have hijacked the truth about the Islamic faith and played the dominant role in deforming the image of Islam around the globe. Puritans believe that aggression against others is justified, and they exploit the doctrine of jihad to achieve their aims. They also justify aggression against women and their patriarchic belligerence by exploiting a number of theological concepts. The common thread that connects the issues of jihad and women is the coveting of power and supremacy. It is the desire to dominate others that causes puritans to so profoundly deform and mutilate the truth about the roles of jihad and women in the Islamic faith.

Around the middle of March 2002, Saudi newspapers reported an incident that took place in Mecca, the Prophet Muhammad's birthplace. According to the official count, at least fourteen young girls burned to death or were asphyxiated by smoke when an accidental fire engulfed their public school.

Parents who arrived at the scene described a horrific situation in which the doors of the school were locked from the outside, and the Saudi religious police, known as the *mutawwa'un,* forcibly prevented girls from escaping the burning school and also barred firemen from entering the school to save the girls by beating some of the girls and several of the civil defense personnel. According to the statements of parents, firemen, and the regular police forces present at the scene, the *mutawwa'un* would not allow the girls to escape or to be saved because they were "not properly covered," and the *mutawwa'un* did not want physical contact to take place between the girls and the civil defense forces for fear of sexual entice-ment, presumably in the midst of crisis. "Not properly cov-ered" meant that the girls were either missing the *niqab,* a veil concealing their faces, or the *'abaya,* a cloaklike wrap cover-ing their bodies.

The governmental institution that is responsible for admin-istering the *mutawwa'un* (known as the Committee for the Promotion of Virtue and the Prevention of Vice) denied that officers had beaten any of the girls or civil defense workers, and also denied that the men had locked the gates of the school and trapped the girls inside.[1] But witnesses told Saudi newspapers that the *mutawwa'un* yelled at the police and fire-men to stay back and beat several firemen as they commanded the girls to go back into the burning building and retrieve their veils before they would be allowed to leave the school. Several parents told journalists that they had seen at least three girls being kicked and beaten with sticks when they attempted to argue with the *mutawwa'un.* Several girls did obey the *mu-tawwa'un* and returned to the school to retrieve their veils, only to be found dead later.

This incident was reported in Saudi newspapers such as the *Saudi Gazette* and *Al-Iqtisadiyya.* In rarely voiced criticism against the religious police, both papers demanded investigations and prosecutions of those responsible. The day after the event, Crown Prince 'Abdullah announced that the government would investigate and punish those responsible. Three days after the event, the Saudi government ordered all newspapers to desist from publishing anything about the tragedy, and to date no one has been prosecuted or fired for the death of the girls. The tragedy was reported in the media extensively in the West, but received very limited coverage in the Muslim world.[2]

I started the chapter with this painfully tragic story because it is revealing at so many levels. There are no words to describe the morally abhorrent depravity of this incident. The *mutawwa'un,* acting under the influence of puritan theology as the school burned, were concerned with one thing and one thing only: that the girls' hair and faces would not be seen in public. In the minds of the *mutawwa'un,* the horror and offense of that transgression was more compelling than the idea of fourteen-year-old girls being burned alive. At the time this incident occurred, many justifiably asked what type of theology—what type of law or insanity—would support such behavior. Others disgustedly waved it away as yet another manifestation of the barbaric religion of Islam.

Although Saudi influence managed to limit the amount of media coverage this incident received in the Arab press, moderate Muslims tried to bring attention to the entirely depraved and base social ethics underlying this event. Sadly, however, although moderate Muslims were appalled by what took place in this most ominous event, they were not surprised by the puritanical logic that led to this tragedy.

I don't think there *is* a theology or law behind the kind of attitude that led to the death of these girls. This morally repugnant incident represents an emotive attitude that trumps theology, law, and even logic. This is so because any of these three—theology, law, or logic—if used would have resulted in saving the lives of these girls. In Islam, the lives of human beings are sacrosanct—the Qur'an clearly proclaims that whoever kills a human being, it is as if he has killed all of humanity.[3] Furthermore, there is no religious obligation that takes priority over the preservation of life. Therefore, at the most basic level, even if one assumes that Islamic law does command strict adherence to rules of seclusion and veiling according to Islamic law and theology, the necessity of preserving human life would clearly override any such rule. The well-established Islamic legal maxim provides: Necessities will render the forbidden permissible (*al-darurat tubih al-mahzurat*)—and the preservation of human life is considered in Islamic jurisprudence to be the most basic and fundamental necessity of all. Preservation of human life, in the order of Islamic values, is a greater priority than even the safeguarding of God's rights (*huquq Allah*).[4]

But even more, the Qur'an itself clearly states that whatever rules of seclusion might have been commanded at one time or another for women, these rules had one and only one justification, and that is the safeguarding of women from molestation or harm.[5] The very objective and logic behind these laws is the *protection* of the welfare and well-being of women. Therefore, the death of these girls was contrary to the raison d'être and every possible rational basis for the laws of seclusion.

Logically, one even wonders why the police did not do something as simple as unlock the gates of the burning school and withdraw all the men from the area so that the girls could escape to safety without being seen by men. If the religious police were sufficiently concerned, they could have even removed their own headgear (known as the *ghutra*) and placed it on the heads of the escaping girls, thus helping them to survive. Not even the puritanical Saudi religious police believe that men are commanded to cover the hair on their head. The custom of Saudi men, including the religious police, however, is to wear a piece of cloth that covers a part of their heads. They could have easily lent this cloth to the girls to save their lives.

But the point is not the Saudi religious police's lack of creative problem-solving; the point is the puritans' abnormal obsession with the seductive powers of women, and their callous disregard for the value of human life—especially the lives of women. The puritan attitude toward women is difficult to make sense of solely on the basis of the textual analysis of religious sources. The puritan attitude is marked with such vehement hostility and disregard that it appears to be aimed at achieving complete dominance, a dominance that is bound to bring on their social death. As far as the puritans and women are concerned, I do not believe that the issue is the sexual lures of women—the issue is power. Puritans promote an aggressive form of patriarchy in which they respond to feelings of political and social defeatism by engaging in symbolic displays of power that are systematically degrading to women. The power exercised over women is so aggressive and total that it leads to their complete marginalization and exclusion from public life. This amounts to the social death of the women living in puritan societies—meaning that as far as the moral consciousness of society is concerned, women are as if dead.

Whether it is the girls who died in Mecca or any of the women who suffer daily from oppressive puritanical laws, all of these women are direct victims of the sense of frustration and disempowerment felt by puritan men over their sense of humiliation and defeat in various political and social contexts. In my experience studying puritan orientations in modern Islam, one finds that women are not targeted and degraded simply because of certain textual interpretations. Rather, there is a certain undeniable vehemence and anger in the treatment of women, as if the more women are made to suffer, the more the political future of Islam is made secure. This is manifested in the puritans' tendency to look at Muslim women as a consistent source of danger and vulnerability for Islam, and to go so far as to brand women as the main source of social corruption and evil. This vehemence and anger is often expressed in terms of describing women as the worst *fitna* (source of enticement and social discord). Furthermore, they claim that women will constitute the vast majority of the residents of Hell, and that most men in Hell will be there because of women.[6]

Consider, for example, the recent truly ominous and disturbing development by one of the highest-ranking puritan jurists. Shaykh Saleh al-Fawzan,[7] a Saudi jurist, issued a *fatwa* (a legal opinion) in which he claimed that not only is slavery lawful in Islam, but that it ought to be legalized in Saudi Arabia. Al-Fawzan went further in accusing Muslim scholars who condemned and outlawed slavery of being ignorant and infidels.[8] This *fatwa* is particularly disturbing and dangerous because it effectively legitimates the trafficking in and sexual exploitation of so-called domestic workers in the Gulf region[9] and especially Saudi Arabia.

The position of slavery had been resolved for most of the twentieth century: slavery was considered unlawful and immoral, and all Muslim countries without exception had made the practice illegal. Importantly, most Muslim scholars had reached the reasonable conclusion that slavery is inconsistent with Qur'anic morality and the ethical objectives of the Islamic faith. In short, the prohibition of slavery was considered a closed matter. So why would a puritan jurist reopen this issue? Even more importantly, why would this jurist accuse the

numerous jurists who considered slavery an ungodly abomi-
nation of being heretics and blind imitators of the West? I
think two points need to be considered. First, as a matter of
regular practice, puritans always accuse all theological arguments aimed at honoring women through the augmentation of
their autonomy and social mobility, as a part of the Western
conspiracy designed to destroy Islam. According to puritans,
any position that is remotely respectful toward women is always treated as foreign and particularly Western. Second, the
timing of this *fatwa* was peculiar; it was issued during the recent American invasion of Iraq.

It is as if the puritans compensate for the loss of autonomy
at the national level by asserting greater male autonomy over
Muslim women. Since puritans believe that the empowerment
of women is part of the Western cultural invasion of Muslim
lands, they seem to act as if political defeat can be compensated by a cultural victory—a supposed victory that comes at
a great expense for women. There ought to be no doubt that
the attempt at reinstituting slavery is a poorly veiled attempt
at formally legalizing the sexual exploitation of women—or,
more specifically, an authorization for puritan men to deal in
the market of trafficking women. The reinstitution of slavery
has nothing to do with the safeguarding of Islam or Islamic
law, and it also has nothing to do with protecting the integrity
of Arab or Saudi cultures, but in the puritan mind, this is a
slap in the West's face. Because puritans believe that the West
pioneered the abolition of slavery and invented the idea that
the practice of slavery is a violation of human rights, they sim-
plistically think that championing the cause of slavery is a
snub to Western moral standards.[10] But since in the puritan
consciousness women are socially dead, the fact that women
would bear the cost of this snub directed at the West is of little
real consequence.

There is one word that sums up the puritan attitude toward women: *fitna*. *Fitna* is a vast term that has many connotations, all of which are decidedly negative. *Fitna* means sexual entice-ment, a source of danger, civic and social discord, a sense of instability and impending evil. Although puritans often praise and celebrate the role of women as mothers, in every other role women are portrayed as deficient and subservient. There-fore, as a wife, she is completely under the tutelage of her hus-band; as a daughter, she is under the tutelage of her father; as a member of society, she is under the tutelage of all men. She is never an independent and autonomous being who shares in equal measure the obligation of fulfilling the Divine covenant. She is never an equal partner who shares fully in the burden of enjoining the good and forbidding the evil, strug-gling to bring the earth closer to Godliness. In the puritan paradigm, she is cast in a role in which she fulfills her obliga-tions only through men—whether as husbands, fathers, or men who control the public space. Consequently, it is hardly surprising that puritans often claim that women will not enter Heaven unless they subserviently obey men on this earth.

The consistent practice of puritans is to collect, publish, and disperse traditions, attributed to the Prophet or the Compan-ions, that are demeaning to women. Such collections act as a foundation for issuing deprecating determinations in regard to women. Muhammad bin 'Abd al-Wahhab himself, the founder of the Wahhabi movement, set the precedent by collecting a group of these women-deprecating traditions and listing them under the subheading "Living with Women."[11] But these women-deprecating traditions, without exception, are of weak authenticity, if not pure fabrications. As I discussed earlier, moderates will rely on traditions attributed to the Prophet, but such traditions must be reliable in the sense that if we can be reasonably sure that the Prophet actually uttered the words attributed to him. The traditions utilized by the puritans invariably are of a single transmission, which means that the possibility exists that the Prophet actually authored them, but the possibility is remote and far-fetched.

The impact of this difference over which traditions to rely upon and which to discard is enormous. By picking and choosing the traditions that appear demeaning to women, puritans are able to impose limitations on women that can only be described as suffocating. For instance, recently I picked up a short book, published in Lebanon, authoritatively titled *Responsa* (*fatawa*) *for Women,* written by a Ph.D.-carrying purported scholar. The author's *responsa* reproduces the same misogynist determinations that have become commonplace in contemporary puritan culture. The following is a partial list of the determinations of this puritan author, listed in the order in which they appear in his book. According to the author,

- A Muslim wife may not worship God by fasting without the permission of her husband because her husband may want to have sex with her during the day.

- A woman may not speak with her fiancé over the telephone because she may seduce him.

- A woman engaged to a man may not go out with him in public because she may seduce him.

- A bride seated with her groom in a car driven by a relative must make sure not to wear perfume because she may seduce the relative driver.

- A woman who wishes to go to the mosque to learn the Qur'an must obey her father if he forbids her from going, and the father need not express any reason for his opposition.

- A man who marries a woman with the intention of divorcing her after having his pleasure with her, but fails to inform her of his intention, does not commit a sin, and the marriage is valid.

- A woman may not refuse her husband sex, except if she is ill. Refusing a husband sex without compelling justification is a grave sin (*kabira*). On the other hand, a husband may refuse his wife sex for any reason or no reason at all.

- As a legal matter, the voice of a woman is not an *'awra* (a privacy that must be concealed from all except *mahrams*—*mahrams* are men of a close blood relation that a woman may not marry them, such as a father or brother). Nonetheless, because of its seductive powers, the voice of women should not be heard in public, or in a private setting where it might cause sexual enticement.

- Women should not mix with men in public ways or forums even if women are wearing the *hijab* (covering their hair).

- Even if wearing the *hijab* women should not travel unaccompanied by a male *mahram*.

- Women may not chew gum because it is seductive.

- Women may not dance in front of other women in a wedding even if there are no men around because it might be sexually arousing to other women.

- Women may not shorten their head hair because doing so is considered imitating men. However, women *must* remove any facial hair, such as a beard or mustache, because it is more feminine to do so, and because a woman must be sexually appealing to her husband (i.e., facial hair on a woman is not sexually appealing).

- Women should not attend funerals or gravesites or convey their condolences to foreign men so as to avoid sexual enticement.[12]

In addition to the above, one will find puritan literature prohibiting women from engaging in any form of public speaking; demanding that women attend sermons or lectures behind a curtain or wall; teaching that a woman's entry into Heaven is hinged on her husband's being pleased with her; claiming that the angels curse any woman who upsets her husband; alleging that an education beyond basic literacy is unnecessary for women; and preaching that women were created to act as a source of temptation and test for men.

Puritans flood the Muslim markets with this genre of literature, which pretends to represent the Divine law. The unfortunate reality is that many Muslims who are not experts in Islamic law are likely to believe that this is genuinely what their religion demands of them. They are likely to believe that this compulsive obsession with sexual enticement is truly the will of God. What is truly incredulous is that at the same time that puritans advocate the total seclusion of women from the public arena, they will also claim that their vision of Islam liberated and honored women by protecting them from the evil gazes of lustful men and from being exposed to humiliation or molestation while in the public arena. Accordingly, women should not work outside their homes, should be forced to veil either their hair or their face, and are not qualified to take positions of leadership.

The moderate position is fundamentally at odds with the puritan approach. At a minimum, the puritan rulings are not objectively mandated by Islamic sources. In fact, moderates argue that a fair and balanced reading of the Qur'an, the traditions of the Prophet, and the precedents of the Companions would not support the claimed Islamicity of the puritan positions. Aside from betraying a profound obsession with sexual enticement and allures, the puritan determinations have the clear effect of denying women their intellect and soul, and they exclude women as viable and necessary contributors to society. They turn women into a heaving bundle of sexual enticement and allure, and then punish them for the sexual fantasies men have projected onto them.

This, in the moderate view, is entirely inconsistent with the history and ethics of Islam and the nature and role of Divinity. In an earlier chapter, I explained the difference between Shari'a and *fiqh,* two terms often used interchangeably to describe Islamic law today. Shari'a, contrary to *fiqh,* is the Divine potential fulfilled in the Divine reality. Shar'ia represents law in its pristine perfection as it exists in God's mind—the ideal, immutable, and eternal laws of goodness, justice, beauty, and ultimately Divinity as conceived in God's mind. And *fiqh* is the human effort to reach this ideal, which is always, by definition, faulty and incomplete. In the case of the relationship between women and men, the Divine ideal—the moral eternal law of Shari'a—is justice; and justice, provided that the circumstances are appropriate, demands equality in value, worth, and opportunity.

This moral principle and objective comes from the Qur'an itself. The Qur'an emphasizes that in the eyes of God, there is no distinction between genders, races, or classes. In God's eyes, women are equal to men because they are rewarded and punished exactly in equal measure, and they have equal access to God's grace and beneficence.[13] In principle, women have rights equal to their obligations, in accordance with what is recognized as just and fair.[14] Of great significance is the fact that when the Qur'an speaks of the solemn duty to enjoin the good and forbid the evil, it obligates men and women in equal measure. The Qur'an states: "The believers, men and women, are aides and support for one another. They enjoin what is right and forbid what is wrong. They keep up their prayers, and give alms [to the poor] and they obey God and His Prophet. God will bestow His mercy upon them. God is almighty and all wise."[15] Hence, according to the Qur'an, men and women are not just equal partners in building the moral fabric of society, but they must fully cooperate by supporting and aiding each other.

This solemn obligation means nothing less than bearing the duty of struggling to come as close to Godliness as one's efforts would make possible. Therefore, the task is to bring men and women to a position where they have an equal opportunity to pursue Godliness in equal measure. To reach that point, however, means becoming engaged in the process of pursuing Godliness. This is not an objective that can be achieved overnight; it has to be a moral goal that men and women patiently pursue.

The thorough and fair-minded researcher will observe that behind every single Qur'anic revelation regarding women was an effort seeking to protect women from exploitative situations and from situations in which they are treated inequitably. In studying the Qur'an it becomes clear that the Qur'an is educating Muslims on how to make incremental but lasting improvements in the condition of women that can only be described as progressive for their time and place. In addition, women at the time of the Prophet Muhammad were very active in the social and political life of the community. And as is commonly known, several wives of the Prophet, after his death, took on the important roles of being teachers and jurists in the community.[16] Significantly, in this context the majority of the Qur'an's progressive reforms came about as a result of social demands *expressed and advocated by women*.

Moderates start by observing that the ideal expressed in the *eternal* law is equality—equality in responsibility before God, and in responsibility on this earth. Furthermore, moderates focus on studying the Qur'anic methodology in bringing about reform and analyzing the progressive, forward motion evident in the Qur'anic text. That is to say, the Qur'an itself anticipates the passage of time and articulates the manner in which Muslims must change in order to adapt to their time.

In this context, through the use of the systematic tools of jurisprudential analysis, the task of *fiqh* is to seek how to make earthly reality as close as possible to the Divine ideal. The Qur'an introduced reforms that were appropriate within the confines of the social reality existing at the time the Qur'an was revealed, and in doing so the Qur'an achieved justice. Moderates recognize that the Qur'an sought to empower women by setting in motion a process according to which women gained greater rights in direct proportion to their social status—a social status that they (women) played the critical role in defining. Moderate Muslims believe that since the Qur'an is their teacher, the burden is on them, as men and women, to set in motion the same process of helping women achieve an upward trajectory of empowerment and reach results appropriate for each generation and its time. But the Qur'an makes a point to illustrate that social change comes when those who are entitled to a right demand it. Therefore, it is imperative that women play the critical role in initiating the process of change. Since men and women are, as the Qur'an puts it, aides and supporters to each other in enjoining the good and forbidding the evil, they must also be partners in helping women achieve their due rights.

This necessarily means that the rules of law that apply to women cannot be static and unchanging. Islamic law has to keep charging forward to achieve the moral objectives expressed in the Qur'an. To achieve justice, there has to be a constant effort to achieve a more authentic proportionality between duties and rights in the lives of Muslim women. So, for instance, if within the social dynamics of the time, women carry a financial responsibility equal to men, it is more consistent with Shari'a to allow women an equal share to men in inheritance. Puritans define the social status of women by strictly limiting the rights and duties of men and women for every age and place, and then coercing women to accept their predetermined status in society. Moderates, on the other hand, recognize that social status shifts according to human consciousness and knowledge, and thus they strive to achieve justice through a legal proportionality between rights and duties. Puritans read the Qur'an verse by verse on matters relating to women, and from each verse they come up with an uncompromising and unchanging legal rule that is set in stone forever. But what they always ignore is the moral message and the ethical objectives of the Qur'an.

For moderate Muslims, it is clear that there are ethical and moral objectives that the Qur'an unfailingly pursues. For moderates, the Qur'an does not set a bunch of unconnected and unwavering rules applicable to women, but addresses particular problems that arose in specific historical contexts. Moderates read the Qur'an as having illustrated an ethical and moral methodology on how to deal with situations that at one time were abusive and dismissive toward women.

I will give a few examples to illustrate the moderate's approach. These examples will also help explain why the moderates and puritans reach conclusions that are so dissimilar about the relationship of Islam to women:

Consider the law of inheritance in the Qur'an, which in various circumstances dictates that women inherit only half of what men inherit. According to various sources, in pre-Islamic Arabia, the only class of individuals qualified to share in the inheritance were people who fought in battles. Since normally men fought in battles and women did not, in pre-Islamic Arabia women were excluded from receiving any inheritance. After Muslims established a city-state in Medina, on several occasions women *did* participate in battles that Muslims fought, and so a controversy arose. The men of the city insisted that women should continue to be disqualified from any possible inheritance because women were not *expected* to fight. In other words, the men argued, in effect, that if women go to battle, they do so as volunteers, and therefore, the pre-Islamic rule should not be amended to allow these fighting women a share of the inheritance. After all, the men argued, if these women had chosen to stay home, no one would have blamed them.

A number of women in Medina, however, strongly disagreed with the men's reasoning, and they were vocal about their opinions. The protesting women complained to the Prophet Muhammad that although they may not have participated in every battle, they, as women, contributed in material and crucial ways to the well-being of the city-state in Medina, which put the men in a better position to fight, and therefore, they saw no reason for being excluded from inheritance. After listening to the women's argument, the Prophet told them that he was unable to give them an immediate response and asked them to wait because God might reveal something to him about this matter. Shortly thereafter, the Prophet received revelation giving women a share of the inheritance that often is half of the share received by men.[17]

Not surprisingly, men protested. They argued that it was unfair that most women did not take part in battle and yet women, depending on their relationship to the deceased, were entitled to a share equal to that of men or, more often, half of that received by men. In response to the men's protest, a Qur'anic revelation addressing men and women instructed: "Do not covet what God has favored some of you with over others. For men is a share in accordance with what they earned and for women is a share in accordance with what they earned. And ask God for His favors for God is all knowing."[18] What happened here was that women were given a part of what they demanded. As to the protests of the men, the Qur'an reprimands them by saying, in effect: "Behave yourselves and don't envy women the share they got!"

Interestingly enough, puritans often cite this Qur'anic verse: "Do not covet what God favored some of you with over others," as a way of suppressing women's rights—effectively, as a way of telling women not to desire more rights than they have been given. But understood in its proper context, the Qur'anic verse takes on an entirely different meaning.

It is important to notice that the verse advises people not to begrudge each other the favors that God has bestowed *in accordance with what they have earned*. The verse even goes on to leave open the possibility that one may earn more of God's favors by praying to God for such favors. Far from implying that there is a stable and static condition in which men and women have a set of unchanging, predetermined rights, the verse indicates that there is a dynamic and evolving situation in which men and women gain rights in accordance with what they have earned, and in which, instead of envying and working to undermine each other, people supplicate to God for further rights—further favors. Whatever rights or favors are enjoyed are not bestowed as a matter of status (or gender), but are earned by the dual engagement between the human and the Divine—by work and prayer. Theologically, what this means is that by praying to God, but also by working to earn further rights, people will (with God's help) reach their just deserve. From the point of justice, if people take on certain duties, their rights must change in proportion.

The same dynamic is found in another verse that has often been cited to legitimate inequality between men and women. Puritans always cite this verse as a way of convincing women that they should be obedient and subservient before their husbands. There are two main alternative ways to translate this verse. The verse I am referring to could be read to say: "Men are the *guardians* of women in accordance with the favors God has bestowed upon some over others, and in accordance with the wealth they spend to provide for others" (emphasis mine). The verse could also be read to say: "Men are the *supporters* of women in accordance with the favors God has bestowed upon some over others, and in accordance with the wealth they spend to provide for others" (again, emphasis mine).[19] In Arabic, the word that I emphasized is *qawwamun* and the variant translations depend on the way that the word *qawwamun* is understood and interpreted—the word could mean "guardians," "supporters," "masters," or "servants." Either way, the important point is that the verse does not define the relationship of men to women in an absolute and noncontingent fashion. Rather, the verse explicitly states that whatever the status—whether as guardians or supporters—it is a status contingent on the actions of human beings (that is, "in accordance with wealth they spend to provide for the others") and on the action of the Divine (that is, by the favors the Divine has bestowed upon one over the other).

The word used in the Qur'an for God's favor is *fadl*. This word and its variant forms are used repeatedly throughout the Qur'an to connote a physical or spiritual blessing or preference granted by God, either as a reward for good deeds or as an act of grace. If one analyzes the well over fifty times that the Qur'an uses the word *fadl,* one will come to realize that the clear and ascertainable fact that both the reward and the grace of God are accessible to *all* seekers. Consistently, the Qur'an calls upon believers to struggle and strive for the reward and grace of God. Once it is realized that God's reward and grace are accessible to all, and are contingent on the efforts of human beings and God's blessing, this materially affects the way we approach the verses cited above. With this understanding, we come to realize that men and women equally qualify for God's grace and reward. The authority given to men over women is not because they are men but because, in a particular historical context, men financially provided for women. But if the circumstances change, and women share financial responsibility with men, authority must be equally shared between the two as well.

Rather tellingly, many of the rights women achieved in early Islam were in response to demands made by women to the Prophet in Medina. A *basic* set of moral rights was offered to women without there being a social demand for such rights. For instance, the Qur'an strictly forbade the morally offensive practice in pre-Islamic Arabia in which poor families murdered their young daughters and offered their souls to the gods, believing that engaging in this sacrificial practice, the gods would send them boys to replace the girls. This was strictly prohibited without regard to social demands because murder is wrong in every condition and situation. However, financial and property rights, as well as some social rights, were often granted by God after women mobilized into a demand group. This is consistent with the Qur'an's principle of accessibility of reward and grace. The Qur'an consistently emphasizes that God does not change a people unless they first change themselves.[20] Put simply, the Qur'an sets out moral goals and ethical objectives, but if people want to advance on the road of morality and beauty, they must change themselves first, and struggle toward acquiring God's blessings and grace.

Another example of a practice that caused suffering and that raised demands for change, and in turn elicited a strong Qur'anic response relates to repeated marriages and divorces done in an abusive way. In pre-Islamic Arabia, a man enjoyed the exclusive right to divorce his wife with or without cause. After the divorce, a woman was compelled to go through something known as the *'idda* (a specific waiting period before she could marry again), during which a husband could remarry his divorcée without a new contract or dowry. Many men started using these privileges as a way to torment women—as a way of spite, a man would divorce his wife, wait until a day or two before the *'idda* period was about to expire, and then remarry his wife again, only to divorce her again immediately so that a new waiting period would begin. This would be done over and over without any limit. This was used as a way of keeping a woman hanging—such a woman would neither be married nor divorced. As long as the husband kept taking his divorcée back shortly before the end of the waiting period, the wife would remain in an impossible situation, never being able to remarry as long as her husband kept exercising his option during the waiting period. In one version of this same practice, husbands would add insult to injury by proclaiming, one or two days before the end of the waiting period, *"La'ibt"* ("I was just playing, jesting, or fooling around").

Several women complained to the Prophet about these practices and asked for a solution, and the Prophet asked them to wait until he received revelation on the matter. The Qur'anic response to these practices was manifold, and as is typical of Qur'anic methodology, the Qur'an limited the potential for abuse without fundamentally changing the existing social structure. Condemning those who divorce and remarry women out of a desire to torment and harass them, the Qur'an exclaimed that a husband should either live with his wife in kindness and honor, or divorce her also in kindness and honor; but in all situations, those who hold on to their wives in order to torment or harass them have committed a great sin and they have become among those who are unjust toward themselves.[21] In addition, while not eradicating the practice of *'idda,* the Qur'an limited the process to two times. A husband and wife may divorce and return to each other during the waiting period, but only two times. If there is a third divorce, they cannot remarry during the waiting period.[22] As to those who insulted their wives by telling them they were just jesting, the Qur'an describes such behavior as sinful and responds by saying: "Do not mock the words and decrees of your Lord."[23] It is interesting that mocking a divorced wife is equated in the Qur'anic discourse with the sin of mocking the words, decrees, and will of the Lord. It is as if this demeaning way of dealing with divorced women is considered directly offensive to God.

The repeated Qur'anic dynamic was to honor the demands of women and empower them to the extent possible within the prevalent sociohistorical context at the time. But I think it is fair to say that whatever particular rights were granted women at one time or another, even without there being a demand for change, the Qur'an consistently and systematically condemned conditions that were oppressive and abusive toward women. There is a condition in Qur'anic language called *'istid'af* (abusive and oppressive treatment that renders a person powerless). The ethical lesson consistently and systematically taught by the Qur'an is that placing women in oppressive and abusive conditions—*'istid'af*—is fundamentally at odds with Islamic morality and with the very idea of submission to God. There are numerous examples of this:

In pre-Islamic Arabia, in the seventh century and earlier, one of the prevailing abusive practices was to consider a wife as part of the inheritable legacy of a deceased man. Accordingly, a brother would typically inherit his deceased brother's wife, but he did not inherit the wife as *property*. Rather, the brother would have an option to marry the wife if he so desired, and the wife would not be free to marry again until the brother had decided whether or not to exercise his option. The resulting practice was that brothers having the option would refuse to release the wife unless she paid him a sum of money for her freedom, or, if the wife received a marriage proposal, the brother would usurp the dowry in return for granting the wife a release. Of course, this practice created a class of oppressed and highly dependent women and the Qur'an strictly prohibited the taking of women as hostages. In addition, more generally, the Qur'an forbade the tyrannizing of women in order to usurp their money, and laid out a broad principle that when men live with women, the basis for their cohabitation must be kindness and equanimity.[24]

Another widespread social practice with an oppressive effect on women involved the taking of the dowry. Normally upon marriage, the groom would pay the bride a dowry, the amount of which she was supposed to decide with input from her family. Fathers, however, got into the habit of taking dowries themselves, without consulting with their daughters. This created a strong potential for abuse because fathers had an incentive to marry their daughters off to the person paying the highest dowry. This practice undermined the very purpose for dowries in Islam, which were supposed to provide women with some form of financial security. In response, the Qur'an ordered men to refrain from usurping women's dowries and went further by advising men that it is immoral to covet money they have given women (*'ann tib nafs*), and that it is also immoral to connive to take back money that was given to women in goodwill.[25] Not surprisingly, considering the practices of the age, the idea that there was to be a distinction between the property of fathers and husbands on the one hand, and daughters and wives on the other, was nothing short of shocking. Nevertheless, the distinction was necessary to address actual abuses confronting the early Muslim community.

Divorce presented a whole separate set of problems. Among the pervasive and highly abusive practices was that upon divorcing women, men would seek to take back whatever money or property they had given them during the course of the marriage. In addition, quite often upon divorce, men would make alimony payments or other forms of support conditional. If, for whatever reason, men became displeased with the demeanor or conduct of their divorced wives, they would refuse to make any postmarriage payments. The Qur'an emphasized that it was a serious sin to take money given to wives during the course of a marriage, and it could be done only under a limited and restricted set of conditions.[26] As to alimony, the Qur'an asserted: "And for divorced women make fair provision—this is a duty upon the God-fearing and pious."[27] In other words, the Qur'an removed the element of discretion from the hands of men and made a correlation between obedience to God, piety, and submission to God and the removal of the condition of *istid'af* in which these women found themselves.

In each of these examples, the Qur'an reformed social conditions that were oppressive and exploitative toward women. Importantly, in the process of implementing the needed social reforms, the Qur'an also established or promoted broadly applicable moral and ethical principles that transcend any particular context or circumstance. In other words, as the Qur'an solved the social problems that confronted the women living in Medina at the time of the Prophet, it also affirmed moral and ethical principles that are universal in scope.

I think it is clear that in the modern age it is impossible for any country to develop if half of its population is marginalized and secluded. Women constitute more than half of the Muslim world's population, and most of the Muslim countries are poor and underdeveloped. In the majority of these impoverished countries, the labor and active participation of women in public life is a requisite for development. Countries like Saudi Arabia are in a very different situation. Because of their wealth, they can afford to preach the seclusion of women—many households in the oil-rich countries can afford to subsist on single incomes. The point is that the puritans' positions are not only gender-biased but also class-biased. Most Muslims cannot afford the puritan vision of Islam.

The type of marginalization and seclusion of women advocated by puritans today is unprecedented in Islamic history. I focus on the issue of women and provide specific examples from the Qur'an because puritan propaganda, supported by petro-dollars, has managed to make many Muslims forget their own heritage and civilization. In just the few previous examples, it is clear that women played a very active role in the early Medina state of the Prophet. But even more, up to the sixteenth century, Islam had produced thousands of women jurists and scholars, who used to stand in the mosques of Damascus and Cairo and teach hundreds of male jurists. Because Muslims have largely forgotten their own heritage, puritans find it easy to accuse anyone who seeks to recognize women's rightful place in Muslim society of being a Westernizer.

The fact is that far from being Westernizers, moderates are fully anchored in the theology and jurisprudence of Islam. Their views, in my opinion, are far more anchored in Islamic morality and history than the puritans' reactive and often vindictive attitudes toward women. The difference between moderates and puritans often comes down to an issue of respect toward women as dignified and autonomous beings. For example, all puritans agree that regardless of a woman's convictions, the state should compel *and coerce all* women to wear the veil. Moderates disagree amongst themselves on whether the veil is Islamically mandated or whether it is a religious duty upon women, but all moderates agree that in all cases it should be a woman's autonomous decision whether to wear the veil or not, and that her choice must be respected. The moderates' pro-choice position is based on the Qur'anic teaching that there ought to be no compulsion in religion.

CONCLUSION

Religions, like all strong convictions, are a powerful force—they have the ability to thrust people toward an abyss of hate or carry them to unprecedented heights of love and enlightenment. This force is a potential that exists in all of what represents a religion: its texts and history, its creed and mythology, its rituals and symbols. What comes out of this potential depends on those who are able to give effect to the force of religion on earth. While a religion is owned, at least in theory, by a deity, the reality is that unless that deity is present here on earth, managing and regulating how the potential is used, it is left to those who describe themselves as the followers of that religion to exploit the potential in any particular way. The question, once that potential is used, is: Who bears the responsibility—on whom do we place the responsibility for what has been done in the name of this religion?

The answer to this question is actually much harder than some might realize. But the response is also what explains so many of the differences between the puritans and the moderates of Islam. How would the puritans answer this question? I think that the puritans would think that it is the wrong question—how can one differentiate between a religion and the responsibility for it? Puritans would say religion is not represented by anything other than its texts and rituals, and the sincere follower would read the text and do the rituals.

And that is all. To God goes the credit and the gratitude (not the responsibility) for the religion and all that is accomplished and done in its name.

For moderates, the puritan position is not only naive, but problematic. What makes up a religion is more than text and ritual, and what takes place because of the text and ritual is not a full manifestation of Divinity. God and God's will are too magnanimous to be fully expressed in text and ritual, and what takes place because of them is fully human. The responsibility for what humans do in God's name must fall on the shoulders of human beings.

Puritans and moderates both seek to be fully engaged with God. Both are not willing to live their lives on earth without Divine guidance, and both think of God as Ever-Present, and fully engaged in what human beings do or do not do. Both believe in God as the Supreme, the All-Powerful, the All-Knowing, the Benevolent, the Merciful, the Compassionate, the Giver and Taker, the Judge and Punisher, and the Just.

Yet what separates the puritans and moderates is vast. Much of what separates them has to do with trust and accessibility. Moderates believe that God entrusted humans with the power of reason and the ability to ascertain between right and wrong. But the trust placed in human beings is enormous—so enormous that human beings and human beings alone bear the responsibility for their own actions. This in turn justifies accountability in the Hereafter. The trust placed in human beings is not just to enforce or implement the set of instructions given to humans by God. Rather, God provided human beings with guidelines and goals, and left it up to them to discover the necessary and adequate laws.

Puritans, on the other hand, do not believe that the trust placed in human beings was so vast and indistinct. God gave human beings the law, which in most instances is specific and detailed, and trusted them to enforce it. Thus the true Divine gift to human beings was not the ability to reason but the ability to comprehend and obey. Not surprisingly, then, puritans are convinced that God micromanages the affairs of human beings by giving concrete and specific laws that regulate a great deal of what human beings say and do. Moderates believe the exact opposite: most matters of the affairs of life are left to human discretion with which they are to do the best they can provided that they observe general moral guidelines.

At the core of the dispute between puritans and moderates is not just the accessibility of God but what kind of accessibility. Moderates are skeptical that God's will is fully accessible to human beings—human beings can make their best efforts to know what God wants, but they can rarely be absolutely sure that they have succeeded in knowing what God wants. To do so, moderates believe, is dangerous because there is a risk that human beings will arrogantly impute to God their own flawed and limited knowledge. But while moderates believe that God's will is not easily accessible, they believe that God's benevolence, mercy, compassion, and love are accessible to many. By becoming engaged in the search to know God, to submit body and soul to God—in this highly personal interrelationship—God reciprocates the human effort, and the human being could love God and be loved by God.

With puritans, it is nearly the opposite—God's will is accessible through God's law, not love. God's law is the full expression of God's will. One is not engaged in *knowing* God; one is engaged only in *obeying* God. Puritans hardly mention love as a desirable or even possible engagement between God and human beings. As a pure act of benevolence, God might love his servants, but there is no reciprocity in this relationship. In the puritan framework, people should properly fear God, not love Him. And even if they do love God, they gain no special knowledge, intimacy, proximity, or familiarity from that love. God remains the emotionally inaccessible Supreme Commander that expects obedience, not love. Ironically, however, puritans also believe that God is completely accessible through law. If one knows the laws of the Supreme Commander, one knows the Supreme Commander. Moderates believe that this is belittling toward God—as if all there is to know about the Divine is His laws, or as if this is the only part of God that is relevant to human beings and the rest of God is simply irrelevant.

Moderates, perhaps unlike Sufis, do not believe that loving God can lead to a complete unity with God. For moderates, while one should privately build a partnership with God, it is dangerous and wrongful to pretend that through law the Divine Will can achieve complete unity with the human will.

To pretend that the human and Divine could be one and the same does not lead to the elevation of either and, in fact, deprecates both. Moderates believe that puritans cling to a set of inaccessible and unaccountable rules, and pretend that such rules are the soul and heart of Islam. This creates the false impression of being in control of the Heavens but, meanwhile, the command of the earth slips away. In periods of intense fluctuation and insecurity, clinging on to a system of rules for security and stability is sociologically understandable. The problem, however, is that history is relentless in its progress, and the high cost of this false sense of security is marginalization and irrelevancy to a constantly moving and developing world.

If these were theological disputes without practical effects as to the way Islam is lived and experienced today, perhaps these issues would not be so urgent. But they *do* make a difference, and the difference is often monumental and tragic.

Those who have traveled in Muslim countries will find that the lived Islam—the Islam that people actually practice and experience—is very much consistent with what I have described as the moderate view. In most countries, women have the choice to wear the veil or not to wear it; in most Muslim countries, women attend colleges at all levels, and serve as lawyers, doctors, and judges; in most Muslim countries, women are partners in their households, not servants or slaves; people enjoy all types of non-Western and Western music; in most countries, women mix freely with men in schools, markets, workplaces, and theaters; most countries don't force their citizens to worship or fast; most people believe that they can love and be loved by God; and most Muslims associate whatever is harsh and cruel with that which is un-Islamic. If you tell most any Muslim a story of misery and suffering and then ask them if they believe that it is consistent with Islam, instinctively most Muslims will give you an unequivocal no.

So then, what is the problem? Why can't we claim the puritan phenomenon as ineffective and move on? The problem is several-fold. Puritans do not care for the lived Islam—either Islam as it is lived now, or what lived in history. The sociological and anthropological forms of Islam, whether of today or of the past, are declared irrelevant and even deviant. Puritans do care, however, about an *imagined* Islam—either as an imagined past in the form of mythology, or an imagined future in the form of a promised utopia. Puritans believe that people should be made to fit the law and not the other way around. In other words, Muslims should be coerced to live according to the law, and that the law should not be made to serve the people. This has been the experience with the Taliban in Afghanistan, and the experience currently with Saudi Arabia.

The problem is that this puritan orientation has been nurtured and spread by the country in control of the two holy cities of Mecca and Medina, and that with the financial backing the puritans have received, they have been able to make alarming inroads throughout the Muslim world. It is not an exaggeration to say that there is a real danger that the puritans will be able to redefine the nature of the Islamic religion. Worst of all, puritans have managed to commit remarkably horrific acts of violence that have shocked the conscience of all people, Muslim and non-Muslim. The traditional forces that used to confront and marginalize such extremist groups were the jurists. At one point in time, these jurists played a critical role in defining the power dynamics within civil society, but today that role has become marginal, subservient, and entirely dependent on the government's will.

So what of the future? Which way will Islam go? If history is any indicator, then it should provide us some comfort. Despite the historical mistakes made in the religion's name, Islam founded a great civilization that inspired the humanistic revolution that took place in the West. In fact, without the accomplishments of the Islamic civilization, it is doubtful that the European Reformation and all that followed from it would have ever taken place. Furthermore, if one were to compare all the humanistic accomplishments achieved in Islam's name in the premodern age with the abuses committed in Islam's name today, the latter would pale in comparison. If one assesses the overall contributions of the Islamic faith to humanity, it would be clear to any fair-minded and objective observer that the good inspired by this religion far outweighs the bad.[1] Therefore, when we think about the future, shouldn't this provide us with grounds for optimism?

Well, yes and no. It is painfully obvious that regardless of how rich, humanistic, and moral the Islamic tradition was in the past, this will be of very limited usefulness if it is not believed and acted upon by Muslims today. The future depends on how modern Muslims choose to understand their past, and how they will develop and assert it. The real issue is not whether the Islamic legacy was humanistic; the issue is whether Muslims believe that the impact of Islam upon the world today ought to be humanistic. By *humanistic,* I mean characterized by a religious orientation that focuses on ending human suffering and that believes that human well-being and progress is a Godly task.

In my view, religious humanism is exemplified in the belief that the pursuit of goodness on earth is part of realizing the goodness of God, and seeking beauty in life is part and parcel of reflecting the beauty of God. Imperatively, generating and spreading love is inseparable from the Qur'anic instruction to come to know one another. Religious humanism means that through the act of loving God, the believer radiates compassion and care toward all creation. As early theologians like Ibn Abi al-Dunya used to put it, love is but a luminous state, and in this luminous state, it is as if the believer glows with compassion and mercy toward all of creation. Therefore, the act of loving God transforms the Divine command to "come to know the other" (*ta'aruf*) into an ethical imperative to strive to create the necessary moral and material conditions in which people can come to love one another. God's appeal to human beings to engage in *ta'aruf,* or knowing the other, is not a call for a heartless process of collecting data about other human beings. It is, however, Divine guidance and an exhortation to believers to realize that essential to knowing and loving God is to know and love God's viceroys on earth. According to the Qur'an, human beings inherited the earth and are charged with preserving and protecting this Divine inheritance, and as such, human beings occupy the lofty status of being the viceregents of the Divine. This theology is at the heart of the religious humanism of Islam.

Secular humanism and modernity are powerful universal forces that pose their own challenges to all religious convictions.

The universal challenge and obligation that confront all religions in the modern age is how to harness and direct the powerful force of religion toward the pursuit of goodness and beauty in life. The modern age, with its aggressive secular movements, poses numerous challenges to all religions by threatening to marginalize and extinguish the role of religion altogether. Modernity embodies pervasive and insistent universalisms such as human rights, self-determination, prohibitions on the use of force, basic rights for women, and ethnic, national, and religious rights; complex global economic systems; and many other international institutions that compose the structure of our modern world. Unless religions can contribute to and enrich human life in decisive and clear ways within this existing universal structure, religion will either be forced to the sidelines of history, or be forced into a confrontation with the powers of modernity—powers that will often be violent and destructive.

Puritans and moderates are opposite poles that are *both products* of modernity and that also *respond* to modernity. Both orientations react to modernity, the one by rejecting it and the other by embracing it. There are some orientations in Islam that do not seem to be touched by modernity and do not respond to it, such as the conservatives or traditionalists, but I do not believe that they are significant in shaping the future of Islam. I believe that the future of Islam will be shaped by either the puritans or the moderates. I hope that Islam is not doomed to suffer the megalomania of pretenders who claim to rule on God's behalf or those who assume the pretense of applying a set of objective rules that claim to embody the Divine Will.

In part because of the forces of secular humanism and modernity, Islam is forced to confront powerful and formidable challenges. But there is also no question that Islam is going through a transformative period that grows increasingly acute. It grows more acute mostly because in the case of Islam, the natural and inevitable process of growth and change keeps getting postponed. In every period—colonialism, modernity, and postmodernity—there were changed realities, circumstances, and meanings that were constantly shifting, mutating, and evolving. Each period confronted Muslims with stark challenges that mandated change and reform. For many reasons, all that changed was the rhetoric and dogma used, but the realities of the religion remained the same. Now enough pressure has built and we have reached a truly transformative point because the ever-increasing pressure that has not been properly dealt with has now produced an aggressive malignancy known as puritanism. With this malignancy, there is no longer a question of whether there *will* be a change. The only question is what direction the coming change will take. Will the compass bear toward the puritan direction or the moderate direction? That is the question.

I believe that both Muslims and non-Muslims have a role to play in forming the future of Islam. I will address the Muslim role first and then the non-Muslim role.

Earlier I noted the pivotal importance of taking a critical stance toward one's own tradition. Many Muslims are offended by the idea of reform because they wrongly believe that this implies that Islam is somehow faulty or incomplete. But reform is not about correcting God; reform is about improving our relationship with God, and about better serving the trust that has been given to us. God has given us a trust—that much most Muslims can agree on. Reform is about improving our understanding of the nature of that trust and also better serving the objectives of the trust. In other words, the critical reflection that I am calling for is about, first, reassessing in light of new challenges and changed conditions our understanding of the nature of the trust placed in us by God; and second, once we develop a conception of that trust, assessing whether we are doing our duties toward that trust.

In this book, we have studied two approaches toward understanding and serving that trust: the puritan and the moderate. Muslim scholars may emerge with a third alternative that is completely different. The possibility of a third choice or a different approach altogether is a matter that can be dealt with in other works. The issue that confronts most Muslims right now is: As to the two opposite poles that currently exist, to which pole do they wish to direct their faith?

I believe that Muslims can meet the formidable challenge of modernity by anchoring themselves in a humanistic understanding of Islam, and from that point gain the power to leap and thrust forward in the moral and ethical direction God has given them. In doing so, Muslims will not only contribute positively in shaping the ethical direction that our world will take, but they will also remain true to the spirit of the Islamic message. In this process, it is important that Muslims be well grounded in their history, to absorb its lessons, study its continuities and potentialities, and analyze it critically. History teaches, but it does not dictate inevitabilities. Analyzing historical dynamics can yield a considerable amount of wisdom in dealing with the future, but staying frozen and immobile in the moment, clinging for security to a mythical idealized past or to static rules and regulations while refusing to change because of anxiety and fear about what the future may bring is most unwise. It is this anxiety and fear that pervades so much of what the puritans believe in and do. Modernity has made them insecure, and they have responded to this insecurity in a variety of ways, much of it ugly and destructive.

For those Muslims who refuse to associate Islam with the destructive, ugly, and inhuman acts we have witnessed recently, I think that the choice has been made. The problem, as alluded to earlier, is that the puritans are aggressive, zealous, vocal, and well funded. For moderate Muslims or for those Muslims who incline toward the moderate orientation, there is no choice but to be as aggressive, zealous, and vocal in representing what we believe to be the more authentic and true Islam. Puritans speak loudly with acts of violence. Moderates have to speak more loudly with acts of peace. For instance, moderates should get into the habit of organizing massive demonstrations denouncing the violence of the puritans. Puritans fill the markets with their literature, beautifully printed but cheaply priced. For every puritan book written, there must be ten moderate books written in response. Puritans have established numerous seminaries and centers to promote their thought. Moderates must get into the habit of doing the same. Suffice it to say that before the 1970s, there were about five institutions focused on producing moderate scholarship, like the institute established in Pakistan by Fazlur Rahman. Today, there are none.

Puritans are able to do all of this for two reasons: they have money, and they have a jihad attitude about the spreading of their creed and thought—they deal with the propagation of their faith as a holy struggle and so they do it with unrelenting zeal. Moderates lack both of these elements.

Earlier I noted that all the Islamic seminaries and universities in the premodern period were established by private endowments in the form of *waqf* (charitable trusts). Moderate Muslims have no real chance of winning unless they rekindle this charitable tradition. Put bluntly, moderate Muslims must spend generously on the propagation of moderate Islam, and they must do so with an attitude of jihad. It is due time that moderate Muslims realize that they are in a state of war with puritan Muslims. The power of moderate Muslims must come from the belief that their cause is Divine and holy. While puritans wage violent jihad, to win this war, moderates must engage in the superior form of jihad—a peaceful jihad. Unless moderate Muslims realize that they are in a state of intellectual jihad over the future of Islam, they will never match the unrelenting zeal of the puritans.

To save the soul and reputation of Islam, moderates have a dual obligation. First, they must become educated as much as possible about Islam and the Shari'a. Only then can moderates have an equal claim to legitimacy and potentially attain the legitimate power to define Islam. Second, they must consider themselves in a state of defensive jihad to protect their religion from the onslaught of deformed interpretations and disinformation perpetuated by puritans against Islam. *To win this very real war that has done inestimable damage to so many Muslims and to the truth of the Islamic faith, it is absolutely imperative that moderates declare a counter-jihad against the puritan heresy.* This is not a call for the shedding of blood; it is a call for matching the zeal of puritans through unrelenting intellectual activism. *This is a counter-jihad to reclaim the truth about the Islamic faith and win the hearts and minds of Muslims and non-Muslims all around the world.*

As for non-Muslims, what can they do? First and foremost, learn and understand, because nothing helps the puritans' cause as much as Western ignorance, prejudice, and hate. As discussed, much of the puritan framework relies on the notion that the West despises Islam and conspires to destroy it. Practically every book published in the West exhibiting prejudice and hatred toward Muslims is translated into Arabic, and the puritans quote from this type of hate literature extensively as justification for the puritans' worldview. It is not an exaggeration to say that Islam-hating texts written in the West act as recruitment manuals for the puritans. Furthermore, Western writings that advocate a bipolar view of the world by contending that there is an inevitable clash between the Judeo-Christian tradition on the one hand and the Islamic tradition on the other, confirm the puritan worldview, and literally serve as propaganda material for them.

There is no doubt that Islam-haters and Islamophobes will continue to write this drivel, but the average non-Muslim can help by not buying these books, creating a financial disincentive for prominent publishers to distribute material that essentially reproduces the hateful worldview of the puritans. At the same time, it is of crucial significance that non-Muslims support the work of moderate Muslims by purchasing and distributing their works. This is the only way that non-Muslims can help overcome the formidable financial resources of the puritans. If non-Muslims purchase and read moderate Islamic literature, not only will they help overcome the financial vulnerability of moderates, but they will also find much common ground with moderate Muslims upon which to build partnerships to promote goodness and Godliness on earth.

In addition, I believe it is imperative that citizens living in Western democracies bring considerable pressure upon their governments to stop lending support to any state, whether Egypt, Syria, Saudi Arabia, Tunisia, Israel, or any other country, that uses torture. The practice of torture is literally a factory and processing line for the production of puritans. It is also undeniable that bringing a swift end to the occupation of Iraq and finding a just and fair solution to the Palestinian problem will help dry up the sources of recruitment for puritanism.

All of the recommendations I have made are based on my practical sense of what would help in giving the upper hand to moderates in the fight for the soul of Islam. But it is not my practical calculations that I ultimately rely on. As a man of faith, in the final analysis I rely on that faith. I believe, as the Qur'an teaches, that Islam is intended as a mercy for all humankind, and that the earmark of a Muslim is moderation. Thus Islam and Muslims should be the means through which all humans should see the mercy and compassion of God demonstrated. If the two foundational values of Islam are mercy and moderation, and these foundational values are remembered and rekindled in the hearts of most Muslims, then extremism will have no quarter, and the shared pursuit of Godliness among all humankind can progress in earnest. There is no other choice.

ACKNOWLEDGMENTS

In the Islamic tradition, it is said that one seasoned intellect is the product of a thousand years. However, it takes much more than one intellect to produce and publish a book such as this, and for that I have many people I wish to thank and acknowledge. First, I wish to thank my parents, Medhat Abou El Fadl and Afaf El Nimr, my first teachers, who taught me the importance of learning and knowledge and, by example, moderation and balance. I am grateful to my wife, Grace, who was instrumental in reading, editing, and helping this book to its completion, along with our newborn son and her parents in tow. I also wish to thank my son Cherif for reading and commenting on the text. I am grateful to my brother Tarek and his family, who provided me with the tranquil environment and sustenance needed through the writing process. I thank my executive assistants, Naheed Fakoor and Omar Fadel, for their invaluable help and support. I owe a debt of gratitude to Muhammad Farid for his belief in my work and for his generous ongoing support. I give special thanks to Lesley Karsten DiNicola for her friendship and for introducing me to the excellent group of editors and staff at Harper San Francisco. I feel especially fortunate to have worked with Steve Hanselman, Gideon Weil, Anne Connolly, and Miki Terasawa at Harper. I am especially thankful for the incredible support of UCLA Law School, and particularly

Dean Michael Schill and Associate Dean Ann Carlson, for their friendship and ongoing support. Lastly, I wish to thank the many people who have contacted me over the years to ask for assistance in understanding the differences in Islamic conceptions of moderation and extremism. It is in large part their search for the authentic, moderate Islam that inspired this work, and I hope that I have, at least in some small way, contributed to a clearer vision of what I learned is the true Islam—the Islam of moderation. May God accept. I thank Farukh Rashid, Saeed Mirza, and Rabea Chaudhry for taking on the arduous task of preparing the index to this edition.

NOTES

INTRODUCTION

1 Peter G. Riddell and Peter Cotterell, *Islam in Context: Past, Present, and Future* (Grand Rapids, MI: Baker Academics, 2003), have two chapters on the radical and moderate Islamist worldviews, 164–94.

CHAPTER 1: ISLAM TORN BETWEEN EXTREMISM AND MODERATION

1 Ralph Ketcham, *The Idea of Democracy in the Modern Era* (Lawrence, KS: University Press of Kansas, 2004), 30–39.

CHAPTER 2: THE ROOTS OF THE PROBLEM

1 See Gary R. Bunt, *Islam in the Digital Age: E-Jihad, Online Fatwas and Cyber Islamic Environments* (London: Pluto Press, 2003), 124–80.

2 On the interesting historical phenomenon when Shi'i jurists trained in Sunni seminaries and law, see Devin Stewart, *Islamic Legal Orthodoxy: Twelve Shiite Responses to the Sunni Legal System* (Salt Lake City: University of Utah Press, 1998).

3 For a description of the disintegration of the Shari'a, see Wael Hallaq, "Can the Shari'a Be Restored?" in *Islamic Law and the Challenges of Modernity*, ed. Yvonne Haddad and Barbara Stowasser (Lanham, MD: Rowman and Littlefield, 2004), 21–53.

4 The best sources on the reformists of this period remain: Albert Hourani, *Arabic Thought in the Liberal Age 1798–1939* (Cambridge: Cambridge University Press, 1983), and Daniel Brown, *Rethinking Tradition in Modern Islamic Thought* (Cambridge: Cambridge University Press, 1999).

5 For other studies on the thought of the moderates, see John Cooper, Ronald Nettler, and Mohamad Mahmoud, eds., *Islam and Modernity: Muslim Intellectuals Respond* (New York: I. B. Tauris, 2000); Omid Safi, ed., *Progressive Muslims*

(Oxford: Oneworld Press, 2004). For those interested in reading excerpts from the original sources written by moderate Muslims, see Charles Kurzman, ed. and trans., *Liberal Islam: A Source Book* (Oxford: Oxford University Press, 1998).

6 On many occasions I give two dates: the first date is according to the Islamic Era and the second is according to the Common Era. The Islamic calendar, which commenced from the year in which the Prophet migrated from Mecca to Medina, relies on the lunar year.

7 See Yusuf bin Ahmad al-Dijjawi, "al-hukm 'ala al-muslimin bi'l kufr," *Nurr al-Islam* (also known as *Majallat al-Azhar: The Azhar University Journal*) 1, no. 4 (1933): 173–74.

8 Muhammad Ibn Qayyim, *A'lam al-Muwaqqi'in* (Beirut: Dar al-Jil, n.d.), 3:3.

9 Said K. Aburish, *Nasser: The Last Arab* (New York: Thomas Dunne Books, 2004), 141. Arab secularists, such as the cited author, often recognize Nasser's interferences with Azhar University, which led to extensive curriculum changes and also to the organizational restructuring of the thousand-year-old seminary. But they believe that these interferences led to necessary reforms. In reality, these interferences completely undermined the authority and credibility of Azhar University.

CHAPTER 3: THE RISE OF THE EARLY PURITANS

1 Several writers have noticed the literalist and extremist nature of 'Abd al-Wahhab's writings. For instance, see Hamid Algar, *Wahhabism: A Critical Essay* (Oneonta, NY: Islamic Publications International, 2002); Henry Bayman, *The Secret of Islam: Love and Law in the Religious Ethics* (Berkeley: North Atlantic Books, 2003). Recently, an apologetic work has tried to defend the founder of Wahhabism against the charges of rigidity, literalism, and extremism: see Natana Delong-Bas, *Wahhabi Islam: From Revival and Reform to Global Jihad* (Oxford: Oxford University Press, 2004). This is not the place to discuss the glaring omissions, mistakes, and misrepresentations that plague this book. I would be remiss, however, not to note my strong disagreement with most of what is printed in this curious work.

2 Amin al-Rihani, *Tarikh Najd wa Mulhaqatih* (Beirut: Dar al-Rihani, 1973): 35–36.

3 The connection between Wahhabism and Bedouin life is clear in a work like John Lewis Burckhardt, *al-Badw wa al-Wahhabiyya* [Notes on the Bedouins and Wahhabis], trans. Muhammad al-Asyuti (Beirut: Dar Swidan, 1995), hereinafter Burckhardt, *Notes;* al-Sayyid Muhammad al-Kuthayri, *al-Salafiyya bayn Ahl al-Sunna wa al-'Imamiyya* (Beirut: al-Ghadir li'l Tiba'a, 1997), 509, discusses the connections between Bedouin life and Wahhabism, and describes Wahhabism as a Bedouin creed.

4 The massacre of Muslim jurists by Wahhabis is described in Ibrahim al-Rawi al-Rifa'i, *Risalat al-'Awraq al-Baghdadiyya fi al-Hawadith al-Najdiyya* (Baghdad: Matba'at al-Najah, 1927): 3–4.

5 'Abd al-Wahhab, "al-Risalah al-Ula," in *Majmu'at al-Tawhid* (Damascus: al-Maktab al-Islami, 1962), 34–35; 'Abd al-Wahhab, "Kashf al-Shubuhat: al-Risalah al-Thalitha," in *Majmu'at al-Tawhid,* 104; also see 'Abd al-Wahhab, "Bayan al-Najah wa al-Fakak: al-Risalah al-Thaniya 'Ashra" (collected by Hamad al-Najdi), in *Majmu'at al-Tawhid,* 356–57.

6 'Abd al-Wahhab, "al-Risalah al-Thaniya," in *Majmu'at al-Tawhid,* 4–6; 'Abd al-Wahhab, "Asbab Najat al-Sul: al-Risalah Thamina," in *Majmu'at al-Tawhid,* 208–12; 'Abd al-Wahhab, "Bayan al-Najah wa al-Fakak: al-Risalah al-Thaniya 'Ashra," (collected by Hamad al-Najdi), in *Majmu'at al-Tawhid,* 382–83; 'Abd al-Rahman bin 'Abd al-Wahhab, "Bayan al-Mahajja: al-Risalah al-Thalitha 'Ashra," in *Majmu'at al-Tawhid,* 453.

7 See the treatise written by Muhammad b. 'Abd al-Wahhab's son, who was a devout follower of his father: 'Abd al-Rahman b. 'Abd al-Wahhab, "Bayan al-Mahajja: al-Risalah al-Thalitha 'Ashra," in *Majmu'at al-Tawhid,* 466–93.

8 For an example of a list containing acts the commission of which would make a Muslim an infidel, see 'Abd al-Wahhab, "Bayan al-Najah wa al-Fakak min Muwalat al-Murtaddin wa Ahl al-Shirk: al-Risalah al-Thaniya 'Ashra" (collected by Hamad b. 'Atiq al-Najdi), in *Majmu'at al-Tawhid,* 413–16. Also see Aziz Al-Azmeh, *Mohammed Bin Abdel-Wahhab* (Beirut: Riad El-Rayyes Books, 2000), 77–89.

9 In the Islamic faith, the belief in the Trinity is a form of associating partners with God.

10 See 'Abd al-Wahhab, "al-Risalah al-Ula," in *Majmu'at al-Tawhid,* 30–31, 68; 'Abd al-Wahhab, "Bayan al-Najah wa al-Fakak: al-Risalah al-Thaniya 'Ashra" (collected by Hamad al-Najdi), in *Majmu'at al-Tawhid,* 394, 400, 421–23, 433.

11 See 'Abd al-Wahhab, "al-Risalah al-Ula," in *Majmu'at al-Tawhid,* 30–31, 68; 'Abd al-Wahhab, "Bayan al-Najah wa al-Fakak: al-Risalah al-Thaniya 'Ashra" (collected by Hamad al-Najdi), in *Majmu'at al-Tawhid,* 394, 400, 421–23, 433. Also see 'Abd al-Wahhab, *Mu'allafat al-Shaykh al-Imam Muhammad bin 'Abd al-Wahhab* (Riyadh: al-Maktaba al-Su'udiyya, n.d.), 1:281–310.

12 'Abd al-Wahhab, *Mu'allafat al-Shaykh al-Imam Muhammad bin 'Abd al-Wahhab* (Riyadh: al-Maktaba al-Su'udiyya, n.d.), 1:312–29.

13 Muhammad bin 'Abd al-Wahhab, "Awthaq al-'Ura: al-Risalah al-Sadisa," in *Majmu'at al-Tawhid,* 171.

14 See Sayyid Qutb, *Milestones on the Road* (Bloomington, IN: American Trust Publications, 1991); Ahmad S. Mousalli, *Radical Islamic Fundamentalism: The Ideological and Political Discourse of Sayyid Qutb* (Syracuse: Syracuse University Press, 1993).

15 'Abd al-Wahhab, "Bayan al-Najah wa al-Fakak: al-Risalah al-Thaniya 'Ashra," (collected by Hamad al-Najdi), in *Majmu'at al-Tawhid,* 358–68, 375, 412.

16 For instance, this is obvious in the Saudi-sanctioned history of the Wahhabi movement: Munir al-'Ujlani, *Tarikh al-Bilad al-'Arabiyya al-Su'udiyya*—the copy available to me does not provide a publisher or place and date of publication.

17 Al-Rihani, *Tarikh Najd,* 229–43. Hamid Algar, *Wahhabism,* 37–40, argues that the claim that the Wahhabis were inspired by Arab nationalism is anachronistic. I disagree because it is clear that Arab nationalism was on the rise in the nineteenth century.

18 Several Shi'i scholars have noticed the inconsistencies of Wahhabism and written treatises on the subject, but very few Sunni scholars have done the same. One very notable example is Muhammad al-Ghazali in his *al-Sunnah al-Nabawiyya Bayn Ahl al-Fiqh wa Ahl al-Hadith* (Cairo: Dar al-Shuruq, 1989). In this book, al-Ghazali, a prominent Egyptian jurist, spoke about a Bedouin form of Islam that was camouflaging itself as the only true form of Islam and was threatening to take over the Muslim world. For political reasons, al-Ghazali did not explicitly mention Wahhabi Islam. Al-Ghazali is discussed in considerable detail later in this chapter.

19 The Najdi influence on Wahhabism is apparent in a pro-Wahhabi text such as Rashid Rida, ed., *Majmu'at al-Hadith al-Najdiyya* (Qatar: Matabi' al-'Uruba, 1963). Also see Mohamed Al-Freih, "Historical Background of the Emergence of Muhammad Ibn 'Abd al-Wahhab and His Movement" (Ph.D. diss., University of California at Los Angeles, 1990), on the tribal nature of Arabia and the competition between Hijaz and Najd, and 'Abd al-Wahhab's role in this competition; see esp. p. 350.

20 In Sunni Islam, the expression "Rightly Guided Caliphs" refers to the four Companions who ruled the Muslim nation after the death of the Prophet Muhammad. In consecutive order they are: Abu Bakr (d. 13/634), 'Umar (d. 23/644), 'Uthman (d. 35/656), and 'Ali (d. 40/661). In addition, many Muslims consider the Umayyad Caliph 'Umar bin 'Abd al-'Aziz (d. 101/720) to be the fifth Rightly Guided Caliph, although he was not a Companion of the Prophet. These leaders are referred to as the "Rightly Guided" as an expression of the deep respect and honor in which they are held. Sunni Muslims believe that these four caliphs were

able to establish a just and equitable polity similar to the polity established by the Prophet in Medina.

21 See 'Abd al-Wahhab, "al-Risalah al-Ula," in *Majmu'at al-Tawhid*, 36, 70–72; 'Abd al-Wahhab, "Kashf al-Shubuhat: al-Risalah al-Thalitha," in *Majmu'at al-Tawhid*, 117–18; 'Abd al-Wahhab, "Bayan al-Najah wa al-Fakak: al-Risalah al-Thaniya 'Ashra" (collected by Hamad al-Najdi), in *Majmu'at al-Tawhid*, 403–9. The same arguments by 'Abd al-Wahhab are collected in Husayn Ghannam, *Tarikh Najd* (Riyadh: Matabi' al-Safahat al-Dhahabiyya, 1381): 40–43.

22 On the Abu Bakr precedent and its historical origins, see Abou El Fadl, *Rebellion and Violence in Islamic Law* (Cambridge: Cambridge University Press, 2001), 34–61.

23 Among the cruel acts committed by the Wahhabis was the butchering of the children of Muslims whom they considered to be infidels. See al-Rifa'i, *Risalat al-Awraq al-Baghdadiyya*, 3.

24 Muhammad b. 'Abd Allah b. Humaydi al-Najdi, *al-Suhub al-Wabila 'ala Dara'ih al-Hanabila* (Beirut: Maktabat al-Imam Ahmad, 1989), 275. The same claims are made by al-Sayyid Ahmad bin Zini Dahlan, *Khulasat al-Kalam fi Bayan 'Umara' al-Balad al-Haram* (Cairo: Maktabat al-Kulliyyat al-Azhariyya, 1977): 229–30.

25 Sulayman b. 'Abd al-Wahhab, *al-Sawa'iq al-Ilahiyya*, 60–61, 120. Ibn Humaydi reports the stories of some jurists who were assassinated by the followers of 'Abd al-Wahhab; see Ibn Humaydi, *al-Suhub al-Wabila*, 276–80, 402, 405.

26 Sulayman b. 'Abd al-Wahhab, *al-Sawa'iq al-Ilahiyya*, 9, 34–35. Dawud al-Musawi al-Baghdadi, *Kitab Ashad al-Jihad fi Ibtal Da'wa al-Ijtihad* (Cairo: al-Babi al-Halabi, n.d.), 40–41, describes 'Abd al-Wahhab as an ill-educated man who empowered ignorant people to pontificate about Islamic law. On Muhammad b. 'Abd al-Wahhab's education, see Michael Cook, "On the Origins of Wahhabism," *Journal of the Royal Asiatic Society* 3, no. 2 (1992).

27 See, in support of his argument that 'Abd al-Wahhab's behavior was unprecedented, Sulayman b. 'Abd al-Wahhab, *al-Sawa'iq al-Ilahiyya*, 21, 25, 30–32, 38.

28 Sulayman b. 'Abd al-Wahhab, *al-Sawa'iq al-Ilahiyya*, 16, 72; Ibn Humaydi, *al-Suhub al-Wabila*, 275.

29 Addressing the Wahhabis, Sulayman states: "*Wa taj'alun mizan kufr al-nass mukhalafatakum wa mizan al-Islam muwafaqatakum*" ("You [Wahhabis] make the measure of people's faith their agreement with you and the measure of their disbelief, their disagreement with you."). Sulayman b. 'Abd al-Wahhab, *al-Sawa'iq al-Ilahiyya*, 54; also see 14, 42.

30 Al-'Ujlani, *Tarikh al-Bilad al-'Arabiyya al-Su'udiyya,* vol. 1, pt. 2, 279–81.

31 Dahlan, *Khulasat al-Kalam,* 230. This practice is vividly and painfully described in a letter signed in 1792 by a group of Shafi'i, Maliki, Hanafi, and Hanbali jurists sent to the Ottoman authorities pleading for help against Wahhabi atrocities. That letter is reproduced as the first of two historical documents in al-'Ujlani, *Tarikh al-Bilad al-'Arabiyya al-Su'udiyya,* vol. 1, pt. 2, letters "dhal" to "Ghin."

32 See the treatise by the *mufti* of Mecca at the time, Ahmad bin Zini Dahlan, *al-Dawla al-'Uthmaniyya min Kitab al-Futuhat al-Islamiyya* (Istanbul: Hakikat Kitabevi, 1986), 2: 229–40. For a description of the atrocities, also see Algar, *Wahhabism,* 24–26.

33 Sulayman bin 'Abd al-Wahhab, *al-Sawa'iq al-Ilahiyya,* 17–19, 62–64, 70–71, 74–75, 80–82, 92, 100–102, 110–12. For Rashid Rida's view on the merit of the first three centuries of Islam, see Muhammad Rashid Rida, *Majallat al-Manar* (Mansura, Egypt: Dar al-Wafa', 1327), 28:502–4 (hereinafter Rida, *al-Manar*). Rida's assessment of the merits of the first three centuries was similar to 'Abd al-Wahhab's.

34 Sulayman b. 'Abd al-Wahhab, *al-Sawa'iq al-Ilahiyya,* 48–49.

35 Sulayman b. 'Abd al-Wahhab, *al-Sawa'iq al-Ilahiyya,* 121–42.

36 Burckhardt, *Notes,* 250.

37 The treatise is reproduced in Husayn Ibn Ghannam, *Rawdat al-Afkar wa al-Afham Li Murtad Hal al-Imam wa Ti'dad Ghazawat Dhwi al-Islam* (Riyadh: al-Maktaba al-Ahliyya, 1949), 1:111–13.

38 Muhammad Amin Ibn 'Abidin, *Hashiyat Radd al-Muhtar* (Cairo: Mustafa al-Babi, 1966), 6:413; Ahmad al-Sawi, *Hashiyat al-'Allamah al-Sawi 'ala Tafsir al-Jalalayn* (Beirut: Dar Ihya' al-Turath al-'Arabi, n.d.), 3:307–8. Also see Ahmad Dallal, "The Origins and Objectives of Islamic Revivalist Thought, 1750–1850," *Journal of the American Oriental Society* 113, no. 3 (1993): 341–59; al-Rihani, *Tarikh Najd,* 43–44. The same accusation of being the Khawarij of modern Islam is made in Sulayman b. 'Abd al-Wahhab, *al-Sawa'iq al-Ilahiyya,* 10, 28, 50–51; Yusuf b. Ahmad al-Dijjawi, "Tawhid al-Uluhiyya wa Tawhid al-Rububiyya," *Nurr al-Islam* (also known as *Majallat al-Azhar: The Azhar University Journal*) 1, no. 4 (1933): 320, 329; al-Sayyid Muhammad al-Kuthayri, *al-Salafiyya bayn Ahl al-Sunna wa al-'Imamiyya* (Beirut: al-Ghadir li'l Tiba'a, 1997), 345–52.

39 See Dallal, "The Origins and Objectives of Islamic Revivalist Thought, 1750–1850," 341–59.

40 D. Van der Meulen, *The Wells of Ibn Sa 'ud* (London: Kegan Paul International Publications, 2000), 35–36.

41 Al-Freih, "Historical Background," 339–51.

42 On the saga of British involvement in Arabia and British support of Al Sa'ud, see Efram Karsh and Inari Karsh, *Empires of Sand: The Struggle for Mastery in the Middle East, 1789–1923* (Cambridge, MA: Harvard University Press, 1999), esp. pp. 171–98.

43 On the intimate alliance between Al Sa'ud and the British, see Algar, *Wahhabism*, 37–45; James Wynbrandt, *A Brief History of Saudi Arabia* (New York: Checkmark Books, 2004), 176–93; and Nasir al-Faraj, *Qiyam al-'Arsh al-Su'udi: Dirasa Tarikhiyya li'l-'Ilaqat al-Su'udiyya al-Britaniyya* (London: Al-Safa Publishers, n.d.).

44 Gerald de Gaury, *Rulers of Mecca* (London: Harrap, 1951), 275. The author argues that Ibn Sa'ud's alliance with the Wahhabis was forged out of conviction.

45 On the destruction of the intellectual diversity in the two holy sites, see Algar, *Wahhabism*, 44.

46 On the atrocities committed in Karbala, see Algar, *Wahhabism*, 24.

47 For heart-wrenching descriptions of the Wahhabi atrocities committed in Karbala and other places, see al-Sayyid Muhammad al-Kuthayri, *al-Salafiyya bayn Ahl al-Sunna wa al-'Imamiyya* (Beirut: al-Ghadir li'l Tiba'a, 1997), 327–39.

48 Ahmad bin Zini Dahlan, *Futuhat al-Islamiyya ba'd Mudiy al-Futuhat al-Nabawiyya* (Beirut: Dar Sadir, 1997), 2:234–45. Algar, *Wahhabism*, 42; Van der Meulen, *The Wells of Ibn Sa'ud*, 33–34; Geoff Simons, *Saudi Arabia: The Shape of a Client Feudalism* (Palgrave, UK: Macmillan, 1998), 151–73. For historical surveys on these and subsequent events, see Joseph Kostiner, *The Making of Saudi Arabia: From Chieftaincy to Monarchical State* (Oxford: Oxford University Press, 1993), 62–70, 100–117; Joseph A. Kechichian, *Succession in Saudi Arabia* (New York: Palgrave Press, 2001), 161–68; Richard Harlakenden Sanger, *The Arabian Peninsula* (Freeport, NY: Books for Libraries Press, 1954), 27–35.

49 Van der Meulen, *The Wells of Ibn Sa'ud*, 65–68; Kostiner, *The Making of Saudi Arabia*, 117–40; Wynbrandt, *Saudi Arabia*, 184–86.

50 Algar, *Wahhabism*, 39.

51 Simons, *Saudi Arabia*, 152–59; Kostiner, *The Making of Saudi Arabia*, 119; Van der Meulen, *The Wells of Ibn Sa'ud*, 62–113.

52 Algar, *Wahhabism*, 43. For a detailed accounting of the destruction of historical sites by the Wahhabis see, Yusuf al-Hajiri, *al-Baqi' Qisat Tadmir Al Sa'ud li'l-Athar al-Islamiyya bi'l-Hijaz* (Beirut: Mu'assasat al-Baqi', 1990). Burckhardt, *Notes*, 244–50; al-Sayyid Muhammad al-Kuthayri, *al-Salafiyya bayn Ahl al-Sunna wa al-'Imamiyya* (Beirut: al-Ghadir li'l Tiba'a, 1997), 331.

53 Algar, *Wahhabism*, 25–28.

54 Al-Rihani, *Tarikh Najd*, 38–39.

55 Burckhardt, *Notes*, 244.

56 See, on these events and others, Michael Cook, *Commanding Right and Forbidding Wrong*, 180–91; Van der Meulen, *The Wells of Ibn Sa'ud*, 104–13. Reportedly, the Egyptian media severely criticized the Wahhabis over this incident; see Rida, *al-Manar*, 27:463–68.

57 Al-Rihani, *Tarikh Najd*, 39.

58 De Gaury, *Rulers of Mecca*, 276.

59 On the aggressive policies of Saudi Arabia in spreading the Wahhabi creed in the Muslim world, see Nabil Muhammad Rashwan, *al-Islam al-Su'udi Dur al-Su'udiyyin fi Ifsad Din al-Muslimin*. Rather tellingly, no place, date of publication, or publisher's name is given.

60 Aburish, *Nasser*, 162, 256–57, 303.

61 On this process, and on the use of *talfiq* and *maslaha* in modern Islam, see Noel Coulson, *A History of Islamic Law* (Scotland: Edinburgh University Press, 1994), 197–217. Also see Rida, *al-Manar*, 17:372–84.

62 For a critical and similarly grim assessment by a Muslim intellectual of the impact of apologetics upon Muslim culture, see Tariq Ramadan, *Islam, the West and the Challenges of Modernity*, trans. Said Amghar (Markfield, UK: Islamic Foundation, 2001), 286–90. For an insightful analysis of the role of apologetics in modern Islam, see Wilfred Cantwell Smith, *Islam in Modern History* (Princeton: Princeton University Press, 1977).

63 For an example of this apologetic literature, see Muhammad Qutb, *Islam: The Misunderstood Religion* (Chicago: Kazi Publications, 1980). For a valuable discussion of Islamic apologetics and its impact, see Smith, *Islam in Modern History*.

64 Olivier Roy, *Globalized Islam: The Search for A New Ummah* (New York: Columbia University Press, 2004), 232–57. The author notes the convergence between Salafism and Wahhabism as well.

65 The influence of fascist theory upon Qutb has been noted by other writers. See Roxanne L. Euben, *Enemy in the Mirror: Islamic Fundamentalism and the Limits of Modern Rationalism* (Princeton: Princeton University Press, 1999), 199, n. 181; Aziz Al-Azmeh, *Islam and Modernities* (London: Verso Press, 1996), 77–101. On Qutb see Ahmad S. Mousalli, *Radical Islamic Fundamentalism: The Ideological and Political Discourse of Sayyid Qutb* (Lebanon: American University of Beirut, 1992).

66 Hasan al-Hudaybi's book is titled *Du'a la Quda* [Counsels Not Judges] (Cairo: Dar al-Fikr al-Arabi), 1965.

67 The same fate met the work of the liberal Salafi Hasan Ashmawi, *Qalb Akhar min Agl al-Za'im* [Another Heart of the Leader], which was published in 1970 but largely ignored.

68 See Johannes Jansen, *The Neglected Duty: The Creed of Sadat's Assassins and Islamic Resurgence in the Middle East* (New York: Macmillan, 1986).

69 Emmanuel Sivan, *Radical Islam: Medieval Theology and Modern Politics* (New Haven: Yale University Press, 1985), 21–22.

70 Gilles Kepel, *Muslim Extremism in Egypt: The Prophet and Pharaoh,* trans. Jon Rothschild (Los Angeles: University of California Press, 1984), 203–4.

71 Olivier Roy, *Globalized Islam: The Search for a New Ummah* (New York: Columbia University Press, 2004), 250, notes the fact that Islamic militants criticized and condemned Qutb.

72 He rejected the four schools of jurisprudence, and also rejected all plurality of opinions in the Islamic juristic tradition. Shukri Mustafa considered most of Islamic history a corrupt aberration and, therefore, he asserted that it is necessary to return to the original sources of Islam (Qur'an and Sunna), and reinterpret their meaning. But as was the case with 'Abd al-Wahhab, he insisted on his individual right to read the Qur'an and Sunna literally and to establish conclusively the meaning of those texts. In a way that is reminiscent of 'Abd al-Wahhab's approach, as far as Shukri Mustafa was concerned, his groups' reading and understanding of the text was decisive, and anyone who disagreed with their understanding was a heretic and apostate. According to Shukri and Faraj, the saved group—the group of true believers—must wage an unrelenting war against all vestiges of *jahiliyya* wherever they may exist [Gilles Kepel, Jihad: *The Trial of Political Islam* (Cambridge: Harvard University Press, 2002), 85; David Sagiv, *Fundamentalism and Intellectuals in Egypt 1973–1993* (London: Frank Cass, 1995), 47–49; Johannes J. G. Jansen, *The Dual Nature of Islamic Fundamentalism* (Ithaca, NY: Cornell University Press, 1997), 76–80]. Practically identical to Wahhabi theology, both Shukri and Faraj believed that all Muslims, other than their own followers, are *mushrikin* (polytheists) and it is not only permissible but obligatory to wage warfare against them, that the men ought to be killed, that women and children ought to be killed or enslaved, and that their properties have no sanctity. However, the historical context did not favor the plans of military conquest of people like Shukri and Faraj. They could not imitate the violent exploits of 'Abd al-Wahhab because, like their counterparts in many Muslim countries, they clashed with powerful states that crushed them.

73 For one of the rare books by a Sunni author arguing that Wahhabism is fundamentally inconsistent with the Salafi creed, see Ahmad Mahmud Subhi, *Hal Yu'ad al-Madhhab al-Wahhabi Salafiyyan* (Alexandria: Dar al-Wafa', 2004).

74 On the Saudi control over the Hajj and its effect see David Long, *The King-dom of Saudi Arabia* (Tampa, FL: University Press of Florida, 1997), 93–106.

75 For a description of the efforts made by the Saudi government to propagate Wahhabism around the globe see Stephen Schwartz, *The Two Faces of Islam: The House of Sa'ud from Tradition to Terror* (New York: Doubleday, 2002), 181–225; Dore Gold, *Hatred's Kingdom* (Washington, DC: Regnery Publishing Inc., 2003); Algar, *Wahhabism*, 49–66. For the propagation of Wahhabi thought in the United States see Freedom House Report, *Saudi Publications on Hate Ideology Fill American Mosques* (Washington, DC: Center for Religious Freedom, 2005).

76 For examples of such works, see Muhammad Fathy Osman, *al-Salafiyya fi al-Mujtama'at al-Mu'asira* [Salafis in Modern Societies] (Kuwait: Dar al-Qalam, 1981). The author equates the Wahhabis and the Salafis and also engages in lengthy and unequivocal praise of 'Abd al-Wahhab and his movement; see esp. pp. 31–87. Interestingly, the author was a professor in Saudi Arabia when he wrote the book. Another unabashed defense of the Wahhabi movement by a lib-eral scholar is Muhammad Jalal Kishk, *al-Sa'udiyyun wa al-Hall al-Islami* [The Saudis and the Islamic Solution] (West Hanover, MA: Halliday, 1981). This book, however, is a bit more balanced than Osman's work. Interestingly, Kishk was the recipient of the influential King Faysal award. An Arabic book published in Lon-don critically analyzed and illustrated the many uncomfortable facts about Wah-habism that Kishk's book conveniently ignored. See Khalifa Fahd, *Jahim al-Hukm al-Sa'udi wa Niran al-Wahhabiyya* (London: al-Safa Publishing, 1991). As the au-thor demonstrates, many Muslim and non-Muslim writers from the Muslim and non-Muslim world were handsomely rewarded for writing pro-Wahhabi texts.

77 On *Ahl al-Hadith*, see Khaled Abou El Fadl, *Speaking in God's Name: Is-lamic Law, Authority, and Women* (Oxford: Oneworld Publications, 2001), 114; Khaled About El Fadl, *And God Knows the Soldiers: The Authoritative and Au-thoritarian in Islamic Discourses* (Lanham, MD: University Press of America, 2001), 48, 78.

78 Muhammad al-Ghazali, *al-Sunnah al-Nabawiyya Bayn Ahl al-Fiqh wa Ahl al-Hadith* (Cairo: Dar al-Shuruq, 1989).

79 *Manaqib Abu Hanifa*, 350.

80 On the selective citing of *hadith* by Wahhabis to support idiosyncratic posi-tions see al-Sayyid Muhammad al-Kuthayri, *al-Salafiyya bayn Ahl al-Sunna wa al-'Imamiyya* (Beirut: al-Ghadir li'l Tiba'a, 1997), 477–79.

81 Muhammad bin 'Abd Allah al-Salman, *Rashid Rida wa Da'wat al-Shaykh Muhammad bin 'Abd al-Wahhab* (Kuwait: Maktabat al-Ma'alla, 1988).

82 For example, the *fatawa* of Rashid Rida were collected and published in six volumes in 1970 by a publisher known as Dar al-Jil. Saudi Arabia compensated

Dar al-Jil so that it would hold on to the copyright but not distribute or sell the book. I located a copy of the six volumes sold in Egypt. The market value of the volumes was four thousand dollars, which is an exorbitant price in the Egyptian market.

83 The first poem praising 'Abd al-Wahhab and the second poem condemning him are printed in al-Imam Muhammad bin Isma'il al-Amir al-Husayni al-San'ani, *Diwan al-Amir al-San'ani* (Beirut: Dar al-Tanwir, 1986), 166, 173.

84 The following is a partial list of books attacking al-Ghazali: Muhammad Jalal Kishk, *Al-Shaykh al-Ghazali bayn al-Naqd al-'Atib wa al-Madh al-Shamit* (Cairo: Maktabat al-Turath Islami, 1990); Ashraf bin Ibn al-Maqsud bin 'Abd al-Rahim, *Jinayat al-Shaykh al-Ghazali 'ala al-Hadith wa Ahlihi* (al-Isma'iliyya, Egypt: Maktabat al-Bukhari, 1989); Jamal Sultan, *Azmat al-Hiwar al-Dini: Naqd Kitab al-Sunnah al-Nabawiyya bayn Ahl al-Fiqh wa Ahl al-Hadith* (Cairo: Dar al-Safa, 1990); Salman bin Fahd 'Uwda, *Fi Hiwar Hadi' ma 'a Muhammad al-Ghazali* (Riyadh: n.p., 1989); Rabi' bin Hadi Madkhali, *Kashf Mawqif al-Ghazali min al-Sunna wa Ahliha wa Naqd Ba'd Ara'ihi* (Cairo: Maktabat al-Sunna, 1410); Muhammad Salamah Jabr, *Al-Radd al-Qawim 'ala man Janab al-Haqq al-Mubin* (Kuwait: Maktabat al-Sahwa al-Islamiyya, 1992), esp. 100–108. Also see Abu 'Ubaydah, *Kutub Hadhdhar minha al-'Ulama'*, 1:214–28, 327–29.

85 For example, at the time of the controversy, even the influential Egyptian jurist Yusuf al-Qaradawi, who was al-Ghazali's colleague and friend, remained conspicuously silent; but a few years after al-Ghazali died, he wrote two books, one about al-Ghazali's life and the other about the controversy. In both books, he defended al-Ghazali's piety and knowledge, but he stopped short of criticizing the Wahhabis; see Yusuf al-Qaradawi, *al-Imam al-Ghazali bayn Madihih wa Naqidih* (Beirut: Mu'assasat al-Risalah, 1994); Yusuf al-Qaradawi, *al-Shaykh al-Ghazali kama 'Araftuh: Rihlat Nisf Qarn* (Cairo: Dar al-Shuruq, 1994).

CHAPTER 4: THE STORY OF CONTEMPORARY PURITANS

1 My two books *And God Knows the Soldiers* and *Speaking in God's Name* are primarily concerned with this phenomenon.

2 On the humanistic legacy of the Islamic civilization, see Lenn E. Goodman, *Islamic Humanism* (Oxford: Oxford University Press, 2003); George Makdisi, *The Rise of Humanism in Classical Islam and the Christian West* (Edinburgh: Edinburgh University Press, 1990); Marcel Boisard, *Humanism in Islam* (Bloomington, IN: American Trust Publications, 1987).

3 I have already mentioned the early puritanical creed of the Khawarij (literally, the secessionists), who in the first century of Islam slaughtered a large number of Muslims and non-Muslims and were responsible for the assassination of

the Prophet's cousin and Companion, the Caliph 'Ali bin Abi Talib. As noted earlier, the descendants of the Khawarij exist today in Oman and Algeria, but after
centuries of bloodshed, they became moderates, if not pacifists.

CHAPTER 5: WHAT ALL MUSLIMS AGREE UPON
  1 Qur'an 29:46.
  2 Qur'an 2:285.
  3 Qur'an 3:84.
  4 Qur'an 42:13.
  5 As discussed later, many Muslims believe that the highest and most true form
of submission is love.
  6 The most comprehensive study on the subject in the English language is by
Michael Cook, *Commanding Right and Forbidding Wrong in Islamic Thought*
(Cambridge: Cambridge University Press, 1997). For an abridged study on the
topic, see Michael Cook, *Forbidding the Wrong in Islam: An Introduction* (Cambridge: Cambridge University Press, 2003).

CHAPTER 6: GOD AND THE PURPOSE OF CREATION
  1 Most of these attributes are mentioned in the Qur'an, and they are known as
the names of God (*asma' Allah al-husna*).
  2 Somewhat inconsistently, puritans agree that on a few issues or on a narrow
set of points, the Shari'a need not be precise and clear, and on those particular issues or points Muslims may legitimately disagree with each other. I will discuss
this point further in the chapter on law.
  3 For instance, see Qur'an 2:27; 2:205; 5:32.
  4 Qur'an 2:27.
  5 Qur'an 2:195; 2:222; 3:76; 3:134; 3:146; 3:159; 5:13; 5:42; 9:108; 49:9;
60:8; 9:108.
  6 Qur'an 2:190; 2:205; 3:57; 16:23; 22:38; 28:77; 31:18; 42:40; 57:23.
  7 Qur'an 3:31; 2:152.
  8 Qur'an 2:165; 7:56; 9:24; 20:39.
  9 Qur'an 2:186; 50:16; 56:85.
  10 Qur'an 22:40.
  11 Qur'an 5:64.
  12 Qur'an 9:67; 58:19; 59:19; also see 7:51; 32;14; 45:34.
  13 Qur'an 2:272; 6:90; 88:21–22; 12:104; 16:44; 36:69; 38:87; 51:55; 68:52;
73:19; also see 87:9; 80:4
  14 Qur'an 25:43; 28:50; 30:29; 45:23; 47:14.

15 Common throughout the Middle East, and in particular in Syria, Jordan, and Pakistan, honor killings are killings where a male family member, often a brother or father, kills a female member of his family, often a sister or daughter, for having engaged in any "inappropriate" sexual relations. Because the inappropriate sexual relations in which the female engaged shamed the family, the act of killing her is said to reinstate her family's honor in the eyes of society and God.

CHAPTER 7: THE NATURE OF LAW AND MORALITY

1 On the very selective readings of Hanbali sources by Salafi and Wahhabi groups, see al-Sayyid Muhammad al-Kuthayri, *al-Salafiyya bayn Ahl al-Sunna wa al-'Imamiyya* (Beirut: al-Ghadir li'l Tiba'a, 1997), 352–54, 473–501.

2 Remarkably, puritan Shi'i movements are no less selective and opportunistic with the Ja'fari school of thought. Despite the sectarian differences, puritan Shi'is and puritan Sunnis, although they are extremely intolerant of one another and despise one other, adopt the same substantive positions and reach nearly identical conclusions.

3 *Sahih al-Buthari* is a multivolume compendium of Sunna and *hadith* arranged by topic. This compendium was collected Muhammad bin Isma'il al-Bukhari (d. 256/870), and it is considered to be the most reliable and accurate collection of Prophetic traditions by Sunni Muslims.

4 See the discussion of the al-Ghazali controversy in Chapter 3.

5 Qur'an 88:21–22.

6 Al-Suyuti, *Asbab al-Nuzul,* commenting on 2:256.

7 Qur'an 2:256; 10:99; 18:29.

CHAPTER 8: APPROACHES TO HISTORY AND MODERNITY

1 Shi'i Muslims honor and respect 'Ali, the Prophet's cousin, and they also admire 'Umar 'Abd al-'Aziz, but they are critical of the first three caliphs because they believe that 'Ali, as a member of the Prophet's family, had a stronger claim to governance than they did. The label "Rightly Guided Caliphs" was invented in part as a response to Shi'i criticisms, in order to affirm the equal worth of four caliphs and thus defend Abu Bakr, 'Umar, and 'Uthman against Shi'i challenges to their political legitimacy as rulers.

2 To name just a few, Saudi Arabia, Egypt, Syria, Jordan, Algeria, Tunisia, Sudan, Mauritania, Pakistan, Uzbekistan, and Indonesia all have despotic regimes, and they have abysmal human rights records; and all these countries have produced more than their fair share of puritans.

3 At-will employment is a legal expression connoting an employment relationship according to which the employer retains or fires an employee at his/her sole

will and discretion. Most employment relationships in the United States are at-will.

CHAPTER 9: DEMOCRACY AND HUMAN RIGHTS

1 Among others, Samuel Huntington used the expression "false universalisms" in arguing that the Western belief in the universality of Western values is both immoral and dangerous. See Samuel Huntington, *The Clash of Civilizations: Remaking of World Order* (New York: Touchstone Press, 1996), 310.

2 Qur'an 17:70.

3 Qur'an 4:97.

4 Qur'an 3:64.

CHAPTER 10: INTERACTING WITH NON-MUSLIMS AND SALVATION

1 Qur'an 49:13.

2 Qur'an 11:118–19.

3 Qur'an 10:99.

4 Qur'an 2:145.

5 Qur'an 5:49.

6 Qur'an 29:46.

7 Qur'an 16:125.

8 Qur'an 3:64.

9 For instance, Qur'an 25:63; 28:55; 43:89.

10 Qur'an 5:2.

11 Qur'an 5:43–48.

12 Qur'an 5:69; 2:62.

13 Qur'an 3:128–29. Also see 88:21–22.

14 Qur'an 22:67–68.

15 Qur'an 21:107.

16 Qur'an 2:105; 3:74; 35:2; 38:9; 39:38; 43:32.

17 Qur'an 22:34.

18 Qur'an 5:69; 2:62.

19 Qur'an 3:199.

CHAPTER 11: JIHAD, WARFARE, AND TERRORISM

1 Christendom, or more accurately Western Christendom, as a legal and theological concept defined by the papal authority in Rome, played a critical role in the four Crusades, which were sanctioned by the pope, and also in what has been called the military missionizing of pagan tribes in the regions of northeastern Ger-

many, the territories of the Slav, Liv, and Lett tribes, and the rest of Eastern Europe. Military missionizing was a polite expression invented by historians to describe the widespread practice, sanctioned by the pope, of forcing pagan and heathen tribes to convert to Christianity. These forced conversions were described by papal authorities and Catholic apologists as defending and extending the lands of Western Christendom. See Geoffrey Hindley, *The Crusades: Islam and Christianity in the Struggle for World Supremacy* (New York: Carroll and Graf, 2003), 159–67.

2 In the medieval world order, these options were not unusual. The paying of tribute to avoid military conflict was an accepted practice to the extent that when in 1147, in the context of fighting the pagan Slavs, Bernard of Clairvaux urged Christian forces not to accept tribute while stating, "We utterly forbid that for any reason whatsoever a truce should be made with these peoples, either for the sake of money, or for the sake of tribute, until such a time as, by God's help, they shall be either converted or wiped out"—historians and Christian theologians considered this statement very extreme and problematic. As in the Islamic context, the paying of a monetary sum by the weaker to the stronger party was the usual practice even in concluding peace treaties. See Jonathan Phillips, *The Crusades, 1095–1197* (London: Pearson Education, 2002), 71–72.

3 On this subject, see Khaled Abou El Fadl, "Islamic Law and Muslim Minorities: The Juristic Discourse on Muslim Minorities from the Second/Eighth to the Eleventh/Seventeenth Centuries," *Islamic Law and Society* 1, no. 2 (1994): 141–87.

4 On this subject, see Khaled Abou El Fadl, "The Rules of Killing at War: An Inquiry into Classical Sources," *The Muslim World* 89, no. 2 (1999): 144–57; Khaled Abou El Fadl, "Holy War Versus Jihad: A Review of James Johnson's 'The Holy War Idea in the Western & Islamic Traditions,'" *Ethics and International Affairs* 14 (2000): 133–40.

5 Qur'an 6:54; 43:89; 36:58. The expression "God has decreed mercy upon God's Self" is rather ambiguous, and it inspired a considerable debate in the Islamic tradition. Muslim scholars agreed that at a minimum the expression is intended to emphasize the critical importance of mercy in Islam. If God has committed Himself to be merciful in all matters, those who seek to pursue Godliness in their lives must do the same. Confronted by any challenge or problem, they must commit themselves to act in the most merciful way, and they should not be misled by anger, hostility, or vengeance to abandon mercy as the rightful course of action in any given situation.

6 Qur'an 5:8.

7 Qur'an 5:2.

8 For instance, Qur'an 2:190; 5:87; 7:55.

9 Qur'an 2:192–93.

10 Qur'an 2:195.

11 Qur'an 41:34–36.

12 Qur'an 7:199.

13 Qur'an 6:108.

14 Qur'an 22:40.

15 Qur'an 5:64

16 For instance, see Qur'an 2:27; 2:205; 5:32.

17 Qur'an 2:27.

18 Qur'an 13:25.

19 Qur'an 22:39; 60:8; 2:246.

20 Qur'an 2:190; 2:194; 5:87

21 Qur'an 60:9.

22 Qur'an 8:61.

23 Qur'an 4:90.

24 Qur'an 4:94.

25 Qur'an 4:90.

26 For those interested in this abrogation argument and its logic, see Abid Ullah Jan, "The Limits of Tolerance," in *The Place of Tolerance in Islam,* ed. Joshua Cohen and Ian Lague (Boston: Beacon Press, 2002): 42–50.

27 Qur'an 6:164; 17:15; 35:18; 39:7; 53:38.

28 Today, Saudi Arabia and to a lesser extent Iran and Nigeria are the only Muslim countries that enforce the stoning penalty. Most Muslim countries have found stoning to be cruel and shocking to the modern conscience. Puritans consider this a sign of moral weakness, while moderates consider it to be a form of moral growth.

CHAPTER 12: THE NATURE AND ROLE OF WOMEN

1 On the modern origins of the *mutawwa'un,* and their often violent practices, see Michael Cook, "The Expansion of the First Saudi State: The Case of *Washm,*" in C. E. Bosworth and others, eds., *Essays in Honor of Bernard Lewis: The Islamic World from Classical to Modern Times* (Princeton: Princeton University Press, 1989), 672–75; and Ameen Fares Rihani, *The Maker of Modern Arabia* (New York: Greenwood Publishing, 1983), 203. William Gifford Palgrave, *Personal Narrative of a Year's Journey Through Central and Eastern Arabia* (London: Gregg Publishers, 1883), 243–50, 316–18, reports that during the reign of King Faysal bin Turki (r. 1249–1254/1834–1838 and 1259–1282/1843–1865), in response to a cholera outbreak, twenty-two so-called zealots were selected to combat vice in Mecca and elsewhere. Apparently, this was beginning of the system

of the *mutawwa'un*. Also see Michael Cook, "On the Origins of Wahhabism," *Journal of the Royal Asiatic Society* 3, no. 2 (1992).

2 On the tragedy, its causes, and its aftermath, see Eleanor Doumato, "Saudi Sex-Segregation Can be Fatal," http://www.projo.com/opinion/contributors/content/projo_20020331_ctdou31.1032e23f.html (Mar. 31, 2002); Tarek Al-Issawi, "Saudi Schoolgirls' Fire Death Decried," *Washington Times*, Mar. 18, 2002, at http://www.washtimes.com/world; Mona Eltahwy, "They Died for Lack of a Head Scarf," *Washington Post*, Mar. 19, 2002, at http://www.washingtonpost.com/ac2/wp-dyn?pagename=article&node=&contentId=A47458-2002Mar18&notFound=true; "Muslims Allow Girls to Burn to Death in So-Called Moderate Saudi Arabia," *The Welch Report*, Mar. 18, 2002, at http://www.welchreport.com/pastnews_c.cfm?rank=287; "Saudi Police Stopped Fire Rescue," *BBC News*, Mar. 15, 2002, at http://news.bbc.co.uk/2/hi/middle_east/1874471.stm.

3 Qur'an 5:32.

4 On the doctrine of necessity (*darura*) see Subhi Mahmassani, *The Philosophy of Jurisprudence in Islam,* trans. Farhat Ziadeh (Leiden: E. J. Brill, 1961), 152–59; Mohammad Hashim Kamali, *Principles of Islamic Jurisprudence* (Cambridge, UK: Islamic Texts Society, 1991), 267–81. Also see Khaled Abou El Fadl, *Speaking in God's Name: Islamic Law, Authority and Women* (Oxford: Oneworld Press, 2001), 196–97; Khaled Abou El Fadl, "Constitutionalism and the Islamic Sunni Legacy," *UCLA Journal of Islamic and Near Eastern Law* 1, no. 1 (Fall/Winter 2001–2002): 86–92.

5 Qur'an 33:59.

6 For a systematic analysis of this issue, see Abou El Fadl, *Speaking in God's Name*, 170–249.

7 The honorific title *shaykh* does not always refer to jurists. Sometimes it is a designation given to the elderly or to respected members of society. Every jurist is a *shaykh*, but not every *shaykh* is a jurist.

8 Ali Al-Ahmed, "Author of Saudi Curriculums Advocates Slavery," http://www.arabianews.org/english/article.cfm?qid=132&sid=2, Dec. 4, 2003.

9 These domestic workers are typically female and they come from a variety of countries, including India, Bangladesh, the Philippines, and Sri Lanka.

10 Puritans ignore the fact that it was not just Western countries that championed the various international conventions prohibiting the practice of slavery. All of the world's nations became signatories to international treaties prohibiting slavery in all its forms. The prohibition of slavery is a *universal* ethical norm.

11 See Muhammad bin 'Abd al-Wahhab, *Mu'allafat al-Shaykh al-Imam Muhammad bin 'Abd al-Wahhab: Qism al-Hadith* (Riyadh: Jami'at al-Imam Muhammad bin Sa'ud al-Islamiyya, n.d.), pt. 4, 141–51.

12 Al-Sadiq 'Abd al-Rahman al-Ghiryani, *Fatawa min Hayat al-Mar'ah al-Mus-limah* (Beirut: Dar al-Rayyan, 2001): 47, 59–60, 62, 63, 77, 82–83, 86–87, 111–12, 116–17, 122, 130, 137–38, 146, 149.

13 Qur'an 4:32.

14 Qur'an 2:228.

15 Qur'an 9:71.

16 On the active role of women in Medina at the time of the Prophet, see Muhammad Ibn Sa'd, *The Women of Medina* (London: Ta-Ha Publishers, 1997). The Prophet's first wife, Khadija, was much older than he was. After Khadija died the Prophet took several wives, all of whom he married for political reasons or to provide them social security and safety.

17 See al-Suyuti, *Asbab al-Nuzul,* in his discussion of *Surat al-Nisa'*.

18 Qur'an 4:32.

19 Qur'an 4:34.

20 Qur'an 13:11; 8:53; 12:11.

21 Qur'an 2:231. These traditions and others discussed below are discussed in the major Qur'anic commentaries and in all of the books on the topic of occasions for revelation. For a source that succinctly summarizes these traditions, see al-Suyuti, *Asbab al-Nuzul,* which mentions these traditions in commenting on 2:229 and 2:231.

22 Qur'an 2:229.

23 Qur'an 2:231.

24 Qur'an 4:19. The occasion for revelation is mentioned in al-Suyuti, *Asbab al-Nuzul,* in his discussion of *Surat al-Nisa'*.

25 This is mentioned in al-Suyuti, *Asbab al-Nuzul,* discussing verse 4:4.

26 Qur'an 2:229; also see al-Suyuti, *Asbab al-Nuzul,* commenting on this verse.

27 Qur'an 2:241; also see al-Suyuti, *Asbab al-Nuzul,* commenting on this verse.

CONCLUSION

1 For a book that succinctly summarizes the enormous humane contributions of the Islamic civilization and their impact on the Western civilization, see D. M. Dunlop, *Arab Civilization to AD 1500* (Harlow, UK: Longman, 1971).

INDEX